Favourite Food

Valerie Childs

Photographed by Neil Sutherland

Colour Library Books

Compiled by
Valerie Childs

Photographed by
Neil Sutherland

Designed by
Philip Clucas

Edited by
Trevor Hall and Bron Kowal

Editorial Director
David Gibbon

Production Director
Gerald Hughes

Publishing Director
Ted Smart

CLB 1657
© 1987 Colour Library Books Ltd, Guildford, Surrey
Text filmsetting by Words & Spaces, Rowlands Castle, Hants
Printed and bound in Barcelona, Spain by Cronion, S.A.
ISBN 0 86283 582 8

Favourite Food

Contents

INTRODUCTION 6

SOUPS AND STARTERS 8

FISH DISHES 32

BEEF, LAMB AND PORK 38

POULTRY AND GAME 66

VEGETABLES AND SALADS 84

PASTA RECIPES 112

SWEET AND SAVOURY PANCAKES 118

ICES AND COLD PUDDINGS 124

HOT PUDDINGS 164

CAKES AND BISCUITS 178

A LEISURELY BREAKFAST 196

PICNICS AND BARBECUES 200

A COCKTAIL PARTY 216

CHRISTMAS FARE 223

A CHINESE MEAL 230

MEXICAN SPECIALITIES 238

A WEDDING CAKE 242

A PINK PARTY 244

A CHILDREN'S PARTY 250

INDEX 254

Introduction

Compiling a book of so many wide-ranging recipes has proved a lengthy, but exciting and rewarding, challenge. But even with the luxury of almost three years in which to collect, test, prepare, style and photograph them, I could never have achieved this without the generous help of many people, whose kind and willing cooperation I should now like to acknowledge.

First, two very close friends who between them contributed a large number of recipes for this book and gave me an immense amount of help – Nicola Smart, for her tremendous energy, her ideas and enthusiasm; and Penny Booth, for the benefit of her enviable catering experience and for allowing us free use of her newly-modernised kitchen.

Secondly, Koon Eng Choong, for providing the recipes for the Chinese meal, and Angela and Peter Astwood for contributing several – mainly Indian – recipes; Rosemary Barrett, for inviting us into her lovely kitchen; and Dorothy Jordan for the use of her house – and her garden for outdoor barbecue shots; and both of them for supplying recipes and helping with the cooking and preparation. Also Katherine Baird, Edith Caughey, Valerie Day, Angela Helszajn, Angela Hughes, Ted and Mary Key, Romey Lowe, Stephanie Lund and Pat Sheehy, all of whom very kindly supplied one of more of their own favourite recipes.

Thanks also to the many people who allowed their homes and gardens to be used for location photography: especially Anne Noakes, Pauline Altham and Rosemary Derby; Tricia and John Fleming for the loan of their boat, Rosie Charles for her pool-side location, and Malcolm Hillier for the use of his Cheyne Walk house, where Turner once lived.

I am indebted to several friends who lent interesting props and decorative items, which were of invaluable help during photography: Ruth Harris and Elaine Maggs, especially for their lovely tableware and fascinating antique table dishes, plates and ornaments; and Dorothy Cain for her delightful family heirlooms and for her assistance with preparing some of the dishes.

My thanks again to many of these people – and especially to my mother Joan Childs – who also helped with the actual cooking and preparation of recipes and all the ancillary work that is often taken for granted. In addition I am very grateful to Gillian Sutherland, who also assisted with the photography; to Robert Bland for his editorial work; and to Pamela Parry, who not only contributed the recipe for her delicious Cassoulet, but who so accurately typed and so competently proof-read all the recipes.

I must also express my gratitude to the many suppliers, whose names appear in the acknowledgements at the back of this book, for the cooperation, hard work and spare hours that have contributed to the impact of the wonderful pictures that accompany the recipes.

And finally Neil Sutherland, who took all the photographs. His technical experience and creative ideas made my job easier, and allowed our twenty-year-old friendship to remain unscathed even during those fortunately rare moments when food, weather and camera equipment refused to do the expected.

Valerie Childs

Soups and Starters

CELERIAC REMOULADE WITH PROSCIUTTO (PARMA HAM)

Prosciutto, or Parma ham as it is often called, is the best known Italian raw cured ham. It is often served with melon but for a change try celeriac, that rather gnarled, pungent but delicious root vegetable available from October to May/June.

SERVES 4

1 large celeriac
150ml/¼ pint mayonnaise
1 dessertspoon Dijon mustard
Salt and pepper
225g/8 oz thinly sliced Prosciutto (Parma ham)
Parsley to garnish

Peel the celeriac and cut into julienne strips and put into a bowl of acidulated water (a few drops of vinegar to prevent the celeriac discolouring).

Meanwhile, bring to the boil a pan of salted water, also with a few drops of vinegar, add the drained celeriac and cook for no more than 2 – 3 minutes. Tip the vegetable into a colander over the sink and rinse under a cold tap. Pat dry with a cloth and allow to cool. Blend together the mayonnaise and mustard, season to taste and fold into the celeriac.

Arrange the Prosciutto on individual plates, put a spoonful of the celeriac remoulade on each and garnish with chopped parsley.

WATERCRESS, AVOCADO AND BACON SALAD

A good, garlicky French dressing goes well with this salad.

SERVES 4

2 bunches of watercress
1 ripe avocado
3 rashers bacon
3 tablespoons croûtons
Black pepper
French dressing with garlic

Slice off the end of the stalks of watercress and pick over, discarding any yellow leaves or particularly thick stalks. Wash and pat dry. Divide out onto 4 plates.

Meanwhile, cut the bacon into small pieces and fry or grill until crispy. Fry cubes of bread in oil and butter mixed, until golden. Just before serving, peel and slice the avocado and arrange on the watercress together with the bacon and croûtons. Pour on a little French dressing and season with a few twists of freshly ground black pepper.

WHITE BEAN AND TUNA FISH SALAD

"Tonno e fagioli" is a favourite dish from the Tuscany region of Italy. Served with crusty bread it makes a robust first course.

SERVES 4

250g/9½ oz can haricot or cannellini beans OR
    225g/8 oz dried white beans
198g/7 oz can tuna fish
3 tablespoons olive oil
1 tablespoon lemon juice
1 teaspoon white wine vinegar
1 teaspoon Dijon mustard
1 clove garlic, crushed
Salt and pepper
1 small onion
Black olives
1 tablespoon chopped parsley

Drain off the brine from the can of beans. If dried ones are used soak them overnight, drain off the liquid, cover the beans with fresh cold water and bring gently to the boil. Simmer for 5 minutes and turn off the heat. 1½ – 2 hours later they should be tender. Add the salt at this stage. Drain off the oil or brine from the tuna and flake the fish.

Combine the oil, lemon juice, wine vinegar, garlic and salt and pepper to make the dressing and pour over the beans. Combine the beans and tuna fish and garnish with a few rings of raw onion, the black olives and chopped parsley.

Tomato, Avocado and Mozzarella Salad with Basil (top left), Watercress, Avocado and Bacon Salad (centre left), White Bean and Tuna Fish Salad (centre right) and Celeriac Remoulade with Prosciutto (bottom).

TOMATO, AVOCADO AND MOZZARELLA SALAD WITH BASIL

A lovely summer starter, evocative of holidays in Italy. If you can obtain fresh basil the difference to the salad is startling. The plants themselves are becoming more widely available and are a useful addition to a sunny kitchen window-sill. Planted out, they become a tempting target for slugs and, in any case, are too tender to survive British winters.

Tomatoes – the fat Mediterranean ones have the most flavour
Mozzarella – sold in most supermarkets – keep it in a polythene bag in a bowl of water in the refrigerator
Avocado – ripe but firm – sprinkle cut slices with lemon juice to delay discolouration
Olive oil or your favourite salad oil
Salt and pepper
Fresh basil (dried will do)

Arrange slices of tomato, avocado and mozzarella on individual plates. Drizzle on a little olive oil, add some chopped basil and encourage your guests to season the dish with plenty of freshly ground black pepper and rock salt.

Serve with plenty of crusty bread.

BLENDER GAZPACHO

A quick and easy version of the refreshing Spanish soup, which can be made with either 2 lb ripe tomatoes, skinned and seeded, or tinned tomatoes as below.

SERVES 8

2 x 425ml/15 oz tins peeled tomatoes
½ cucumber
2 green peppers
1 clove garlic (more if preferred)
6 – 8 spring onions
1 thick slice of white bread
4 tablespoons oil (olive or preferred salad oil)
900ml/1½ pints chicken stock
1 teaspoon caster sugar
Salt
Ground black pepper
Chopped parsley
300ml/½ pint tomato juice (optional, but improves colour and taste)

Into a large bowl, pour the tomatoes and juice. Peel and cut up the cucumber. Halve, deseed and chop green peppers. Trim and chop spring onions. Crush the clove of garlic. Cut crust off the bread and soak for a few minutes in a little cold water. Add all the ingredients to the tomatoes, first squeezing the water from the bread. Pour in the oil. Ladle this mixture into your blender bit by bit with some small piece of vegetable remaining. Stir in cold chicken stock. Season with salt and pepper and chill for several hours. Ideally, make the day before.

Just before serving sprinkle with chopped parsley.

Serve with small dishes of finely chopped green pepper, spring onions, cucumber and croutons (small cubes of bread fried until golden). Your guests can help themselves to the garnishes, sprinkling liberally onto their soup.

RED PEPPER SOUP

A soup with a wonderful colour and taste.

SERVES 6

1 tablespoon vegetable oil
1 medium onion, finely chopped
3 large red peppers, deseeded and finely chopped
900ml/1½ pints chicken stock
300ml/½ pint tomato juice
Salt and black pepper
Chopped parsley to garnish (optional)

Heat the oil in a medium-sized pan, add the onion and cook for a few minutes until soft and trasparent. Transfer the onion to a blender or food processor together with the chopped red peppers and a little of the stock. Blend until smooth, return to the pan and add the rest of the stock and the tomato juice and season to taste. Bring to the boil and simmer for 15 minutes.

CREAM OF CHAYOTE SOUP

Many exotic vegetables are found at the greengrocers these days, amongst them the pale green chayote, which resembles the green pepper in shape and size. Made into a soup, the chayote has a delicate flavour, one which will keep your family and guests guessing as to its origin.

SERVES 6

2 large chayotes
1 medium onion, finely chopped
1 clove garlic, crushed
25g/1 oz butter
1 tablespoon flour
900ml/1½ pints chicken stock
Salt and black pepper
2 tablespoons double cream (optional)

Blender Gazpacho (top), Cream of Chayote Soup (left) and Red Pepper Soup (right).

10

French Onion Soup (top), Tomato and Lentil Soup (centre left), Minestrone Soup (centre right), Leek and Potato Soup (below centre) and Winter Vegetable Soup (bottom).

Peel and slice the chayotes and put into a medium saucepan, cover with water, season with salt, bring to the boil and simmer for about 20 minutes until tender. Put the chayote into a blender or food processor with half of the cooking liquid and blend until smooth. Discard the rest of the cooking liquid.

Meanwhile, in another pan, melt the butter and gently cook the onion and garlic until the onion softens. Remove from the heat, stir in the flour and cook for a further minute, stirring continously. Gradually add the chicken stock until the mixture is smooth. Add the puréed chayote, season to taste and cook for a further five minutes. Just before serving, stir in the double cream.

MINESTRONE SOUP

A wonderful soup for using up vegetables and, with plenty of crusty bread and butter, a meal in itself. Vary the ingredients according to what you have in the kitchen.

SERVES 6

1 tablespoon butter
1 tablespoon oil
50g/2 oz bacon, de-rinded and finely chopped
1 large onion, finely chopped
2 leeks, finely chopped
2 sticks celery, diced
2 large carrots, diced
2 tomatoes, fresh or tinned, chopped
1 clove garlic, crushed
50g/2 oz cabbage, finely shredded
1.5 litres/2½ pints stock (I often make up the
     amount with a tin of commercial tomato
     soup – children love the flavour it gives)
2 tablespoons tomato purée
¼ teaspoon mixed herbs
¼ teaspoon dried basil
Salt and black pepper
50g/2 oz spaghetti

TO SERVE
Parmesan cheese

In a large saucepan, heat together the butter and oil and add the bacon. Cook for a minute or two before adding the onion and garlic, leeks, celery, carrots and tomato. Fry gently for 10 minutes, covered, stirring occasionally to prevent the vegetables from sticking. Pour in the stock and tomato purée, herbs and salt and pepper. Simmer for about 1 hour before adding the cabbage and spaghetti. Cook for a further 30 minutes. Adjust the seasoning if necessary.

Serve with grated Parmesan cheese.

FRENCH ONION SOUP

Served piping hot, this is a favourite with all the family.

SERVES 6

75g/3 oz butter
700g/1½ lb onions, thinly sliced
1 clove garlic, crushed
½ teaspoon sugar
25g/1 oz flour
1.45 litres/2½ pints good stock
300ml/½ pint dry white wine
Salt and black pepper
1 small French loaf or 3 long crisp rolls, sliced
225g/8 oz Gruyère cheese, grated
Butter for croûtons

In a large saucepan, melt the butter and add the onions, garlic and sugar. Cover and cook gently for 20–30 minutes until the onions are very soft. Remove the lid and continue cooking until they become golden – do not allow them to burn. Sprinkle in the flour. Stir for a minute and gradually blend in the stock and wine. Season with salt and pepper and simmer for 15 minutes.

Meanwhile, spread the slices of bread with butter and bake until golden. When the soup is ready, set

2 or 3 croûtons in ovenproof soup bowls, pour over the piping hot soup and, when the croûtons rise to the surface, sprinkle with grated Gruyère cheese and place under a very hot grill or in a very hot oven until golden brown and bubbling. Serve at once.

WINTER VEGETABLE SOUP

A good warming soup for a cold winter's day. Can be puréed or left as a 'chunky' soup.

SERVES 4

225g/½ lb leeks, thinly sliced
350g/¾ lb parsnips, diced
Small piece of turnip, diced
1 medium potato, diced
1 medium onion, finely chopped
2 tablespoons butter
1.2 litres/2 pints stock
Salt and pepper
Grated nutmeg (about ¼ teaspoon – more or less
     according to taste)
150ml/¼ pint single cream
Parsley to garnish

In a large pan, melt the butter and add the vegetables. Sauté for about ten minutes, stirring frequently. Add the stock and seasonings, bring to the boil and simmer for 15 minutes or until the vegetables are tender.

Liquidize the soup until smooth. Adjust seasoning. Reheat and add the cream just before serving. Garnish with finely chopped parsley.

TOMATO AND LENTIL SOUP

SERVES 4

100g/4 oz lentils
100g/4 oz carrots, diced
100g/4 oz onions, finely chopped
2 stalks celery, finely chopped
2 potatoes, diced
400g/14 oz tin tomatoes
1 tablespoon tomato purée
600ml/1 pint stock
25g/1 oz butter
½ teaspoon sugar
Pinch of basil
1 bay leaf
Salt and pepper
Chopped parsley to garnish

Wash the lentils. In a large pan, melt the butter and sauté the lentils, onions, carrots, celery and potatoes for 10 minutes, stirring frequently to prevent sticking. Add the tinned tomatoes, purée, stock and seasonings, bring to the boil and simmer gently for about 15 minutes until the vegetables are tender. Remove the bay leaf and liquidize the soup until smooth. Return to the pan and reheat. Adjust seasoning if necessary.

Serve sprinkled with chopped parsley.

CREAM OF CARROT SOUP

A simple-to-make soup which is equally good served hot or cold.

SERVES 4

25g/1 oz butter
450g/1 lb carrots, peeled and sliced
1 onion, chopped finely
1-2 cloves garlic, crushed
2 medium-sized potatoes, diced
1 litre/1¾ pints chicken stock
Salt and black pepper
150ml/5 fl oz thick natural yoghurt or cream

GARNISH

Chopped parsley

In a large saucepan, melt the butter and add the carrots, onions and garlic. Cook over a low heat for about 5 minutes, stirring from time to time to prevent the vegetables from sticking. Add the diced potatoes, chicken stock and seasoning and simmer for 20 minutes or until the vegetables are tender. Remove from the heat and allow to cool slightly before liquidizing or sieving the soup. Return it to a clean pan and reheat gently. Add the yoghurt or cream (do not let the soup boil), adjust the seasoning and serve. Sprinkle with the parsley.

To vary this recipe, add the juice and grated rind of an orange.

JERUSALEM ARTICHOKE SOUP

These strange, knobbly vegetables make a delicious soup. Buy large ones if possible, as they are easier to peel.

SERVES 4

25g/1 oz butter
½ kg/1 lb Jerusalem artichokes, peeled and sliced
1 medium onion, finely chopped
1 clove garlic, crushed
900ml/1½ pints chicken stock
1 tablespoon lemon juice
Salt and black pepper
150ml/5 fl oz double cream or thick natural yoghurt

GARNISH

Finely chopped parsley and chives

Melt the butter in a large pan and add the artichokes, onion and garlic. Sauté over low heat

for 10 minutes with a lid on the pan, stirring the vegetables from time to time to prevent them sticking. Pour on the stock and lemon juice, add the seasoning and continue cooking for another 15 – 20 minutes until the vegetables are tender. Remove the soup from the heat and either liquidize it or pass it through a sieve. Return it to a gentle heat in a clean pan. Add the cream or yoghurt but do not let the soup boil.

Serve with a sprinkling of herbs and a few golden croûtons.

LEEK AND POTATO SOUP

SERVES 4

3 large leeks
25g/1 oz butter
1 stick celery
3 medium-sized potatoes
900ml/1½ pints chicken stock
150ml/¼ pint double cream
2 tablespoons chives, finely chopped
Salt and black pepper

Thinly slice the leeks, potatoes and celery. In a large pan, melt the butter and sweat the leeks for a few minutes until soft but not coloured. Add the potatoes, celery and stock, season lightly and bring to the boil. Simmer for about 15 minutes until the vegetables are soft. Blend to a smooth purée, adjust seasoning and add the cream. Reheat gently or serve chilled. Sprinkle with chopped chives.

This soup can also be served unblended – especially good on a cold winter's day.

CURRIED PARSNIP SOUP

A warming, delicious soup, quickly made. Try serving it with a spoonful of smooth chutney sauce.

SERVES 4 – 6

25g/1 oz butter
1 medium onion, finely chopped
675g/1½ lb parsnips, peeled and finely diced
1 teaspoon curry powder (Madras or hot)
½ level teaspoon cumin
1.5 litres/2½ pints chicken stock
Juice of half a lemon
Salt and black pepper
150ml/5 fl oz single cream or natural yoghurt

GARNISH

Chopped fresh herbs and a sprinkling of paprika

Cream of Carrot Soup (top), Curried Parsnip Soup (left) and Jerusalem Artichoke Soup (bottom).

Melt the butter in a large pan and sauté the onion and parsnips over low heat for three minutes. Add the curry powder and cumin and cook for a further 2 minutes, stirring continuously to prevent the vegetables sticking. Pour in the chicken stock and lemon juice, bring to the boil and then reduce heat and simmer the soup for 45 minutes. Remove from the heat, allow to cool slightly and either liquidize the soup or pass it through a sieve. Transfer it to a clean pan and reheat gently, adding the cream or yoghurt at the last minute. Do not let it boil.

Serve with a sprinkling of herbs and paprika.

BAKED AVOCADOS WITH CHICKEN

Avocados are an excellent medium for all kinds of fillings. Their only drawback is that the flesh tends to blacken rather quickly. This can be remedied to a certain extent by rubbing the cut surface with lemon juice or preparing the dish to be served at the very last minute.

Try avocados with a good vinaigrette or various seafoods, such as crab or prawns in a light mayonnaise. For a more slimming idea, pile citrus

Facing page: Smoked Haddock Chowder (top left), Curried Smoked Fish Ramekins (top right) and Coquilles Saint-Jacques (bottom).

Baked Avocados with Chicken (above, bottom right). Also shown are alternative fillings: Citrus Fruits (bottom left), Prawns (top left), Cottage Cheese (top right) and Crab (centre right).

segments onto each half of the avocado and coat lightly with a little oil and lemon juice (or wine vinegar) dressing, or spoon your favourite cottage cheese mixture onto a half and sprinkle with chives.

Avocados can also be baked, although prolonged cooking impairs the flavour.

Try the following recipe as an interesting dinner party starter or light lunch.

SERVES 6

225g/8 oz cooked chicken, diced
3 avocados, firm but ripe
Lemon juice
300ml/½ pint thick white sauce
50g/2 oz Cheddar cheese, grated
25g/1 oz Parmesan cheese, grated
2 tablespoons double cream
Salt and black pepper
50g/2 oz fresh white breadcrumbs

Preheat oven to 400°F/200°C/Gas Mark 6

Make the white sauce, making sure it is quite thick, and add the cheeses, double cream, diced chicken and salt and pepper. Halve the avocados, remove the stones and rub the exposed surfaces with the lemon juice. Pile the sauce onto each half and sprinkle with breadcrumbs. Transfer to a shallow baking dish and cook for 15 minutes only in a preheated oven. If necessary, flash the avocados under a hot grill at the end of the cooking time in order to brown the breadcrumbs. Serve at once.

SMOKED HADDOCK CHOWDER

A hearty soup, a meal in itself, excellent with crusty French bread.

SERVES 4

450g/1 lb smoked haddock
450ml/¾ pint milk
2 medium-sized potatoes, peeled and diced
2 rashers streaky bacon, diced
1 medium onion, finely chopped
25g/1 oz butter
1 tablespoon flour
300ml/½ pint thin cream
Salt and pepper
2 tablespoons finely chopped parsley

Place the smoked haddock in a large saucepan and add the milk. Bring to the boil and simmer for 2 minutes. Remove from the heat, cover and leave to stand for 15 minutes. Drain the fish and reserve the liquid.

In a flame-proof casserole, melt the butter and add the bacon, fry until golden and add the chopped onion. Sauté for 3–4 minutes until it softens. Add the flour, and with a wooden spoon, stir for 2 minutes. Gradually add the fish liquid until a smooth sauce is acquired. Bring to the boil, add the diced potatoes and cook gently for 10–15 minutes, until tender.

Flake the haddock (removing any skin or bones) and add to the soup, season to taste and add the cream. Bring back to the boil and serve at once, sprinkled with finely chopped parsley.

MOULES À LA MARINIÈRE

Wonderful served with crusty French bread to mop up the juices.

SERVES 4 AS A STARTER

2kg mussels (usually sold by the kg bag)
150ml/¼ pint dry white wine
1 medium onion, finely chopped
4 shallots, finely chopped

1 clove garlic, crushed
25g/1 oz butter
Bouquet garni
Beurre manié made with 1 tablespoon butter and 1 tablespoon plain flour
2 tablespoons double cream
Freshly ground black pepper
1 tablespoon freshly chopped parsley

Always eat the mussels the day you buy them. They are at their best between October and March.

Wash the mussels in a sinkful of cold water, discarding any that are broken or open, or any that float to the top. Scrape off any barnacles and remove the hairy beards. Change the water several times whilst doing this to get rid of sand and grit. Melt the 25g/1 oz of butter in a large pan and add the onion, shallots and garlic to soften. Pour in the wine, add the bouquet garni and bring to the boil. Add half the mussels, cover with a lid and cook over a high heat for 5 minutes, shaking the pan at regular intervals. With a draining spoon, lift out the mussels, take off the empty shell from each, keep this first batch hot and repeat for the rest.

Pile the mussels into a dish, strain the liquid through a fine sieve and boil rapidly, reducing it by half. In a cup, combine the tablespoon of butter with the tablespoon of flour to make a paste known as a beurre manié. Stir this into the liquid to thicken it. Add the cream, parsley and black pepper to taste. Pour over the mussels and serve at once.

CURRIED SMOKED FISH RAMEKINS

SERVES 6

400g/1 lb smoked haddock fillets
1 bay leaf
50g/2 oz butter
2 dessertspoons curry paste
1 eating apple, grated
50g/2 oz flour
150ml/¼ pint double cream
25g/1 oz Cheddar cheese, grated
Additional cream for topping (optional)

Put the haddock fillets in a saucepan and cover with 600ml/1 pint boiling water. Add the bay leaf and poach gently for about 5 minutes. Remove the fish and retain the liquid. Melt the butter in a medium-sized saucepan and add the grated apple and the curry paste. Cook for a minute. Stir in the flour and cook for a further minute. Gradually add the liquid from the fish and bring gently to the boil,

Moules à la Marinière

18

stirring continually. Simmer for 5 minutes. Remove from the heat, add the cream and the flaked fish. Spoon the mixture into six ramekins. Sprinkle with grated cheese and a teaspoon of cream. Flash under a hot grill until the cheese is golden and bubbling.

CREAM OF SENEGALESE SOUP

SERVES 6

25g/1 oz butter
1 small onion, finely chopped
1 teaspoon curry powder
900ml/1½ pints chicken stock
175g/6 oz cooked chicken breast, cut into thin strips
4 egg yolks
300ml/½ pint thick cream
Salt and pepper
Chopped parsley to garnish

In a large saucepan, melt the butter and fry the chopped onion for a few minutes until it softens. Add the curry powder and cook for a further 3 – 4 minutes. Pour in the chicken stock and bring to the boil, stirring occasionally. Add the chicken and allow to cool slightly.

In a small bowl, beat the egg yolks together with half the cream until smooth. Add a little of the hot soup, blend and return to the large saucepan. Add the rest of the cream and reheat gently without letting the soup boil. Season to taste and either serve hot or allow to cool and chill in the refrigerator for a couple of hours.

To serve, sprinkle with a little chopped parsley.

PEA AND MINT SOUP

Simple and economical, especially if frozen peas are used. The addition of some cream lifts it from an everyday soup to something more special.

SERVES 6

900g/2 lb peas (frozen are fine)
900ml/1½ pints of chicken stock or water
2 teaspoons sugar
A large handful fresh mint leaves
Salt and black pepper
300ml/½ pint milk
300ml/½ pint cream – optional

Fresh mint to garnish

Tip the peas into a large saucepan. Add the stock or water, sugar and mint. Bring to the boil and simmer for 15 minutes. Liquidize to a smooth purée, return to the saucepan, season to taste, add the milk and bring back to the boil. Remove from the heat and serve in bowls with a swirl of cream and a little finely chopped mint.

CHILLED LETTUCE SOUP

A good recipe for people who grow their own vegetables.

SERVES 4 – 6

25g/1 oz butter
100g/4 oz spring onions, trimmed and chopped
1 large potato (approximately 225g/8 oz)
900ml/1½ pints chicken stock
1 large head lettuce (a bolted lettuce is ideal)
Salt
Freshly ground black pepper

Melt the butter in a large saucepan, add the chopped spring onions and cook over gentle heat until soft but not brown. Peel and dice the potato and add to the pan. Add the stock. Bring to the boil, then lower the heat and simmer for about 15 minutes or until the potato is tender.

Meanwhile, separate and wash the lettuce leaves and shred them coarsely. Add to the saucepan, bring back to the boil and then draw off the heat.

Purée the soup in a blender or food processor, season to taste, cover and leave to cool. Chill until ready to serve. Garnish with a slice of lemon or finely shredded lettuce.

COQUILLES SAINT-JACQUES

Scallops, which are fairly expensive to buy, can be "stretched" by the addition of a few prawns and some mushrooms.

SERVES 4 AS A STARTER

8 cleaned scallops
300ml/½ pint dry white wine
50g/2 oz butter
Half an onion, very finely chopped
100g/4 oz mushrooms, sliced
40g/1½ oz flour
150ml/5 fl oz double cream
Salt and pepper
Sprig of thyme, finely chopped
1 tablespoon parsley, finely chopped
50g/2 oz shelled prawns

TO SERVE

4 scallop shells

TO FINISH

Creamed potato to pipe around the scallop shells made with:
450g/1 lb old potatoes
1 egg yolk
25g/1 oz butter
Salt and pepper

Pea and Mint Soup (top), Chilled Lettuce Soup (centre right) and Cream of Senegalese Soup (bottom).

Remove the orange corals from the scallops and reserve. Slice the white parts into rounds and poach these gently in the dry white wine for 6 – 7 minutes (do not overcook or they will become tough and rubbery). Strain the scallops, reserving the liquid.

In a small saucepan, melt the butter and add the chopped onion, fry for a couple of minutes before adding the mushrooms. Cook for a further 8 – 10 minutes. Sprinkle in the flour and stir for a minute before pouring in the scallop liquid a little at a time in order to achieve a smooth sauce. Cook for about 5 minutes over gentle heat before adding the cream and herbs. Season to taste and add the prawns and scallop corals. Bring gently back to boiling point (do not allow to boil) and divide the mixture between the 4 scallop shells. Pipe a little creamed potato around the edge of each shell and place them under a hot grill so the potato turns slightly golden. Serve at once with brown bread and butter.

ASPARAGUS ON TOAST

SERVES 4

4 slices wholemeal bread
280g/9.8 oz tin asparagus
    OR 350g/12 oz fresh spears
100g/4 oz grated cheese

Toast the bread. Arrange the drained tinned or pre-cooked fresh asparagus on the toast. Cover with grated cheese. Place under a hot grill until the cheese melts and turns golden.

FRESH ASPARAGUS

English asparagus is amongst the best in the world but, unfortunately, has a very short season – from early May to late June. Good quality asparagus however is available at other times from such places as California and Israel.

As well as the fat spears, try the thinner ones known as sprue, they are cheaper, with a good flavour.

1kg/2 lb is enough for four people as a first course.

Cut off the woody parts from the base of the stems and, with a sharp knife, scrape the white parts downwards.

If you do not have an asparagus boiler, either lay the asparagus horizontally in a steamer over a pan of boiling water, or tie in bundles and stand upright in a large saucepan so that the tips are above the level of the rim. You may have to cut more off the stems if you cook them this way.

Cooking time approximately 10 – 15 minutes according to size and age.

Serve warm or hot with melted butter or Hollandaise sauce.
Serve cold, tossed in French dressing.

CUCUMBER MOUSSE

1 large cucumber
175g/6 oz cream cheese
Salt and pepper
150ml/¼ pint boiling water or stock
10g/½ oz gelatine soaked in 3 tablespoons water
2 tablespoons white wine vinegar
1 tablespoon caster sugar
150ml/¼ pint double cream, lightly whipped

Cut off and save a small piece of cucumber for decoration. Peel the rest of the cucumber, dice finely, sprinkle with salt and leave pressed between 2 plates for 30 minutes.

Season the cream cheese with salt and pepper. Dissolve gelatine in 3 tablespoons of hot water in a cup, stirring continuously. (If not completely dissolved, stand the cup in a pan of hot water – do not allow to boil.) Add stock or water to the gelatine and add to the cheese.

Drain the cucumber thoroughly and mix with the vinegar and sugar. When the cheese mixture is quite cold, fold in the cucumber and lightly whipped cream. Put into a mould rinsed out with cold water. Refrigerate.

Serve with melba toast. Decorate with chopped cucumber or a sprig of dill as in photograph.

MANGETOUT STUFFED WITH CRAB

A pretty and light starter or a colourful addition to a tray of finger food.

INGREDIENTS FOR 50 MANGETOUT

50 mangetout
½ red pepper, finely chopped
4 ribs celery, finely chopped
2 tablespoons parsley, finely chopped
2 tablespoons mayonnaise
1 tablespoon lemon juice
1 teaspoon lemon zest
Salt and pepper

Top and tail the mangetout, pulling the strings away from the edges as you go. Cook in a pan of lightly salted water for 2 minutes. Drain and immediately plunge the pods into cold water for some 20 seconds (this helps to retain the bright green colour). Drain again and pat dry on kitchen paper.

Fresh Asparagus (top right), Mangetout Stuffed with Crab (centre left) and Cucumber Mousse (bottom).

Gently slit the mangetout open with a sharp-pointed knife on one side only, creating a pocket for the crabmeat stuffing.

In a bowl, mix together the crab, pepper, celery, parsley, mayonnaise, lemon juice and zest and season to taste. With a small teaspoon, fill the mangetout with the mixture.

CUCUMBER CUPS WITH PRAWNS

SERVES 6

1 large cucumber
150ml/5 fl oz thick natural yoghurt
2 tinned pimentos, finely chopped
1 teaspoon finely chopped mint
225g/½ lb peeled prawns
Salt and pepper
Cayenne pepper

Cut off the stalk end of the cucumber and cut the rest into six equal pieces. Hollow out the centre of each piece, being careful to leave about 5 mm/¼″ around the sides and the base.

In a small bowl, combine the yoghurt, mint and chopped pimentos. Season with salt and pepper and fold in the peeled prawns. Pile this mixture into each cucumber "cup" and sprinkle each with a little cayenne pepper. Transfer to a serving dish and chill for at least 30 minutes. Serve with brown bread and butter.

MELON AND HAM GONDOLAS

SERVES 6

6 slices of ripe melon
6 thin slices of smoked ham (Prosciutto, Parma or Westphalian ham are ideal)
6 wedges of lemon
Black pepper

The melon slices should be free of seeds and skin. There are many varieties available in the shops now. Any of them, providing they are ripe and sweet, make a wonderful combination with the smoked ham, which is simply wrapped around the melon. Garnish each serving with a wedge of lemon and encourage your guests to use freshly ground black pepper.

Clockwise from top left: Cucumber Cups with Prawns; Melon and Ham Gondolas; Sardine-Stuffed Lemons; Smoked Salmon Rolls Stuffed with Smoked Trout Mousse, and Stuffed Eggs with Anchovies and Prawns.

SMOKED SALMON ROLLS STUFFED WITH SMOKED TROUT MOUSSE

SERVES 4

SMOKED TROUT MOUSSE

2 smoked trout yielding about 225g/8 oz flesh
Juice of a lemon
1 tablespoon medium sherry
Few drops of tabasco sauce
Black pepper
150ml/5 fl oz double cream, whipped

4 large slices smoked salmon

Skin and bone the fish and flake the flesh into a food processor or liquidizer together with the lemon juice, sherry and tabasco. Whisk the double cream until thick but not too stiff and fold the fish mixture into the cream. Season to taste.

Use the mousse to stuff the smoked salmon rolls.

Serve with brown bread and butter, garnished with parsley and a wedge of lemon.

SARDINE-STUFFED LEMONS

SERVES 4

4 large lemons
225g/8 oz tinned sardines
175g/6 oz cream or curd cheese
6 tablespoons soured cream
1 teaspoon onion, finely chopped
½ teaspoon paprika
Juice of ½ a lemon
Salt and freshly ground black pepper
Pinch of cayenne pepper
Parsley to garnish

Cut off the tops of the lemons and remove the pulp. Reserve the juice of half of the lemons.

Blend together the sardines, cheese, soured cream and mustard. Add the onion, paprika and lemon juice, and season to taste with the salt, pepper and cayenne pepper. Pile into the lemon shells and garnish each with a sprig of parsley. Set each lemon on a lettuce leaf and serve with hot toast.

WATERCRESS SOUP

SERVES 4 – 6

2 bunches fresh watercress
40g/1½ oz butter
1 small onion chopped
25g/1 oz plain flour
750ml/1¼ pints chicken or vegetable stock
3 – 4 sprigs parsley, chopped
450ml/¾ pint milk
Salt and pepper
Cream (optional)

Wash and pick over the watercress, discarding any yellow leaves. Reserve enough green top sprigs for garnish and chop the remaining cress roughly. Melt butter and cook onion for 3 minutes without browning. Add watercress and continue cooking for another 4 minutes, stirring constantly to avoid browning. Sprinkle in flour and blend well. Stir in the stock and bring to the boil. Add parsley and seasoning, reduce heat and simmer for 15 minutes. Cool slightly and blend until smooth. Add the milk and reheat. Adjust seasoning.

Serve with a spoonful of cream in each bowl and the reserved watercress.

ICED LEBANESE SOUP

SERVES 4 – 6

450ml/¾ pint chicken stock
150ml/¼ pint tomato juice
350ml/½ pint natural yoghurt
150ml/¼ pint single cream
1 clove garlic, peeled
Salt
Freshly ground black pepper

GARNISH

Small cucumber, peeled, seeded and diced
1 hard-boiled egg, finely chopped
1 tablespoon freshly chopped mint

Place all the ingredients into a blender and work until smooth. Chill for a few hours. Just before serving, stir in the garnish.

STUFFED EGGS WITH ANCHOVIES AND PRAWNS

SERVES 4

4 hard-boiled eggs
50g/2 oz peeled prawns
5 anchovy fillets
40g/1½ oz butter
Black pepper
2 tablespoons double cream

GARNISH

Chopped chives
4 stuffed green olives

Watercress Soup.

26

Peel and halve the hard-boiled eggs lengthways and carefully remove the yolks. In a blender or food processor, finely chop the peeled prawns. Remove and put a teaspoonful into the base of each egg white half. Combine the egg yolks, anchovies and butter (which should be slightly soft) in the blender or processor until smooth. Add the double cream and a little freshly ground black pepper to taste and blend for a few more seconds.

If you are feeling energetic, put this mixture into a piping bag and swirl it on top of the prawns. Otherwise use a teaspoon and shape it into a dome. Sprinkle with a few chopped chives and garnish with half a stuffed olive.

SCALLOPS IN VERMOUTH CREAM SAUCE

A sensational starter or a lavish main course which is prepared in minutes

SERVES 4

8 large or 12 small scallops
40g/1½ oz butter
2 tablespoons dry vermouth
Juice of ½ lemon
150ml/¼ pint double cream (must be double)
Salt and pepper
1 tablespoon finely chopped parsley or chives
   for garnish

If fresh, remove scallops from their shells. Frozen scallops, which are now more readily available, should be thawed. Remove the orange roe from the white scallop. Melt the butter in a frying pan and fry the roes for no more than one minute. Remove from the pan and add the scallops. Fry for a further 2 – 3 minutes, turning them once. Remove from the pan and keep warm. To the pan juices add the lemon juice and vermouth and simmer for a few minutes until the liquid is reduced to about one tablespoon. Stir into the double cream and bring to the boil, stirring continuously. Season. Return the scallops

Facing page: Scallops in Vermouth Cream Sauce.

Below: Tomato and Orange Soup.

and roes to the pan and heat through very quickly, then turn out onto a serving dish or individual dishes and garnish with the parsley or chives. Serve at once.

SWEETCORN AND PRAWN SOUP

SERVES 6

2 x 300g/11 oz cans sweetcorn
450ml/¾ pint chicken stock
40g/1½ oz butter
1 small onion chopped finely
1 tablespoon plain flour
600g/1 pint milk
Salt and freshly ground black pepper
100g/4 oz grated hard cheese
225g/8 oz peeled prawns
2 – 3 tablespoons single cream
Chopped parsley

Drain the sweetcorn and place in a saucepan with the chicken stock. Bring to a simmer, cover and cook gently for about 20 minutes. Ladle the stock and corn into an electric blender and blend to a smooth purée.

Melt the butter in the rinsed saucepan over low heat and fry the onion until soft. Stir in the flour then gradually add the milk stirring all the time. Bring to a simmer and cook for 2 – 3 minutes. Slowly add the sweetcorn purée.

STUFFED MUSHROOMS

A tasty first course to make, especially when flat or cup mushrooms are cheap and plentiful.

SERVES 4

450g/1 lb cup or flat mushrooms
4 tablespoons fresh breadcrumbs
25g/1 oz melted butter
2 egg yolks
3 tablespoons cream
1 clove garlic
1 tablespoon each of finely chopped parsley
    and chives
Salt
Freshly ground black pepper
450ml/¾ pint mornay sauce
Grated cheese to taste
50g/2 oz browned breadcrumbs
25g/1 oz melted butter

Preheat oven to 375°F/190°C/Gas Mark 5

Wipe the mushrooms and remove stalks. Allow three to four mushrooms per person according to size. Chop the stalks and any remaining mushrooms, add breadcrumbs, herbs, crushed garlic and seasoning. Bind together with the egg yolks, cream

and melted butter. Fill the mushroom cups with this mixture and place in a greased baking dish.

Coat with the mornay sauce and sprinkle with the cheese, crumbs and melted butter. Bake in a moderately hot oven for approximately 25 minutes.

CARROT AND ORANGE SOUP

Can be served hot or cold.

SERVES 4

1 medium onion, chopped
50g/2 oz butter
450g/1 lb carrots, diced
1 litre/1¾ pints chicken stock
Juice of 1½ oranges
100ml/4 fl oz single cream
Grated rind of one orange
Salt and pepper

Melt the butter in a large pan and gently fry the onion until softened. Add the diced carrots and chicken stock and bring to the boil. Simmer for about 20 minutes until the vegetables are tender. Remove from the heat and purée in a blender or food processor. Return to the pan and add the orange juice, rind and single cream. Season to taste. Reheat without boiling.

TOMATO AND ORANGE SOUP

SERVES 4

50g/2 oz butter
1 medium onion, chopped
2 x 397g/14 oz tins passata (sieved tomatoes)
Juice and rind of one orange
1 teaspoon sugar
1 level tablespoon chopped parsley
150ml/5 fl oz yoghurt or double cream

Melt the butter and add the chopped onion. Cook for 5 minutes without browning. Add the passata, orange juice and rind and simmer for 5 minutes. Add sugar, parsley and seasoning. Cool slightly and blend until smooth, if liked, or leave if a coarse texture is preferred. Add the yoghurt or cream and heat through gently. Sprinkle with extra parsley before serving.

Stuffed Mushrooms.

Fish Dishes

BAKED TROUT

A very fast way to cook trout and fairly foolproof.

Allow one or two trout per person according to the size of the fish.

Preheat oven to 425°F/220°C/Gas Mark 7

Line a baking sheet or roasting tin with foil and brush well with melted butter. Wash and pat dry the trout and dust them with seasoned flour. Lay them on the foil and brush each one with more melted butter. Squeeze lemon juice over each fish.

Bake them in a preheated oven on a high shelf for about 8-10 minutes, basting them once or twice during the cooking. Remove from the oven and serve at once

Pommes Dauphinoises and a green salad or green vegetable go well with the trout. If liked, fry some flaked almonds in a little butter whilst the trout are cooking and sprinkle over the trout before serving.

PAELLA

For hot summer days in the garden, as a change from barbecued food, this classic Spanish dish looks and tastes wonderful.

1 large chicken (about 1.4kg/3 lb) cut into pieces (your butcher will do this for you)
Salt and black pepper
25g/1 oz butter
30ml/1 fl oz vegetable oil
2 cloves garlic, crushed
2 teaspoons paprika
1 green pepper, deseeded and finely sliced
1 red pepper, deseeded and finely sliced
1 large onion, sliced
225g/8 oz prosciutto or smoked ham, cubed
300ml/10 fl oz dry white wine
150ml/5 fl oz tomato purée
2 dozen large, uncooked prawns
2 dozen mussels, washed
55ml/2 fl oz dry white wine
450g/1 lb long-grain rice
1 tablespoon lemon juice
1 teaspoon saffron
1 tablespoon fresh tarragon or 1 teaspoon, dried
1 tablespoon fresh basil or 1 teaspoon, dried
2 bay leaves
1 teaspoon dried oregano
50g/2 oz black olives
1.7 litres/3 pints chicken stock

Melt the oil and butter together in a large pan. Season the chicken pieces with salt and pepper and place in the pan with the garlic and paprika. Brown the chicken on both sides. Add the peppers, onion and prosciutto and sauté for a further minute. Pour over 300ml/10 fl oz of wine and the tomato purée and simmer for 2–3 minutes.

Meanwhile, place the mussels in another pan over high heat, add 55ml/2 fl oz of wine, cover and leave to steam for a couple of minutes, giving them a good shake once or twice. Remove from the pan and strain the liquid into the chicken and prawn mixture.

Stir the rice into the chicken together with the saffron, lemon juice, tarragon, basil, bay leaves, oregano and black olives and pour over the chicken stock. Allow to boil gently for 15 minutes, stirring occasionally to prevent the rice from sticking. Serve the paella in the pan immediately, decorated with the mussels.

Crusty bread and a green salad would complete this colourful dish.

BAKED SALMON TROUT

Thanks to modern fish farming methods, salmon and salmon trout can be enjoyed all year round. Allow approximately 10–15 minutes per pound of fish.

SERVES 8

4–5 lb salmon trout, cleaned but whole

Preheat oven to 300°F/150°C/Gas Mark 2

Place three or four slices of lemon on and inside the fish, together with 2–3 sprigs parsley and 1–2 bay leaves. Wrap loosely in well-buttered foil and set on a baking tray. Bake in the centre of the oven for 40–50 minutes or until the skin is just beginning to show signs of coming away from the flesh. Allow to cool in the foil.

To serve Remove the skin from the body, leaving on the head and the tail. Decorate with

Freshly caught trout – the basis for mouthwatering fish dishes.

32

thinly sliced cucumber, radishes, hard-boiled eggs, prawns and red or black lumpfish roe.

Both salmon and salmon trout are especially delicious with tiny buttered new potatoes, green salad and home-made mayonnaise.

RUSSIAN FISH PIE (COULIBIAC)

SERVES 8

450g/1 lb fresh or frozen salmon
213g/7½ oz tin red salmon, drained
1 tablespoon chopped parsley
350g/¾ lb button mushrooms, sliced
3 eggs, hard-boiled and roughly chopped
Juice 1 lemon
Salt and pepper
1 large packet frozen puff pastry
1 egg beaten

Preheat oven 350°F/180°C/Gas Mark 4

Defrost salmon and puff pastry according to instructions. Cook salmon in buttered foil for 35 minutes. Remove any bones and skin, and flake, adding any juices to the fish. Season well and combine with the drained tinned salmon. Add the lemon juice.

Roll out the pastry to a rectangle 30cm x 25.5 cm/12″ x 10″ and arrange half the salmon along the centre. Add layers of hard-boiled egg, mushrooms and parsley. Top up with the rest of the salmon.

Brush edges of pastry with beaten egg, fold and seal. Turn the pie over so that the join is underneath. Make slits with a sharp knife. Use any surplus pastry to make leaves for decoration. Brush the top with beaten egg.

Cook in a hot oven for 20 minutes until golden brown.

Serve with a green salad or diced vegetables and a Hollandaise sauce.

QUICK HOLLANDAISE SAUCE

A short-cut method of making this rich sauce which is so good served with plain grilled fish, roast meats, asparagus and artichokes. Try it with the Coulibiac (Russian Fish Pie).

175g/6 oz butter
1 tablespoon wine or tarragon vinegar
2 tablespoons lemon juice
3 egg yolks
½ teaspoon caster sugar
Pinch salt
Pinch cayenne pepper (optional)

Melt the butter slowly in a small saucepan and, in

another, heat the vinegar and lemon juice to boiling point. Put the egg yolks, sugar, salt and cayenne in a blender and process for a few seconds. With the motor still running, very gradually add the vinegar and lemon juice mixture. When the butter has reached the boil, add this to the egg mixture in a slow drizzle, also with the motor running, until it is all incorporated and the sauce has thickened.

Serve at once or keep warm by transferring it to a bowl placed in another bowl of hot water. Another idea which works quite well for up to about 2 hours is to keep the hollandaise sauce in a small thermos flask until needed.

SMOKED MACKEREL PÂTÉ

A very easy first course!

SERVES 8

2 smoked mackerel
150ml/5 fl oz soured cream
100g/4 oz cottage cheese
Juice of half a large lemon
Salt and black pepper

Skin the mackerel and take off the flesh, being careful to remove all the bones. Flake the fish and place it in the goblet of a liquidiser or food processor. Then add cottage cheese, soured cream and lemon juice. Switch on and blend until as smooth as required. This pâté is equally delicious smooth or slightly rough. Season to taste. Add more lemon juice if necessary.

Spoon into individual ramekins or a terrine and cover with cling film or foil. Chill until required, serve with crusty bread or hot toast and garnished with lemon slices and watercress.

SMOKED HADDOCK MOUSSE WITH EGG

SERVES 8

450g/1 lb smoked haddock fillet
3 hard-boiled eggs, finely chopped
3 generous tablespoons mayonnaise
2 teaspoons gelatine soaked in
    2 tablespoons water
Freshly ground black pepper to taste
Watercress to garnish

Skin the fish and lightly poach in half milk and half water to barely cover. Cool in this liquid.

Paella.

Facing page: Baked Salmon Trout (centrepiece), with Smoked Haddock Mousse with Egg (above) and Smoked Mackerel Pâté (below).

Above: Russian Fish Pie (Coulibiac) with Quick Hollandaise Sauce.

Flake the fish into a good sized bowl (reserve the cooking liquid), together with the chopped hard-boiled eggs and mayonnaise. Combine well. Dissolve the gelatine (this can be done in a small bowl standing in a saucepan of simmering water until the gelatine becomes clear. Do not boil). Warm the fish liquid and with the gelatine make up a full cup. Cool until just warm and add to the fish and egg mixture. Fold in thoroughly. Turn into an oiled mould or 8 ramekins. Chill for several hours, overnight is best. Serve garnished with watercress.

Beef, Lamb and Pork

ESCALOPES OF VEAL IN A TOMATO AND TARRAGON SAUCE

SERVES 4

4 escalopes of veal, beaten flat and trimmed
Seasoned flour
2 tablespoons oil
1 tablespoon butter
450ml/¾ pint dry white wine
3 tablespoons tinned tomatoes, chopped
3 tablespoons chopped tarragon
1 teaspoon tomato purée
1 teaspoon paprika
Salt and black pepper

Dip the escalopes in seasoned flour. Heat together the oil and butter in a large frying pan until just sizzling. Reduce the heat and fry the escalopes for 2–3 minutes on both sides until golden brown. Add the wine, tomatoes, purée, tarragon, paprika, salt and pepper to the pan and bring to the boil. Again reduce the heat and cook gently for a further 10 minutes, adjusting the seasoning if necessary. Remove the escalopes to a warm serving dish and pour over the sauce. (This can be boiled to reduce and thicken it if necessary.)

PORK CHOPS WITH ORANGE AND GINGER

A simple main course dish with an interesting sweet and sour flavour.

SERVES 4

4 pork chops trimmed
15g/½ oz butter
50g/2 oz soft brown sugar
3 tablespoons wine vinegar
¼ teaspoon ground ginger
Salt
Freshly ground black pepper
1 small orange
2 level teaspoons cornflour

Fry the chops in the butter over a medium heat until golden brown on both sides. Drain off any excess fat.

In a small bowl, combine the sugar, vinegar, ginger and seasonings and pour over the chops. On top of each one place a slice of orange and add to the pan the juice from the remaining orange. Cover the pan with a lid and allow to simmer gently for half an hour.

Remove the chops to a warm serving dish. Drain off the juices into a measuring jug and make up to 150ml/¼ pint with water. Mix the cornflour with a little cold water to a smooth cream, add to the pan juices and return to the frying pan. Reheat, stirring until boiling and thickened. Pour over the chops and serve.

NEW ORLEANS CREOLE JAMBALAYA

SERVES 6

350g/12 oz large frozen prawns
350g/12 oz cooked ham
225g/8 oz garlic sausage
4 tablespoons olive oil
25g/1 oz butter
25g/1 oz lard
1 Spanish onion, finely chopped
2 cloves garlic, crushed
350g/12 oz long-grained rice
2 celery stalks, thinly sliced
1 green pepper, diced
225g/8 oz tin peeled tomatoes, chopped
6 tablespoons tomato purée
1 bay leaf, crushed
½ teaspoon dried thyme or oregano
Large pinch ground cloves
Pinch cayenne pepper
Salt and black pepper
900-1200ml/1½-2 pints chicken stock
150ml/5 fl oz dry white wine
4 tablespoons parsley, finely chopped
12 black olives, stoned

Defrost the prawns, cut the ham into 2.5cm/1″ squares and slice the sausage into 1cm/½″ pieces. Heat the olive oil in a large frying pan and sauté the

Escalopes of Veal in a Tomato and Tarragon Sauce (top left), New Orleans Creole Jambalaya (top right) and Pork Chops with Orange and Ginger (bottom).

prawns, ham and sausage – a batch at a time – until they are golden brown. Remove with a slotted spoon and reserve.

In a large flame-proof casserole, melt together the butter and lard and fry the onion and garlic until the onion has softened and turned transparent. Add the rice and cook gently until the rice also becomes transparent. Next add the ham, sausage and prawns to the rice, together with the celery, green pepper, tomatoes (with their juices), tomato purée, herbs, spices and salt and pepper. Stir gently to mix up all the ingredients.

Meanwhile, in a separate pan, bring the chicken stock to the boil. Pour over the mixture in the casserole (you may not need all the stock at this stage). Cover and simmer over a low heat for 15 minutes or until the rice is tender. (Keep an eye on the dish and top up with more stock if necessary.) Add the white wine and continue cooking for another 5 minutes.

Serve at once, garnished with finely chopped parsley and stoned black olives OR transfer to a warm oven until required.

ROAST RIBS OF BEEF

For a special occasion, ribs of beef (forerib) look good and, because it is cooked on the bone, the meat is especially tasty and tender. Allow 350g/12 oz (uncooked weight) meat and bone per person plus an extra 225g/8 oz. Let the meat come to room temperature before roasting (from the fridge at least two hours) and make sure it goes into a preheated oven.

Roasting times:
35 minutes per kg/15 minutes per pound
for rare meat
45 minutes per kg/20 minutes per pound
for medium meat
65 minutes per kg/30 minutes per pound
for well done meat

A chopped carrot and onion added to the roasting tin, plus any beef bones, will give the gravy a good flavour.

SERVES 6 – 8

2.3kg/5 lb forerib of beef on the bone
A little lard or butter
Freshly ground black pepper
50g/2 oz flour
300ml/½ pint stock (home-made or from a stock cube and a dash of wine if available)
Salt and black pepper

Preheat oven to 425°F/220°C/Gas Mark 7

Set the joint of beef on a rack in a large roasting tin. Rub the meat with softened butter or lard, season it with black pepper and put into the oven at the above temperature for 15-20 minutes in order to sear the meat. Then reduce the oven temperature to 400°F/200°C/Gas Mark 6 for the rest of the cooking time. Baste regularly. Remove the meat

from the oven when sufficiently cooked (according to your individual taste) and transfer to a hot serving dish. Allow to stand for 10-15 minutes before carving.

Pour the excess fat from the roasting tin and set it on top of the oven or hob on a low heat. Add the flour and stir well for 3-4 minutes before adding the stock. Bring to the boil, stirring continually with a wooden spoon, season to taste and simmer for 2-3 minutes. Transfer the gravy to a sauce boat.

Serve with Yorkshire pudding, horseradish sauce or mustard and a selection of seasonal vegetables.

YORKSHIRE PUDDINGS

A must with roast beef, this recipe will make 12 small, individual Yorkshire puddings or "popovers".

100g/4 oz plain flour
1 egg
300ml/½ pint milk and water mixed
½ teaspoon salt
25g/1 oz dripping (use juices from roasting tin)

Preheat oven to 425°F/220°C/Gas Mark 7

In a bowl, sift together the flour and salt. Make a well in the middle and drop in the egg. Gradually mix to a smooth batter using half the liquid. If time allows, leave the mixture to stand for 1 hour then beat in the rest of the liquid.

Grease a bun or patty tin with the dripping and put into a hot oven for a few minutes until the fat is smoking. Remove and pour a little batter into each tin (about ⅔rds full). Return the tin to the oven and bake for 15-20 minutes until the Yorkshire puddings are puffed up and golden brown. Serve immediately.

SMOKY BACON MACARONI CHEESE

SERVES 4

175g/6 oz macaroni (wholewheat could be used)
40g/1½ oz margarine
50g/2 oz flour
600ml/1 pint milk
½ teaspoon ready-made mustard
175g/6 oz Cheddar cheese, grated
1 onion, finely chopped

Roast Ribs of Beef and Yorkshire Puddings.

Above: Leek and Ham Parcels in a Cheddar Cheese Sauce (top), Crispy Chicken Bake (centre left – recipe on page 68) and Smoky Bacon Macaroni Cheese (bottom).

Facing page: Lancashire Hot Pot (top right) and Carbonnade of Beef (bottom left).

4 rashers smoked streaky bacon, chopped
2 sliced tomatoes
Salt and pepper

Preheat oven to 400°F/200°C/Gas Mark 6

Cook the macaroni in a pan of boiling salted water until al dente (still slightly firm). Drain well. Lightly fry the onion and bacon in 10g/½ oz margarine, oil or butter, until onion becomes transparent. Melt the margarine in a pan, add the flour and cook for one minute. Remove from the heat and stir in the milk, a little at a time. Bring to the boil, stirring continuously until the mixture thickens. Cook for a further minute. Remove from the heat, season with salt and pepper and add the bacon, onion, macaroni and 100g/4 oz of the grated cheese.

Pour into an oven-proof dish, top with the remaining cheese and sliced tomatoes. Bake for about 20 minutes until golden.

LEEK AND HAM PARCELS IN A CHEDDAR CHEESE SAUCE

SERVES 4

8 medium-sized leeks
8 thin slices cooked ham
50g/2 oz butter or margarine
60g/2½ oz flour
600ml/1 pint milk
100g/4 oz Cheddar cheese, grated
50g/2 oz white breadcrumbs
Salt and pepper

Thoroughly wash the leeks and boil in salted water for 15 minutes. Drain well. In a small saucepan, melt the margarine or butter, stir in the flour and cook for one minute. Remove from the heat and gradually stir in the milk. Continue to cook until the sauce thickens, stirring all the time. Add 75g/ 3 oz of the grated cheese and season to taste.

Wrap each leek in a slice of ham and place in a shallow oven-proof dish. Pour over the cheese sauce and top with the remaining cheese and the breadcrumbs. Brown under a hot grill.

CARBONNADE OF BEEF (BEEF IN BEER)

The flavour of the beer contributes to a really delicious gravy.

SERVES 4 – 6

900g/2 lb chuck steak cut into 5cm/2″ squares
2 medium-sized onions, sliced
1 clove garlic, crushed
1 tablespoon dripping or oil
1 level tablespoon plain flour
½ teaspoon dried thyme
1 bay leaf
1 teaspoon wine vinegar
Pinch grated nutmeg and sugar
300ml/½ pint Guinness or other brown ale
Salt
Pepper

Preheat oven to 300°F/150°C/Gas Mark 2

Heat the dripping or oil in a large flameproof casserole and when sizzling, brown the meat very quickly on both sides, a few pieces at a time. Remove to a plate. Add the sliced onions to the casserole and fry lightly. Return the meat and dust with the flour. Stir around the meat and onions with a wooden spoon until any juices have been absorbed. Add the ale, garlic, herbs, vinegar, nutmeg and sugar and, if necessary, enough water or beef stock to come halfway up the meat. Stir until boiling. Cover the casserole with a tightly fitting lid and transfer to a preheated oven. Cook for about 2½ hours until tender.

LANCASHIRE HOT POT

A traditional Northern dish, ideal for a cold winter's night.

SERVES 4 – 6

900g/2 lb best end and middle neck of lamb, cut into small, even pieces
25g/1 oz dripping
2 onions, coarsely chopped
4 carrots, scraped and sliced thinly
2 leeks, sliced thinly
900g/2 lb potatoes, sliced thickly
1 tablespoon flour

43

600ml/1 pint stock
1 bay leaf
½ teaspoon dried thyme
Salt and black pepper
Butter

Preheat oven to 350°F/180°C/Gas Mark 4

In a large frying pan, melt the dripping until it is smoking hot and brown the meat a little at a time. Set aside. Fry the onions for about five minutes, add the leeks and carrots and sauté quickly, adding more fat if necessary. Remove the vegetables, stir the flour into the pan juices and cook for a minute before gradually pouring in the stock. Add the bay leaf and thyme and season to taste.

In a large ovenproof casserole, put layers of meat, vegetables and potatoes, ending up with a thick layer of potatoes on top. Season the potatoes as you arrange them. Pour over the stock and put flecks of butter over the top layer of potatoes. Cover with a tight-fitting lid and cook for 2 – 2½ hours. Half an hour before serving, remove the lid, brush the potatoes with a little more butter and turn the oven heat up to 400°F/200°C/Gas Mark 6 so that the potatoes will crisp and brown slightly. (This could be done under a hot grill instead of in the oven.)

STEAK, KIDNEY AND MUSHROOM PIE

This dish is excellent served with creamed potatoes and a green vegetable.

SERVES 4 – 6

675g/1½ lb stewing steak
175g/6 oz kidneys
100g/4 oz mushrooms
2 medium onions, finely chopped
2 level tablespoons seasoned flour
450 – 600ml/¾ – 1 pint water or red wine
400g/14 oz packet of frozen puff pastry
½ teaspoon dried mixed herbs
Salt and freshly milled black pepper
Beaten egg for glazing

Facing page: Chilli Con Carne.

Below: Steak, Kidney and Mushroom Pie.

Preheat oven to 425°F/220°C/Gas Mark 7

Trim the stewing steak and cut into even-sized cubes. Core and dice the kidneys. Roll the steak and kidney in the seasoned flour and place in a large saucepan with the chopped onion, herbs, seasoning and stock or wine. Bring to the boil, remove scum with a slotted spoon and then turn the heat down, cover and simmer for about 1 hour or until the meat is tender when pierced with the point of a sharp knife. Slice the mushrooms and add to the meat and gravy. Let the mixture cool. Spoon the meat and mushrooms into a 900ml/1½ pint pie dish, piling it up in the centre or insert a pie funnel to hold the pastry up. Add 150ml/¼ pint of the gravy.

On a floured work surface, roll out the pastry to an oval at least 2.5 cm/1″ larger than the size of the pie dish. Use the pie dish as a guide to cut the pie lid. Moisten the rim of the pie dish and cut a strip from the edge of the pastry to cover the rim. Moisten the pastry strip and place on the rim. Then moisten the pastry on the rim and place pie lid over the meat. Seal, trim and flute the edges. Glaze the pie with the beaten egg. Decorate the pie with leaves cut from the pastry trimmings and glaze those too.

Place in the preheated oven for 40 minutes, lower the heat to 350°F/180°C/Gas Mark 4. Remove pie from oven, lightly glaze again with the beaten egg, replace in oven and bake for a further 40 minutes to 1 hour. Serve the rest of the gravy separately.

ROAST LOIN OF PORK WITH SAGE AND ONION STUFFING BALLS

SERVES 6

Allow 1 hour per kg/30 minutes per pound – plus 20-30 minutes over

1.4kg/3 lb loin of pork, boned and scored
Oil
Salt and pepper

Preheat oven to 375°F/190°C/Gas Mark 5

Place the loin in a roasting tin. To ensure crisp crackling, brush the surface with oil and rub in salt and pepper. Cook for 1½-2 hours, turning up the temperature for the last 15 minutes to finish off the crackling. Baste the meat occasionally during cooking.

SAGE AND ONION STUFFING BALLS
225g/½ lb onions, finely chopped
8 sage leaves or 1 teaspoon dried sage
100g/4 oz fresh white breadcrumbs
40g/1½ oz butter
1 egg, beaten
Little stock or water
Salt and pepper
Oil or dripping for frying

Melt the butter in a small saucepan and gently sauté the finely chopped onion for 3-4 minutes. Add enough stock or water to just cover the onions, and simmer for 15 minutes. Remove from the heat and add the sage, breadcrumbs and seasoning. Allow to cool slightly before adding the beaten egg. Form the mixture into small balls and fry gently in oil or dripping until golden and cooked. Alternatively, place them around the meat for the last 30 minutes of cooking.

CHILLI CON CARNE

This American interpretation of Mexican food can be made with minced beef, but using cubed chuck steak or good stewing steak makes all the difference. Serve with crusty bread and a green salad.

SERVES 6

675g/1½ lb chuck steak, cut into small cubes
2 tablespoons oil or beef dripping
1 large onion, sliced
1 – 2 cloves garlic
25g/1 oz flour
900ml/1½ pints stock
1 bay leaf
Salt and black pepper
1 tablespoon chilli powder
4 cloves
¼ teaspoon ground cumin
1 teaspoon cayenne
¼ teaspoon dried oregano
¼ teaspoon dried marjoram
¼ teaspoon dried thyme
¼ teaspoon ground coriander
3 tablespoons tomato purée
397g/14 oz can tomatoes, roughly chopped
439g/15½ oz can red kidney beans, drained

Preheat oven to 300°F/150°C/Gas Mark 2

Heat the oil or dripping in a large flame-proof casserole and fry the meat, browning it well. Remove the meat to a side plate. Add the onion and garlic to the casserole and cook for a further 5 minutes. Sprinkle on the flour and stir for a minute before adding the stock and the bay leaf. Bring to the boil, stirring from time to time. Return the meat to the casserole and place in the oven for about 1 hour.

Take the casserole from the oven and again remove the meat with a slotted spoon. Discard the bay leaf and reserve the stock. Take 150ml/¼ pint of the stock and put into a liquidizer together with all the herbs and spices. Liquidize to a smooth paste. In the casserole, heat a little oil and fry this paste for 3 or 4 minutes, stirring continually. Add the chopped

Roast Loin of Pork with Sage and Onion Stuffing Balls.

tinned tomatoes, tomato purée and gradually the reserved stock. Allow to simmer for about 10 minutes before adding the beans and the meat. Either simmer the chilli con carne gently for another 1 hour or return it to the oven for the same length of time.

This dish can be made at least a day in advance, but beware – it tends to get hotter as the days go by. Also freezes well, a boon if it is to be used as a party dish.

VEAL STUFFED WITH HAM AND MUSHROOMS

This dish is very good served with creamed potatoes and French beans.

SERVES 4

100g/4 oz butter
175g/6 oz mushrooms, wiped and finely chopped
50g/2 oz ham, finely chopped
1 teaspoon salt
1 teaspoon black pepper
½ teaspoon freshly grated nutmeg
2 tablespoons dry breadcrumbs
2 tablespoons chicken stock or white wine
4 escalopes of veal, pounded thin
50g/2 oz Emmenthal cheese, grated

SAUCE

2 tablespoons vegetable oil
2 medium-sized onions, thinly sliced
1 large clove garlic, crushed
2 teaspoons fresh parsley, finely chopped
450g/1 lb canned peeled tomatoes
½ teaspoon salt
1 teaspoon black pepper
3 tablespoons grated Parmesan cheese

First make the sauce. In a large saucepan, heat the oil over moderate heat, add the onions and garlic and cook, stirring occasionally, until the onions are soft but not brown. Add the parsley, tomatoes (with their juice), salt and pepper and stir well. Bring to the boil then reduce the heat and simmer the sauce until it has thickened, stirring occasionally.

Meanwhile, in a medium-size frying pan, melt 25g/1 oz butter over moderate heat. When the foam subsides add the mushrooms, ham, seasoning and nutmeg and stir well. Cook, stirring frequently for 3 minutes. Stir in the dry breadcrumbs and stock or wine then remove the pan from the heat.

Lay the veal out flat on the work surface. Divide the stuffing equally among the escalopes and roll them up Swiss roll style, securing them with a cocktail stick or trussing thread.

In a large frying pan, melt the rest of the butter and, when the foam subsides, add the veal rolls and cook

Veal Sauté Marengo (top), Veal Stuffed with Ham and Mushrooms (bottom left) and Veal Escalopes in Lemon Sauce (bottom right).

them for 8 – 10 minutes or until they are browned on all sides.

Meanwhile, remove the saucepan from the heat and stir the Parmesan cheese into the sauce. With a slotted spoon, remove the veal rolls to a flameproof casserole and pour the sauce over the veal rolls. Return the casserole to a low heat and simmer gently for 45 minutes to 1 hour until the veal is tender.

Preheat the grill to high. Remove casserole from the heat and remove cocktail sticks or thread from veal rolls. Sprinkle the Emmenthal over the veal and place under the grill until browned and bubbling. Serve at once.

BEEF FONDUE

An informal way of entertaining

SERVES 4 – 6

900g/2 lb steak (can be fillet, sirloin or rump)
Groundnut oil

ACCOMPANIMENTS

Tomato sauce
Garlic mayonnaise
Curry mayonnaise
Baked potatoes in their jackets with a soured
    cream and chive dressing
Salads

Remove fat and sinews from the meat and cut into bite-sized cubes. If liked, the meat can be marinated in wine and oil in advance.

Half-fill the fondue pot with oil and heat until a cube of bread will brown in less than a minute.

Supply each guest with a long-handled fondue fork and let them cook their own steak to their individual taste.

Tomato Sauce see recipe

Curry Mayonnaise see recipe, reducing quantity by half.

Garlic Mayonnaise – add a little crushed garlic to a quantity of mayonnaise.

VEAL ESCALOPES IN LEMON SAUCE

This dish makes a good main course for an informal dinner. Serve with a green vegetable and sautéed potatoes.

SERVES 4

4 veal escalopes – pounded thin (your butcher
    will do this for you)
4 tablespoons lemon juice
1 teaspoon salt
1 teaspoon black pepper
50g/2 oz butter
175ml/6 fl oz dry white wine or chicken stock

1 tablespoon beurre manié (equal quantities of
    flour and butter mixed together)
1 large lemon, thinly sliced
1 teaspoon parsley, very finely chopped

In a large, shallow dish, marinate the escalopes in 2 tablespoons of the lemon juice for 1 hour, turning occasionally.

Take the escalopes out of the dish then dry them on kitchen paper. Sprinkle on the salt and pepper and leave to one side.

In a large frying pan, melt the butter over a moderate heat. When the foam subsides, place the escalopes in the pan. Fry them, turning once, for 3 – 4 minutes, or until evenly brown. Remove the escalopes to a serving dish and keep them warm while you make the sauce.

Add the remaining lemon juice to the pan together with the wine or stock and bring to the boil, stirring constantly. Boil the sauce for a few minutes until it has reduced slightly. Turn the heat down and return the veal to the frying pan. Cook for 1 minute. Add the beurre manié to the pan a little at a time and cook for a further minute, stirring constantly until the sauce has thickened.

Remove the pan from the heat and pour the sauce over the veal escalopes. Decorate with the lemon slices and parsley. Serve at once.

VEAL SAUTÉ MARENGO

Creamed potatoes or buttered noodles and a green salad go well with this dish. Serve with plenty of French bread to mop up the juices!

SERVES 6

1.4kg/3 lb lean stewing veal cut into 5 cm/2″
cubes
2 teaspoons salt
2 teaspoons black pepper
75g/3 oz butter
60ml/2 fl oz vegetable oil
2 medium-sized onions, thinly sliced
2 garlic cloves, crushed
120ml/4 fl oz white wine
120ml/4 fl oz chicken or veal stock
1 bouquet garni
225g/8 oz can peeled tomatoes
3 tablespoons tomato purée
1 teaspoon paprika
12 small pearl onions, peeled
12 oz button mushrooms, wiped clean
    and quartered
1 tablespoon beurre manié (butter and plain flour
    blended together in equal quantities)

Sprinkle 1 teaspoon of salt and 1 teaspoon of pepper over the veal cubes and set aside.

Beef Fondue with Tomato Sauce, Garlic Mayonnaise and Curry Mayonnaise.

In a large flameproof casserole, melt 50g/2 oz of the butter with the oil over moderate heat. When the foam subsides, add the onions and garlic and fry gently until soft but not brown. Remove onions to a plate with a slotted spoon and turn the heat up. Add the veal cubes and cook them, turning occasionally until they are evenly brown. Add the cooked onions and garlic to the pan and pour in the wine, stock and stir in the bouquet garni, tomatoes, tomato purée and paprika. Bring to the boil, stirring occasionally.

Reduce the heat to low, cover the casserole and simmer for 1½ hours. Add the pearl onions and simmer for a further 30 minutes or until the meat is tender when pierced with the point of a sharp knife.

Meanwhile in a large frying pan, melt the remaining butter over moderate heat and, when the foam subsides, add the mushrooms and cook, stirring frequently, for about 3 minutes. With a slotted spoon, remove the mushrooms from the pan to a deep, warmed serving dish. Then, with the slotted spoon, add the cooked veal and pearl onions to the serving dish. Keep warm while you finish off the sauce.

Remove the casserole from the heat and strain the contents into a medium-sized saucepan, pressing the contents of the sieve with a spoon to extract the flavours. Skim any fat or scum from the surface of the sauce and bring to the boil over moderately high heat. Reduce the sauce by about one third. Add the beurre manié a little at a time, whisking continuously until the sauce has thickened.

Pour the sauce over the veal and vegetables and serve at once.

SAVOURY MINCE CRUMBLE

SERVES 6

CRUMBLE TOPPING
225g/8 oz self-raising flour
100g/4 oz margarine
100g/4 oz Cheddar cheese, grated
Pinch of salt

BASE
1 tablespoon vegetable oil or dripping
675g/1½ lb minced beef
1 medium onion, finely chopped
100g/¼ lb mushrooms, sliced
10g/½ oz flour
300ml/½ pint stock
1 teaspoon mixed herbs
Salt and pepper
1 tablespoon tomato purée

Preheat the oven to 375°F/190°C/Gas Mark 5

Heat the oil in a frying pan and, when hot, add the chopped onion and cook for 3 minutes without browning. Add the mince and fry for a further 3 minutes, stirring occasionally. Add the flour and, after one minute, the stock. Bring to the boil, stirring continuously. Mix in the tomato purée, seasonings and sliced mushroom. Turn the mixture

into a greased oven-proof dish.

TOPPING In a bowl, rub together the flour and the margarine until they resemble fine breadcrumbs. Mix in the Cheddar cheese and the salt. Sprinkle this crumble onto the mince base and bake in the oven for 45 – 60 minutes.

CHILLI HOT POT

A quick and easy supper dish.

SERVES 4

450g/1 lb lean minced beef
1 large onion
1 tin baked beans
300ml/½ pint beef stock
675g/1½ lb potatoes
25g/1 oz dripping/oil
1 teaspoon chilli powder
Salt and pepper
Melted butter

Preheat oven to 350°F/180°F/Gas Mark 4

In a large pan, heat the dripping or oil. Chop the onion and fry for about 5 minutes until soft. Add the minced beef and fry quickly for two or three minutes until browned. Season well with salt and pepper and stir in chilli powder. To this mixture, add the tinned baked beans and turn out into an oven-proof dish.

Peel and slice the potatoes – not too thick – and layer on top of the mince mixture, seasoning each layer with salt and pepper. Pour over the stock and brush the top layer of potatoes with a little melted butter.

Cook for about an hour until the potatoes are tender.

SAUSAGE PLAIT

SERVES 4 – 6

450g/1 lb sausage meat
1 medium onion, finely chopped
1 teaspoon mixed herbs
1 tablespoon chopped parsley
375g/13 oz packet of puff pastry
Salt and pepper

Preheat oven to 425°F/220°C/Gas Mark 7

Combine sausage meat, onion, herbs and salt and pepper in a bowl.

Savoury Mince Crumble (left), Chilli Hot Pot (top centre) and Sausage Plait (right).

Roll out pastry to a rectangle 30cm x 40cm (12″ x 16″) and lay sausage meat down the centre. Make diagonal cuts in the pastry on each side of the sausage meat, about 1cm/½″ apart. Dampen edges. Criss cross from each side over the sausage meat. Brush with a little milk or beaten egg. Bake for 20 minutes at 425°F/220°C/Gas Mark 7 and then lower the heat to 350°F/180°C/Gas Mark 4.

Cook for a further half hour until golden.

LIVER AND BACON CASSEROLE

SERVES 4

450g/1 lb pigs' liver
4 rashers lean bacon
2 large onions
2 cooking apples
100g/4 oz breadcrumbs
1 tablespoon chopped parsley
1 teaspoon salt
Freshly ground black pepper
300ml/½ pint stock

Above: Chop Toad in the Hole.

Facing page: Liver and Bacon Casserole (left) and Kidneys Turbigo (right).

Preheat oven to 375°F/190°C/Gas Mark 5

Slice the liver and cut bacon into small pieces. Peel and chop the onions and apples. Put a layer of the liver and bacon in the base of a greased casserole, followed by some of the breadcrumbs, onions, apples, parsley and salt and pepper. Repeat, finishing with the breadcrumbs. Pour in the stock. Cover the dish and bake for two hours, removing the lid for the final 30 minutes.

KIDNEYS TURBIGO

SERVES 6

8 lamb kidneys
6 chipolata sausages
12 button onions
50g/2 oz butter

25g/1 oz plain flour
450ml/¾ pint stock – beef or chicken
150ml/¼ pint dry white wine
1 dessertspoon tomato purée
3 tablespoons dry or medium dry sherry
1 bay leaf
Salt and pepper
Parsley and croûtons to garnish

Halve the kidneys, removing the white core and any skin. Halve the sausages. Melt the butter in a large, heavy-based pan and fry the kidneys and sausages until they are brown. Remove from the pan and keep hot.

Peel the button onions, leaving them whole and place in a pan of cold water. Bring to the boil and allow to simmer for 5 minutes. Drain.

Using the pan containing the butter and meat juices, stir in the flour and cook for 2 – 3 minutes. Gradually add the stock and wine, stirring the whole time until the sauce is smooth. Bring to the boil and blend in the tomato purée and sherry. Season to taste. Put back into the pan the kidneys and sausages, together with the drained onions and

the bay leaf. Cover with a lid and simmer gently for about 25 minutes.

Remove the bay leaf and transfer the kidneys turbigo to a serving dish and garnish with croûtons and chopped parsley.

Rice or creamed potatoes and a green vegetable are a good accompaniment to this dish.

INDIVIDUAL STEAKS IN PUFF PASTRY WITH MUSHROOM SAUCE

A more economical version of boeuf en croute.

SERVES 4

4 rump steaks – 2cm/¾" thick
Salt and black pepper
75g/3 oz butter
225g/8 oz mushrooms
Pinch of dried thyme
1 tablespoon fresh parsley, chopped
1 clove garlic, crushed
1 glass red wine
2 tablespoons double cream
450g/1 lb puff pastry
1 egg, lightly beaten

Preheat oven to 400°F/200°C/Gas Mark 6

Rub salt and freshly ground black pepper into the steaks.

Melt 50g/2 oz of the butter in a large frying pan over moderate heat and, when sizzling, cook the steaks for 1 minute each side. Remove from the pan and allow them to get cold before putting them in the refrigerator. Meanwhile, finely chop 100g/4 oz of the mushrooms and sauté them lightly in the pan juices. Add the chopped parsley and pinch of thyme and allow to cool.

Roll out the puff pastry until fairly thin and cut into 4 equal-sized rectangles that are large enough to cover the top, sides and tuck under the steaks. Remove the steaks from the refrigerator and place on an oiled baking sheet with space between each one. Put a spoonful of mushroom mixture on the top of each steak and cover with a rectangle of pastry. Decorate, if liked, with any pastry trimmings. Cut a couple of slits in the top to allow the steam to escape. Brush the pastry with a little beaten egg and place the baking sheet in the centre of a preheated oven for 20 – 25 minutes, according to how well done you like your meat. Halfway through cooking, glaze the pastry again with the beaten egg.

Meanwhile melt the remaining butter in the frying pan and add the crushed garlic. Slice the rest of the mushrooms finely and add to the pan, together with the wine and salt and pepper. Cook the sauce until it reduces by roughly one quarter and then, just before serving, stir in two tablespoons of double cream. Serve separately with the steaks.

CHOP TOAD IN THE HOLE

SERVES 6

6 small lamb chops
6 large pork sausages (more if desired)
½ medium onion, chopped
15g/½ oz fat (lard, dripping or oil)

BATTER

1 large or 2 small eggs
75g/3 oz plain flour, sieved with 1 teaspoon baking powder and a pinch of salt
300ml/½ pint milk and water mixed

Preheat oven to 350°F/180°C/Gas Mark 4

In a bowl, whisk together eggs, flour, milk and water until smooth and bubbles appear on the surface. Leave to stand for at least 30 minutes.

Bone chops.

Melt fat in a baking dish in the oven and when hot (5 minutes) arrange chops, sausages and onion in the dish. Cook for 20 minutes until lightly coloured. Pour over batter mixture, increase oven temperature to 400°F/200°C/Gas Mark 6. Cook for a further 15 – 20 minutes until batter is well risen and golden brown.

Serve with a thin gravy made with chop bones, stock cube, 300ml/½ pint water, salt, pepper and a pinch of dried mixed herbs, strained.

STEAK IN GREEN PEPPERCORN SAUCE

These steaks are excellent served with Gratin Dauphinois and a green salad for a special dinner.

SERVES 4

75g/3 oz canned green peppercorns
2 tablespoons prepared French mustard
4 fillet steaks
40g/1½ oz butter
225ml/8 fl oz double cream
½ teaspoon salt
1 tablespoon chopped parsley

Drain the peppercorns and rinse them. Pat dry on kitchen paper and crush them in a pestle and mortar or in small bowl, using the end of a rolling pin. Mix the crushed peppercorns with the mustard and spread this on both sides of the steaks. Melt the butter in a large, heavy-based frying pan over high heat. When the foam subsides, add the

Individual Steaks in Puff Pastry with Mushroom Sauce (top) and Steak in Green Peppercorn Sauce (bottom).

steaks and fry for 2 minutes on each side. This will produce rare steaks. Double the time for medium-rare and allow about 12 minutes for well-done steaks. Remove the steaks from the pan onto a serving dish and keep them warm while you make the sauce.

Add the cream and salt to the pan and cook gently for a few minutes, scraping all the sediment from the bottom of the pan and incorporating it into the sauce.

Remove the pan from the heat and pour the sauce over the steaks. Sprinkle with parsley and serve at once.

HUNGARIAN GOULASH

An ideal dish for a cold winters night that both keeps and freezes well.

SERVES 4 – 6

675g/1½ lb chuck steak cut into 4cm/1½″ cubes
2 large onions sliced
1 clove of garlic crushed
1 tablespoon dripping or oil
25g/1 oz plain flour

Above: Rack of Lamb with Apricot Stuffing.

Facing page: Hungarian Goulash.

50g/2 oz paprika
1 400g/14 oz tin peeled tomatoes
1 tablespoon tomato purée
1 bouquet garni
450ml/¾ pint stock
1 medium sized red or green pepper
1 142ml/5 fl oz carton soured cream
Salt
Freshly ground black pepper
Chopped parsley to garnish

Preheat oven to 300°F/150°C/Gas Mark 2

In a heavy saucepan or flameproof casserole, fry the cubes of meat in the dripping or oil until well browned. Transfer to a plate. Lower the heat and fry the onions and garlic until soft and pale golden-brown. Return the meat to the pan and add the paprika and after about 1 minute the flour. Stir well. Add the tomatoes, tomato purée and stock and bring to the boil, stirring continuously. Season to taste and add the bouquet garni. Transfer to the middle shelf of the oven and cook for a further 2 hours.

Finely shred the green or red pepper – add to the goulash and cook for another 30 minutes. Just before serving, stir in the sour cream to create a marbled effect and sprinkle with the chopped parsley.

RACK OF LAMB (GUARD OF HONOUR) WITH APRICOT STUFFING

SERVES 6

Allow 1 hour per kg/30 minutes per pound – plus 30 minutes over

2 best ends of neck of lamb (interlock the bones)
Flour

APRICOT STUFFING
175g/6 oz dried apricots, soaked overnight
1 small onion, finely chopped
25g/1 oz butter

100g/4 oz fresh white breadcrumbs
50g/2 oz blanched split almonds
2 tablespoons chopped parsley
Salt and black pepper
Juice of ½ lemon
1-2 eggs, lightly beaten

Preheat oven to 375°F/190°C/Gas Mark 5

Make sure the lamb is at room temperature.

To make the stuffing, drain and chop the soaked apricots. Melt the butter in a small pan and sauté the chopped onion for 5 minutes until softened. Put the apricots, breadcrumbs, almonds, parsley, salt and pepper in a large bowl. Add the onion, the beaten eggs and lemon juice. Mix well. Stuff the central cavity of the rack of lamb and place the joint upright in a roasting tin. Lightly dust the outside of the lamb with a little flour. This helps to turn the skin crispy. When cooked, remove the lamb from the oven, transfer it to a hot serving dish and leave to stand for 10-15 minutes before carving.

This is a particularly good dish to try when the new season's lamb reaches the shops, so serve it with a selection of fresh vegetables including new potatoes.

LAMB CHOPS IN CAPER SAUCE

This is a simple but very tasty dish.

SERVES 4

4 large or 8 small lamb chops
25g/1 oz fat
10g/½ oz flour
150ml/¼ pint stock
3 tablespoons medium sherry
Good dessertspoon capers
Salt and black pepper
1 teaspoon brown sugar

Fry the chops on both sides in the fat for 5 minutes. Remove from the pan. Stir the flour into the pan juices and cook for 2 – 3 minutes. Stir in the stock and sherry then add the capers, salt, pepper and sugar. Bring slowly to the boil, stirring continuously. Reduce heat until the sauce is at simmering point. Place the chops back into the pan, cover with a lid and simmer for 15 minutes.

GIGOT D'AGNEAU (LISA'S LAMB IN PASTRY)

This recipe was passed down by an elderly Swiss lady called Lisa. Not only is it a tasty way of serving lamb but it can be prepared well in advance (frozen if necessary) ready just to pop in a hot oven.

SERVES 6 – 8

1.4kg/3 lb boned leg of lamb
Garlic

STUFFING

50g/2 oz butter
100g/4 oz onions, finely chopped
675g/1½ lb mushrooms, finely chopped
100g/4 oz neck of pork, minced
100g/4 oz pie veal, minced
½ teaspoon each of thyme, rosemary and tarragon
1½ glasses white wine
Salt and black pepper

PASTRY

350 – 400g/12 – 14 oz puff pastry
1 egg, lightly beaten

Preheat oven to 375°F/190°C/Gas Mark 5

Insert slivers of garlic into the lamb, set the joint in a roasting tin and place in the oven for 40 – 60 minutes, according to how well done you like your lamb. Set it aside to cool.

For the stuffing, melt the butter in a large pan and add the onions. Cook them for a couple of minutes until they soften. Add the rest of the ingredients, mix well and let them cook gently for 1½ hours with the lid on. Allow to cool. If mixture is too runny, firm it up with fresh white breadcrumbs. Press the stuffing into the space in the leg of lamb left by the bone. Any extra stuffing can be spread on the outside.

Turn up the oven to 450°F/230°C/Gas Mark 8.

Roll out the puff pastry into a rectangle 35x 40cm/14" x 16". Lay the lamb on the pastry, moisten the edges with a little beaten egg and fold the pastry around the lamb, making an envelope. Press the edges together well, making a firm seal. Make 2 or 3 holes in the pastry to allow the steam to escape and cut out some decorative leaves with any spare pastry, attaching them with beaten egg. Brush the whole joint with more egg. Put in the preheated oven for 10 minutes. Remove and brush with the remaining egg. This ensures a deep golden glaze. Cook for a further 20 minutes.

Serve hot.

CASSOULET

Ideal for slow cooking. A story goes that many years ago in France, a cassoulet had been cooking for 20 years! Every time servings were taken from it, more beans, meat and stock was ladled into the big "Cassole d'Issel" or earthenware pot from which the dish takes its name. This recipe is a much simplified version, but one which nevertheless benefits from slow cooking.

SERVES 4

1 x 410g/16½ oz tin flageolets (green kidney beans)
1 x 432g/15 oz tin chilli beans in chilli sauce
1 large onion, peeled and chopped
4 cloves garlic, peeled and crushed with the back of a knife
1 bay leaf
1.2 litres/2 pints chicken stock
225g/8 oz lean pork, cut into thin strips
225g/8 oz lean lamb, cubed
100g/4 oz spicy sausage, chorizo if possible, skinned and diced
1 teaspoonful dried oregano
1 x 400g/16 oz tin tomatoes, chopped
100g/4 oz white or brown breadcrumbs
Freshly ground black pepper

Preheat oven to 250°F/120°C/Gas Mark ¼

Put both lots of beans in a large pan together with the chopped onion, garlic, bay leaf and stock. Bring to the boil, cover and simmer for 30 minutes. Drain beans and reserve the stock.

Gigot d'Agneau (top) and Lamb Chops in Caper Sauce (bottom).

Put a layer of the bean mixture into the base of a large casserole and season with pepper. Cover with the pork, another layer of beans and pepper, then add the lamb, more beans and the sausage. Sprinkle with oregano, pour the tomatoes over the sausage and cover with a final layer of beans. Pour the reserved stock into the casserole until it just covers the top layer of beans. Sprinkle half the breadcrumbs over the beans. Cover with a lid.

Place the casserole on a baking tray near the bottom of the oven and cook on lowest heat for at least 10 – 12 hours – as long as 24 hours if you like! Top up with more stock from time to time if necessary.

Before serving, remove lid, push down the crust which will have formed, sprinkle the rest of the breadcrumbs on the top and turn up the oven to 300°F/150°C/Gas Mark 2. Return cassoulet to the oven and cook, uncovered, for a further 45 minutes.

Serve with a green salad and hot French bread or rolls.

PORK WITH PAPRIKA CREAM SAUCE

SERVES 6

Above: Normandy Veal with Apples and Calvados.

Facing page: Pork Escalopes Baked in Cider with Horseradish and Apple (top left), Pork with Paprika Cream Sauce (top right) and Pork Chops Baked in Foil (bottom left).

675g – 900g/1½ – 2 lb pork fillet
1 tablespoon vegetable oil
25g/1 oz butter
1 large onion, finely chopped
1 tablespoon paprika
1 tablespoon plain flour
150ml/¼ pint medium sherry
300ml/½ pint chicken stock
225g/½ lb button mushrooms, sliced
150ml/5 fl oz double cream or thick yoghurt
Salt and pepper

In a heavy based pan, heat together the oil and butter. Cut the pork into bite-sized pieces and fry quickly, turning once. Add the onion and paprika, reduce the heat and cook for 3 – 4 minutes. With a wooden spoon, stir in the flour, cook for a further minute and add the sherry and stock. Bring to the boil and simmer gently for 30 – 40 minutes until the meat is tender.

Meanwhile, in another pan, sauté the mushrooms for three to four minutes. Add to the pork and season to taste with salt and pepper. Pour in the double cream or yoghurt and serve.

NORMANDY VEAL WITH APPLES AND CALVADOS

This recipe is delicious and easy to prepare, and works equally well with pork fillet instead of veal. However, allow 10-15 minutes cooking time if you do use pork.

4 x 100g/4 oz veal escalopes, beaten thinly
100g/4 oz butter
2 dessert apples
50g/2 oz mushrooms, wiped and sliced thinly
4 tablespoons Calvados
2 tablespoons lemon juice
150ml/5 fl oz double cream or Greek yoghurt
Salt and pepper
1 tablespoons chopped fresh chives or parsley

Peel, core and thinly slice the apples. Melt the butter in a large frying pan and, when it starts to foam, add the apple and sliced mushrooms and sauté gently until tender and just starting to brown. Reserve and set aside. Season the escalopes with salt and pepper, add to the pan and fry quickly on both sides.

In a small saucepan, warm the Calvados, set it alight and pour it over the veal. Gently move the frying pan so the liqueur is evenly distributed, until the flame dies down. Reduce the heat and add the cream or yoghurt, the lemon juice and the apples and mushrooms. Cook for a further 2 – 3 minutes, stirring continuously until the sauce starts to thicken. Do not boil. Transfer the escalopes to a hot serving dish, adjust the seasoning in the sauce if necessary and pour the sauce over the meat. Garnish with the chives or parsley.

BEEF STROGANOFF

SERVES 4

675g/1½ lb rump or fillet steak
100g/4 oz butter
1 medium onion, peeled and thinly sliced
225g/½ lb mushrooms, sliced
25g/1 oz flour
1 level tablespoon tomato purée
1 x 300g/10.6 oz can consommé, or equivalent
   amount of good beef stock
Salt
Freshly ground black pepper
150ml/5 fl oz soured cream
1 tablespoon finely chopped parsley

Cut the meat into strips approximately 7.5 x 2.5 cm/3" x 1". Melt 50g/1 oz of the butter in a large pan and fry the onion for 3–4 minutes until soft. Remove and add the meat a little at a time until it is sealed on all sides. Remove. Add the rest of the butter and fry the mushrooms for 2–3 minutes. Remove.

Stir the flour into the pan juices, followed by the tomato purée and cook for one minute. Add the consommé or stock, stirring continuously until smooth. Return the steak, mushrooms and onion to the pan, adjust the seasoning and heat through thoroughly. Transfer to a warm serving dish and gently stir in the soured cream, creating a marbled effect. Sprinkle with chopped parsley.

PORK CHOPS BAKED IN FOIL

For those people who hate washing-up this is one solution! Try this also with lamb chops parcelled up with vegetables of your choice.

SERVES 4

4 large pork chops
225g/½ lb button mushrooms
25g/1 oz butter
Salt and black pepper
½ teaspoon dried thyme
Juice of half a lemon
1 tablespoon plain flour
4 tablespoons double cream or Greek yoghurt

Chopped parsley to garnish

4 large pieces of tin foil

Preheat oven to 350°F/180°C/Gas Mark 4

In a frying pan, melt the butter and brown the chops on both sides. Transfer each one to a piece of foil large enough to enclose it loosely. Slice the mushrooms and add to the pan, sauté quickly and pour in the lemon juice. After a minute stir in the flour and cook for another minute or two.

Season the chops with salt and pepper and a pinch of thyme and spoon on the mushroom mixture and then the cream or yoghurt. Wrap up the chops securely, place on a baking sheet or roasting tin and bake for an hour in a preheated oven. (They can be left longer without spoiling too much.) Transfer to a serving plate and sprinkle over chopped parsley.

PORK ESCALOPES BAKED IN CIDER WITH HORSERADISH AND APPLE

SERVES 4

4 pork escalopes weighing
   approximately 75g/3oz each
1 large baking-apple
Juice of ½ lemon
1 teaspoon grated lemon rind
2 tablespoons creamed horseradish
600ml/1 pint medium-dry cider
25g/1 oz butter
300ml/10 fl oz double cream
Salt and pepper

Chopped parsley to garnish

Preheat oven to 375°F/190°C/Gas Mark 5

The escalopes should be beaten nice and thin for this dish.

Firstly, grate the baking apple into a bowl, sprinkle with lemon juice and rind and spread this on one side of the escalopes. Roll each one up and secure with a cocktail stick or skewer. Spread the horseradish along the top of each roll and place in a baking dish. Pour over the cider and cover with baking foil. Place in a preheated oven and bake for about 1¼ hours until tender.

With a slotted spoon, remove the escalopes to a serving dish and keep them warm. Pour the cider and meat juices into a saucepan and boil rapidly over high heat until "syrupy" and reduced to approximately half the original volume. Add the butter in small pieces, reduce heat and add the cream. Heat through thoroughly without boiling. Season to taste and pour over the pork escalopes.

Serve with creamed potatoes and a green vegetable to counteract the richness of this dish.

Chicken and Avocado Pear Salad with Grapes and Tarragon (top left), Beef Stroganoff (centre right) and Coronation Chicken (bottom left).

Poultry and Game

ROAST PHEASANT

When roasting pheasant, choose a young, tender bird; the older ones are better casseroled or pot-roasted. Make sure that the pheasant is at room temperature before putting it in the oven, so that the heat will penetrate the meat evenly.

Cock birds are larger than the hen birds and should feed 4 people. Hen birds, although usually plumper, will only feed 2-3 people.

1 good-sized pheasant (wiped inside and out)
Rashers of unsmoked bacon
Softened butter
150ml/5 fl oz stock
150ml/5 fl oz red wine or port
2 tablespoons redcurrant jelly
25g/1 oz finely grated breadcrumbs

STUFFING
1 tablespoon olive oil
1 small onion, finely chopped
1 cooking apple, grated
Juice of ½ lemon
2 tablespoons softened butter
Salt and black pepper

GARNISH
A bunch of fresh watercress

Preheat oven to 400°F/200°C/Gas Mark 6

To make the stuffing, heat the olive oil in a small pan, add the chopped onion and cook until soft and transparent. Grate the apple into a bowl and quickly sprinkle with lemon juice; add the onion together with the softened butter and season to taste. Mix all the ingredients well. Put the stuffing into the body cavity of the cleaned pheasant, packing it well in. Sew up the cavity with a trussing needle and fine string.

Sprinkle the bird with freshly ground black pepper and cover it with the bacon rashers. Spread with a little softened butter before placing it in a roasting tin.

Put in the preheated oven for about 1 hour, basting the pheasant every 10-15 minutes. Test with a skewer in the thickest part of the inside leg to see if it is cooked. When the juices run clear remove the

Roast Pheasant with Game Chips.

bird from the oven – do not over cook or the meat will be dry and tough. Lift the pheasant onto a carving dish, remove the string and bacon and keep the bird warm.

Skim the roasting juices to remove as much fat as possible and then put the roasting tin over a moderate heat. Add the stock and red wine or port and simmer, stirring continually and incorporating all the roasting bits that may be stuck to the bottom of the tin. Stir in the redcurrant jelly and breadcrumbs and keep stirring until the sauce thickens slightly. Adjust seasoning and then transfer to a sauceboat.

Garnish the pheasant with sprigs of watercress before serving.

Game chips and chestnuts are good accompaniments to the pheasant.

GAME CHIPS

Peel and wash the potatoes and slice thinly into rounds. Plunge into cold water and pat dry. Fry in hot fat for about 3 minutes, remove, allow the fat to regain its original heat (about 385°F/196°C) and fry the chips again for just 1 – 2 minutes until golden. Drain on kitchen paper, sprinkle with salt and serve immediately.

CORONATION CHICKEN

Supposedly invented for the Coronation of Queen Elizabeth II, this dish is excellent for summer parties or lunches, particularly as so much of it can be prepared in advance when the sun isn't shining!

SERVES 6

Meat from one 1.4 – 1.5kg/3 – 3½ lb cooked chicken, cut into chunks

CURRY MAYONNAISE
2 tablespoons olive oil
One small onion, peeled and finely chopped
1 level tablespoon curry powder
150ml/¼ pint chicken stock
1 large teaspoon tomato purée
Juice of ½ lemon
2 level tablespoons apricot jam OR sweet chutney
300ml/½ pint mayonnaise (home made or good
    commercial- NOT salad cream)
3 tablespoons double cream

Heat the oil in a saucepan, add the chopped onion, cover and fry gently for 5 minutes until the onion is soft. Stir in the curry powder and cook for a further two minutes to bring out the flavour. Stir in the stock, tomato purée, lemon juice and jam or chutney. Stir until boiling, then cook for 5 minutes until the mixture reduces and thickens. Allow to cool and then stir in the mayonnaise and cream. This sauce should be of a coating consistency. Arrange chicken pieces in a serving dish and spoon the sauce over.

A rice salad with fresh or tinned pineapple, green pepper and sultanas goes well with this dish.

CRISPY CHICKEN BAKE

SERVES 4 – 6

450g/1 lb cooked chicken pieces, diced
2 x 275g/10 oz cans condensed chicken soup
½ cucumber
1 celery heart
100g/4 oz walnuts, chopped
1 lemon
Salt and pepper
3 small packets crisps, crushed
50g/2 oz grated Cheddar cheese

Preheat oven to 425°F/220°C/Gas Mark 7

Mix the chicken with the canned soup. Dice the cucumber and celery. Grate the lemon rind and squeeze the juice. Add these ingredients, together with the chopped walnuts, to the chicken mixture. Season to taste.

Turn into an oven-proof dish and bake for 20 minutes. Turn off oven, sprinkle on a topping of cheese and crushed crisps and return to the oven for a further 3 – 5 minutes.

CHICKEN AND AVOCADO PEAR SALAD WITH GRAPES AND TARRAGON

A quick and easy summer lunch dish.

SERVES 4 – 6

1 cooked 1.6 – 1.8kg/3 ½ – 4 lb chicken
1 – 2 ripe avocado pears
150ml/5 fl oz mayonnaise
90ml/3 fl oz double cream
1 tablespoon chopped fresh tarragon or ½
    teaspoon dried
2 tablespoons lemon juice
1 crisp lettuce
Salt and freshly ground black pepper
100g/4 oz green grapes (seedless if possible)

Remove the meat from the chicken and cut into bite-sized pieces. Peel and slice the avocados, and sprinkle with the lemon juice. Mix the mayonnaise, double cream and tarragon and season to taste with the salt and pepper.

Wash and shred the lettuce and put into the bottom of an attractive serving dish. Gently combine the chicken and avocado with the mayonnaise dressing. Pile onto the lettuce and garnish with the green grapes. Serve at once.

RABBIT IN MUSTARD SAUCE

SERVES 4

1 x 1.8kg/4 lb rabbit, cleaned and cut into serving pieces
4 tablespoons French mustard
25g/1 oz butter
1 tablespoon oil
1 medium onion, finely chopped
25g/1 oz plain flour
1 scant teaspoon dried thyme
1 scant teaspoon rosemary
450ml/¾ pint dry cider
Salt and freshly ground black pepper

Smear the rabbit pieces with the mustard and set aside for a couple of hours to absorb the flavour. Melt the butter and oil together in a large frying pan and when the foam subsides fry the rabbit pieces, a few at a time, until golden brown. Transfer them to a flameproof casserole.

Add the chopped onion to the frying pan, adding a little more oil if necessary. Fry until soft and then add the flour and herbs, stirring constantly. Cook for 1 – 2 minutes over gentle heat, then add the cider. Stir the sauce well and bring to the boil. Season to taste and pour the thickened sauce over the rabbit pieces. Cover the casserole and simmer gently for 45 minutes to 1 hour until tender.

This dish is delicious served with buttered noodles and a green salad or vegetable. French bread is also a handy accompaniment to mop up all the lovely juices.

CORIANDER CHICKEN

A lovely combination of flavours turns a chicken into something special. This dish can be prepared well in advance and cooked for about an hour just before serving.

SERVES 6

1.8kg/4 lb chicken, skinned (or 2 small chickens)
2 tablespoons lime or lemon juice

Rabbit in Mustard Sauce.

2-3 fresh, hot green chilli peppers, very finely
   chopped
1 bunch fresh coriander leaves (with roots and
   lower stems removed), very finely chopped
¼ teaspoon cayenne pepper
2 x 2.5 cm/1″ cubes of fresh ginger, peeled and
   finely chopped
150ml/5 fl oz plain yoghurt
6 cloves garlic, peeled and crushed
2 tablespoons vegetable oil
Garnish – fresh coriander leaves and lime or
   lemon wedges

Preheat oven to 400°F/200°C/Gas Mark 6

Combine the lime or lemon juice, salt and chilli in a
large bowl and rub this mixture into the chicken,
which has been skinned and pricked all over with a
fork. Set this to one side whilst the marinade is prepared. Put the coriander, cayenne pepper, ginger and
yoghurt into a bowl and mix well. This marinade is
then added to the bowl containing the chicken,
making sure that it is rubbed all over. Cover the bowl
with cling film and set aside for at least 6 hours.
Longer will not hurt, providing it is properly
covered.

Put the vegetable oil in a roasting tin along with
the chicken and marinade mixture. Bake the chicken
in the centre of the oven for 20 minutes. Reduce the
oven temperature to 350°F/180°C/Gas Mark 4 and
continue baking for about 45 minutes or until the
chicken is tender. The chicken needs to be regularly
basted with the pan juices. Skim any fat from the pan
juices with a spoon. Place the chicken on a hot
serving platter, spoon over the sauce and serve
immediately, garnished with the fresh coriander
leaves and wedges of lime or lemon.

Saffron rice is a good accompaniment to this dish.
Try also the okra, or cauliflower with mustard seed.

SPICED ORIENTAL CHICKEN

*A multitude of spices transform an everyday
chicken into a delectable experience.*

SERVES 6 – 8

2 x 1.125kg-1.35kg/2 ½ lb-3lb chickens, skinned
   and pricked with a fork
10 dried curry leaves, crumbled
¾ -1 teaspoon cayenne pepper
2 teaspoons ground coriander
1 teaspoon ground cumin
2-3 fresh hot green chilli peppers, finely chopped
2 x 2.5 cm/1″ cubes fresh ginger, finely chopped
1 cinnamon stick, broken into pieces
1 teaspoon turmeric
5 cloves garlic finely chopped
2 bay leaves, crumbled
2 teaspoons salt
2 Spanish onions, finely chopped
6 tablespoons vegetable oil
300ml/10 fl oz tin coconut milk or 225g/8 oz

finely cut desiccated coconut (unsweetened)
1 teaspoon sugar
2 teaspoons lime juice

FOR SPRINKLING OVER THE CHICKEN JUST
   BEFORE SERVING

½ teaspoon ground coriander
½ teaspoon garam masala
¼ teaspoon freshly ground cloves
½ teaspoon freshly ground cardamoms
½ teaspoon ground cinnamon

Mix together in a large bowl the curry leaves,
cayenne, coriander, cumin, chilli, ginger, cinnamon,
turmeric, garlic, bay leaves, salt, onion and vegetable
oil. Rub this mixture over the 2 skinned chickens.
Leave the chickens in the bowl and cover with cling
film. Allow them to marinate overnight in a cool
place.

Brown the chickens and spice mixture in a large
flame-proof casserole. Add the coconut milk, cover
and simmer gently until the chicken is tender (about
45-60 minutes). Remove the chickens and keep
warm. (If tinned coconut milk is unavailable then it
can be made by pouring 450ml/15 fl oz of boiling
water over the desiccated coconut. Let it stand for 20
minutes, then squeeze the milk out of it.)

Add the sugar to the casserole juices and reduce the
liquid a little, stir in the lime juice and then pour this
sauce over the chickens.

Mix the remaining spices together and sprinkle
over the chickens just before serving.

Saffron rice goes well with this dish and try some
of the side dishes mentioned below.

SAFFRON RICE

*A sweet yellow rice which is delicious with both
English and Indian foods.*

SERVES 4

½ teaspoon saffron threads
2 tablespoons warm milk
225g/8 oz rice (Basmati is particularly good for
   this dish)
50g/2 oz butter
2 cardamom pods
2.5 cm/1″ cinnamon stick
300ml/½ pint water
½ teaspoon salt
75g/3 oz sugar
25g/1 oz blanched flaked almonds
25g/1 oz sultanas

Preheat oven to 300°F/150°C/Gas Mark 2

Spiced Oriental Chicken (top), with Saffron Rice,
Cauliflower with Mustard Seed, Coconut, Okra,
Cucumber Salad with Yoghurt and Mint, Dhal, Cashew
Nuts, and Coriander Chicken (bottom).

Place the saffron in a heavy-based frying pan over medium heat and stir around until the threads darken. Remove from the heat. Add the saffron to the warmed milk in a small bowl and leave for 2-3 hours.

Wash the rice well, soak it for at least half an hour and allow to drain for the same amount of time.

Melt the butter in a large flame-proof casserole over medium heat, add the cardamom pods and cinnamon stick and stir them around very quickly before adding the rice. Cook the rice for 3-4 minutes, stirring to prevent it sticking. Add the water and salt and cook the rice gently until all the water is absorbed, again stirring with a wooden spoon. Add the saffron milk, almonds, sultanas and sugar. Combine all these ingredients well before putting the casserole in the oven, covered with a lid or tinfoil. Cook for a further 30 minutes, remove from the oven and serve. Remember to take out the cardamom pods and cinnamon stick.

CAULIFLOWER WITH MUSTARD SEED

1 large cauliflower
6 tablespoons vegetable oil
1 tablespoon whole black mustard seeds
2 teaspoons whole fennel seeds
1 teaspoon whole cumin seeds
¼ teaspoon turmeric
4 cloves garlic peeled and finely chopped
2 fresh green chilli peppers, finely chopped
1 teaspoon salt
Cold water

Cut cauliflower into small florets, wash and drain them. Heat the oil in a large, heavy-based frying pan over medium heat. When hot add the mustard, fennel and cumin seeds. When the mustard seeds start to pop (after a few seconds) add the garlic, salt and chilli and stir-fry until lightly browned. Add a few tablespoons of water and the cauliflower and cook for about 5 minutes until the cauliflower is cooked but still firm. Add extra water if necessary to prevent the pan from drying out.

DHAL

225g/½ lb split lentils or yellow split peas
3 tablespoons ghee or unsalted butter
1 small onion, finely chopped
1 teaspoon ground cumin
1 teaspoon ground coriander
¼ teaspoon turmeric
½ teaspoon chilli powder
2 red chilli peppers (seeds removed)
2 cardamoms
5cm/2" piece of cinnamon stick
2 cloves garlic, finely chopped
900ml/1½ pints cold water

Wash the lentils or peas thoroughly and drain. Heat the ghee over a medium heat and add the chopped onion. When it begins to colour add the cumin, coriander, turmeric, chilli powder and peppers, cardamom, cinnamon and garlic. Stir once and add the lentils or peas together with 900ml/1½ pints of cold water. Bring to the boil, cover and simmer gently until cooked (about 15 minutes). The thickness of the dhal will depend upon the amount of water added.

COCONUT

Put freshly grated coconut into a frying pan over medium heat. Stir constantly until the coconut is golden. Season with a little salt and transfer to a serving dish.

Alternatively, use unsweetened desiccated coconut toasted in the bottom of a low oven.

OKRA (LADIES' FINGERS)

Take 450g/1 lb okra, rinse, pat dry and cut off both ends. Bring a small amount of salted water to the boil (enough to just cover the okra), plunge in the okra, turn down the heat and simmer until tender (less than 10 minutes – be careful not to overcook it). Serve at once.

ROAST SADDLE OF VENISON WITH SPICED PEARS

This is an impressive main course for a special occasion, such as New Year's Eve. Venison is now more readily available at some butchers and supermarkets. It is a lean meat and benefits from being marinated for 24 – 48 hours before cooking.

SERVES 8 – 10

MARINADE

300ml/½ pint good oil
300ml/½ pint wine vinegar
600ml/1 pint white wine
Bouquet garni
A few parsley stalks
Rind of ½ an orange
8 crushed juniper berries
1 sliced onion
1 stick celery
1 clove garlic, crushed

In a saucepan bring the above ingredients to the boil. Simmer for 5 minutes and, when cool, pour over the meat. Turn the meat several times during the marinating.

Roast Saddle of Venison with Spiced Pears.

1 saddle venison (6 – 7 lbs)
4 – 5 ripe pears, according to numbers being
   catered for
Butter
Salt and pepper
2 teaspoons cinnamon

Preheat oven to 375°F/190°C/Gas Mark 5

Roasting time 15 minutes per lb.

Remove the venison from the marinade and pat dry with paper towels. Lay the meat in a roasting tin, rub the surface with butter and sprinkle with salt and pepper. Cover with foil and roast for 2 hours, basting the meat frequently. Remove foil and cook for a further hour, continuing to baste.

30 minutes before end of cooking time slice pears in half , dot with butter and sprinkle with cinnamon. Add to the roasting tin. Baste together with the meat.

Using a skewer, test for tenderness in the chest part of the venison.

CHICKEN HAM AND LEEK PIE

The addition of cream and egg yolks at the end of the cooking time makes this pie extra special.

SERVES 6 – 8

1 x 1.4kg/3 lb chicken
1 onion
1 bay leaf
Parsley stalks
Salt and black pepper
100g/ ¼ lb cooked ham (in small pieces)
450g/1 lb leeks
25g/1 oz butter
300ml/½ pint chicken stock
1 tablespoon parsley
350-400g/12-14 oz puff pastry
150ml/¼ pint double cream
1 egg, lightly beaten for glazing

Preheat oven to 450°F/230°C/Gas Mark 8

Put the cleaned chicken in a large saucepan together with the onion, bay leaf, parsley stalks and salt and pepper. Cover with cold water and bring gently to the boil. Allow to simmer for about 45

Above: Chicken, Ham and Leek Pie.

Facing page: ingredients for Partridge Casserole.

minutes until the chicken is tender. Leave it to cool in the pan. Meanwhile, wash and trim the leeks and cut into 4cm/1½″ pieces. Melt the butter in a small pan and gently sauté the leeks for about 5 minutes. Remove from the heat. Take the cooled chicken out of the pan, remove the skin and strip off the flesh. Cut it into good-sized pieces. Put the chicken, ham, leeks and parsley into a large pie dish with plenty of seasoning. Pour over 300ml/½ pint of the stock from the chicken.

Roll out the pastry slightly larger than the size of the pie dish. Use the trimmings to line the rim of the dish. Dampen them and put on the pastry lid. Trim and seal the edges together firmly. Any surplus pastry can be used to make decorative leaves. Cut a few slits in the pastry to allow the steam to escape. Brush the pastry well with beaten egg.

Bake in the centre of a preheated oven for 15 minutes, remove and glaze again with beaten egg. Reduce the temperature of the oven to 400°F/200°C Gas Mark 6. Return the pie to the oven for another 20 minutes.

When the pie is ready, i.e. the top is golden brown, remove it from the oven and carefully lift off a segment of pastry and pour in the cream which has been gently warmed together with any of the beaten egg.

Serve the pie with creamed potatoes and a green vegetable.

PARTRIDGE CASSEROLE

SERVES 4

175g/6 oz bacon, cubed
25g/1 oz oil or lard
2 young partridges, quartered
1 onion, chopped
1 carrot, sliced
2 sticks celery, sliced
2 medium cooking apples, sliced
10g/½ oz flour
185ml/6 fl oz cider (or dry white wine)
185ml/6 fl oz stock
75g/3 oz seedless raisins
1 bouquet garni
Salt and black pepper
150ml/¼ pint cream or yoghurt

To finish: triangular-shaped croûtons

Heat the oil or lard in a heavy-based casserole and add the bacon. Fry gently until brown and remove. Sauté the partridge quarters until well browned on all sides. Remove.

Add the vegetables and apple slices and fry for five minutes. Add the flour and stir for a minute before adding the cider, stock, bouquet garni and raisins. Season to taste. Return the partridges to the casserole. Cover with a lid and cook slowly for 25 – 30 minutes until the meat is tender. Remove the partridge quarters to a hot serving dish and keep warm.

If the sauce is too runny, boil to reduce. Lower heat and add the cream or yoghurt. Adjust seasoning. Discard the bouquet garni and pour the sauce over the partridges. Surround them with the croûtons.

CHICKEN PROVENÇALE

Crusty bread and a green salad go well with this informal supper dish.

SERVES 4

1 teaspoon salt
1 teaspoon black pepper
1 clove garlic, crushed
1.8kg/4 lb chicken, cut into serving pieces
3 tablespoons olive oil
1 medium onion, finely chopped
225g/½ lb mushrooms, halved
25g/1 oz flour
175ml/6 fl oz white wine
110ml/4 fl oz chicken stock
3 tomatoes, peeled, seeded and coarsely chopped
½ teaspoon basil
6 black olives, halved and stoned
4 anchovy fillets, chopped
2 anchovy fillets, halved

Preheat oven to 325°F/160°C/Gas Mark 3

Rub the salt, pepper and crushed garlic into the chicken pieces and set aside. Melt the oil in a large flameproof casserole and, when hot, sauté the chicken pieces, turning them often until they are evenly browned. Reduce the heat, add the chopped onion and cook for about 20 – 25 minutes, until the chicken is tender. Remove the chicken to an ovenproof casserole and keep it warm in the oven whilst making the sauce.

Halve the mushrooms, add to the original casserole and sauté for 2 – 3 minutes. Stir in the flour and cook for half a minute before gradually pouring in the wine and stock. Bring the sauce to the boil, stirring continually. Add the tomatoes,

basil, olives and chopped anchovies. Bring to the boil again then reduce the heat and simmer for 10 minutes. Remove the chicken from the oven and pour over the sauce. Garnish with the halved anchovies. Serve immediately.

CHICKEN BREASTS WITH CREAM AND FRESH TARRAGON

This is a good dish to prepare, especially when fresh tarragon is plentiful. It is also very quick to cook.

SERVES 4

4 chicken breasts
50g/2 oz butter
2 tablespoons fresh tarragon leaves
150ml/¼ pint white wine
150ml/¼ pint double cream
Salt and black pepper

Melt the butter in a large frying or sauté pan and, when foaming, add the chicken breasts (this can be done 2 at a time). Sauté the breasts for about 3-4 minutes a side or until cooked. Remove to a warm serving dish. Add the wine and tarragon to the pan juices and boil rapidly until the sauce reduces and thickens slightly. Reduce the heat and pour in the cream. Reheat gently without boiling, season to taste, put the chicken breasts back into the pan for another minute and then serve immediately.

BLUE STILTON CHICKEN

4 chicken breasts, skinned, boned and beaten flat
100g/4 oz Blue Stilton (or Danish Blue) cheese
75g/3 oz butter
2 tablespoons thick cream
1 tablespoon parsley, finely chopped
8 rashers bacon
25g/1 oz oil
25g/1 oz butter
150ml/¼ pint dry white wine
150ml/¼ pint chicken stock
1 dessertspoon cornflour
Salt and pepper
Wooden cocktail sticks or small skewers

In a bowl, cream together the cheese and butter then add the cream to make a spreading consistency. Add the parsley.

Spread the cheese mixture on one side only of the chicken breasts, leaving a narrow border. Roll the breasts up, wrap each one in 2 bacon rashers and secure with a cocktail stick or skewer.

In a flameproof casserole, melt the oil and butter together and, when sizzling, brown the chicken breasts on each side until golden. Pour in the wine,

Chicken Provençale (top left), Chicken Breasts with Cream and Fresh Tarragon (top right) and Blue Stilton Chicken (bottom).

chicken stock and seasoning (go gently with the salt because the cheese stuffing will be quite salty). Bring to the boil, cover and simmer gently for about 40 minutes, turning occasionally. When cooked, remove the chicken to a hot serving dish and take out the sticks or skewers.

Blend the cornflour in a cup with a little cold water and add to the pan juices. Stir until the sauce thickens, adjust seasoning if necessary and pour over the chicken. Serve at once.

PIGEONS IN RED WINE

This dish, served with creamed potatoes and a green vegetable, is suitable for a winter supper or dinner party.

SERVES 4

6 rashers of streaky bacon, chopped
1½ tablespoons oil
2 medium onions, finely chopped
4 pigeons
300ml/½ pint chicken stock
300ml/½ pint red wine
1 bay leaf
1 scant teaspoon thyme
100g/¼ lb mushrooms, thinly sliced

Preheat oven to 350°F/180°C/Gas Mark 4

In a large casserole, heat the oil and fry the bacon until crisp. Using a slotted spoon, remove the bacon to a plate. Add the onion to the oil and cook until soft. Remove. Add the pigeons to the oil, turning frequently, until the skin is slightly crisp. Add the chicken stock and red wine so that the liquid almost covers the birds. Add the cooked bacon, onion, bay leaf, thyme and mushrooms and, placing the pigeons breast-side down, cook in a moderate oven for approximately 1½ hours. Test with a sharp knife. The meat should feel very tender.

Remove the pigeons to a warm serving dish. To the sauce add a beurre manié (i.e. 1 dessertspoon butter worked together on a plate with 1 dessertspoon plain flour), beating well with a wooden spoon. This will thicken the sauce, some of which can be poured over the pigeons. Serve the rest in a warm sauce boat.

Below: Pigeons in Red Wine.

Facing page: Chicken Kiev (left) and Chicken Kromeskies (right).

CHICKEN KROMESKIES

A good way of using up left-over chicken!

SERVES 4

225g/½ lb cooked chicken meat, diced or
   minced
10g/½ oz butter
50g/2 oz mushrooms, finely chopped
300ml/10 fl oz Béchamel sauce
1 egg yolk
Salt and black pepper
4 rashers of bacon, derinded
Fritter batter
Oil or fat for deep frying

Melt the butter in a frying pan, add the finely
chopped mushrooms and cook for 2–3 minutes.
Add the chicken, Béchamel sauce, egg yolk and
seasoning, mix well and cook over a fast heat until
the mixture starts to leave the sides of the pan.
Leave to cool.

Cut each rasher of bacon in half and stretch each
piece with a knife blade. Divide the cooked
chicken mixture into 8 even portions and shape
into croquettes on a floured board. Wrap a piece of
bacon around each one, dip in fritter batter and fry
in deep fat until golden brown.

Serve hot with home made tomato sauce.

CHICKEN KIEV

*Boned chicken breasts are readily available in
supermarkets these days, alternatively your
butcher will happily bone them for you.*

SERVES 4

4 chicken breasts about 200g/7 oz each
100g/4 oz unsalted butter
Grated rind and juice of a small lemon
2 cloves garlic, crushed
2 tablespoons parsley and tarragon, mixed and
   finely chopped
Salt and black pepper
25g/1 oz seasoned flour
1–2 eggs, beaten
100g/4 oz fresh white breadcrumbs
Oil or fat for deep frying

GARNISH

Lemon wedges
Watercress

Cream together in a bowl the butter, lemon rind and
juice, garlic, herbs and season to taste with salt and
pepper. Shape the butter into a rectangular block,
wrap it in foil or greaseproof paper and chill until
solid.

Flatten the chicken breasts and season with salt

and pepper. Cut the chilled butter into 4 fingers and put one on each chicken breast. Fold the edges over neatly and roll each one up tightly. Dust with seasoned flour. Beat the eggs lightly and brush over the meat, then coat each chicken breast in breadcrumbs. Pat the breadcrumbs on firmly. Repeat the egg and breadcrumb process and then refrigerate the chicken for at least 30 minutes so that the coating sets.

Heat the oil or fat to 180°C/350°F in a deep fat fryer and lower in the chicken breasts gently, 2 at a time. Fry for 12 – 15 minutes until they are golden brown. Drain them on kitchen paper and keep hot whilst frying the rest.

Serve with new potatoes and a green vegetable. Garnish with a lemon wedge and watercress.

Give your guests sufficient warning that the garlic butter is quite likely to spurt out if the first incision is not a careful one.

DUCK BREASTS IN BLACK CHERRY SAUCE

SERVES 4

4 duck breasts
Salt and freshly milled black pepper
175g/6 oz morello cherry jam
150ml/¼ pint red wine
Watercress

Preheat oven to 350°F/180°C/Gas Mark 4

Rub the duck breast with the salt and lightly season with black pepper. Gently prick the skin of the duck breasts. Place in the oven and cook for 20 – 25 minutes (depending on the size) until cooked.

Meanwhile, simply place the jam and wine in a saucepan and bring to the boil, then simmer for about 10 minutes.

To serve the duck, place it on a bed of watercress and spoon over a little of the sauce. Serve the rest separately in a sauce boat.

Mangetout and new potatoes go very well with this dish.

TURKEY ESCALOPES IN AN ORANGE AND LEMON SAUCE

4 x 150-175g/5-6 oz turkey escalopes
25g/1 oz butter
1 tablespoon good cooking oil
10g/½ oz butter
1 dessertspoon flour
150ml/5 fl oz chicken stock
Juice of half a lemon
Juice of half an orange
Salt and black pepper
Zest of 1 orange, cut in julienne strips
Zest of 1 lemon, cut in julienne strips
Chopped parsley

Flatten the escalopes slightly.

In a large frying pan, melt the butter and sauté the turkey escalopes, two at a time, for about 4-5 minutes on each side until cooked. Remove them to a hot serving dish and keep them warm.

Melt the 10g/½ oz butter in the pan, add the flour and cook for a further minute before gradually adding the chicken stock and fruit juice. Stir well (any lumps can be worked out with a balloon whisk) until a smooth sauce is achieved. Season with salt and black pepper. If the sauce is too thick, thin down with a little more stock or cold water.

Meanwhile, boil the zest in a little water for about a minute – this reduces the bitterness. Drain well.

To finish, pour the sauce over the turkey escalopes and garnish with the orange and lemon zest and a little chopped parsley.

POUSSINS IN A CURRY SAUCE

SERVES 4

4 poussins
50g/2 oz butter
1 teaspoon good cooking oil
1 medium onion, finely chopped
1 clove garlic, crushed
1 dessertspoon curry powder
150ml/¼ pint chicken stock
1 dessertspoon mango chutney
Squeeze of lemon juice
25g/1 oz sultanas
1 rounded teaspoon cornflour
Cold water

Preheat oven to 350°F/180°C/Gas Mark 4

Put 50g/2 oz butter and the oil in a roasting tin and put into the oven. When sizzling, remove from the oven, add the poussins and baste well. Return the tin to the oven and roast the birds for about 35 minutes, basting at regular intervals until they are cooked. Test with a skewer inserted into the fattest part of the leg. If the liquid runs clear, the poussins are cooked. Remove from the roasting tin and keep them warm.

Drain off any excess fat from the tin and place it over a medium heat. Add the chopped onion and garlic and sauté for a few minutes until softened. Reduce the heat, add the curry powder and stir well for 2 – 3 minutes. Pour in the chicken stock and stir

Poussins in a Curry Sauce (top), Duck Breasts in Black Cherry Sauce (bottom left) and Turkey Escalopes in an Orange and Lemon Sauce (bottom right).

until it is bubbling. Add the squeeze of lemon juice, chutney and sultanas.

In a cup, blend the cornflour with a little cold water and add it to the sauce. Mix well and cook for a few more minutes. Pour over the poussins or serve separately.

Poppadums and little castles of rice are appropriate accompaniments.

COQ AU VIN

SERVES 4

100g/4 oz streaky, rindless bacon, cut into cubes
1.4kg/3 lb chicken pieces
25g/1 oz butter
12 button onions, peeled and left whole
2 bay leaves
2 cloves garlic, crushed
1 bouquet garni
225g/½ lb mushrooms, sliced
900ml/1½ pints full bodied red wine
50g/2 oz beurre manié (1 tablespoon plain flour blended with 25g/1 oz softened butter)
Salt and black pepper

GARNISH

Fried bread croûtons
Parsley

Preheat oven to 350°F/180°C/Gas Mark 4

Fry the bacon until it has browned and rendered its fat and, with a slotted spoon, remove from the pan. Next add the butter to the fat and melt over gentle heat. When the foam subsides, add the chicken joints and fry until golden on both sides. Remove them to a large flame-proof casserole. Fry the button onions until a little brown and then lightly fry the mushrooms.

Add the onions and mushrooms to the casserole

together with the bacon, crushed garlic, bay leaves and bouquet garni. Pour over the red wine and season with black pepper and a little salt. Bring to a steady simmer over gentle heat. Add pieces of the beurre manié until the sauce thickens, cover the casserole and continue cooking over a low heat OR place in a moderate oven until the chicken is tender – about 45 – 60 minutes.

Remove bay leaves and bouquet garni and garnish with fried bread croûtons and chopped parsley.

GRILLED QUAIL WITH SAUTÉED MUSHROOMS

A quick and easy way of cooking these delicious small game birds.

SERVES 4

4 quail
1 cup white breadcrumbs
100g/4 oz butter
175g/6 oz mushrooms
1 glass of sherry
4 slices bread cut into 4 rounds and fried until
    golden in a mixture of oil and butter

Parsley to garnish

Melt half the butter, brush over the quail and dip them in the breadcrumbs. Grill under medium heat for 10 minutes each side.

Sauté the mushrooms in 50g/2 oz of the butter, add the sherry and cook for 2 minutes.

Serve on the crôutes of fried bread.

Facing page: Coq au Vin.

Below: Grilled Quail with Sautéed Mushrooms.

Vegetables and Salads

WILD RICE SALAD WITH RADICCHIO

The pumpkin seeds give a crunchy contrast to the rice and are readily obtainable at health food shops.

1 packet of wild rice and long grain mix
Few pumpkin seeds
1 radicchio lettuce
Small quantity French dressing
100g/4 oz frozen prawns
Cayenne pepper
100g-175g/4 – 6 oz mushrooms (button)
4 spring onions
2 carrots, grated
1 apple, chopped
½ a cucumber
Watercress to decorate

Cook rice according to packet instructions, and leave to cool Add pumpkin seeds. Chop spring onions and mix with mushrooms. Marinate in French dressing, overnight if liked. Defrost prawns.

Mix together the carrot and apple and toss in French dressing. Cut cucumber into cubes. Place the rice mixture in the centre of a large plate and dribble a little dressing over.

Place 8 radicchio leaves around the rice and fill each with the other ingredients.

Shake the cayenne over the prawns and decorate the dish with the watercress.

Serve with a bowl of herb and garlic mayonnaise.

NEW POTATO SALAD WITH FRANKFURTERS

Garlic sausage could be substituted for the Frankfurters.

SERVES 4

750g/1½ lb new potatoes
4 Frankfurters, sliced
1 small onion, finely chopped
2 tablespoons parsley, finely chopped
Salt and black pepper
Vinaigrette dressing

Scrub the potatoes but leave on their skins. Boil for 15 – 20 minutes in salted water until tender. Drain

and transfer to a bowl together with the onion, salt and pepper. Cut the potatoes into thick slices, add the Frankfurters and pour on enough vinaigrette to coat and moisten the potato well. Toss gently and, when cool, sprinkle with parsley.

POTATO SALAD

SERVES 6

900g/2 lb potatoes
French dressing
3 – 4 tablespoons good mayonnaise
Salt and pepper
1 – 2 tablespoons chopped raw onion

GARNISH

Plenty of chopped chives or chopped spring , onions or parsley

Peel and dice the potatoes. Boil in salted water for 5 – 10 minutes (be careful the potatoes do not become mushy and break up). Drain well and drizzle on enough French dressing to coat the potatoes well. Allow to cool and add the chopped onion, salt and pepper and gently fold in the mayonnaise.

Garnish with chopped chives, spring onions or parsley.

SALAD NIÇOISE

An ideal first course or substantial summer lunch dish served with crusty French bread. The ingredients can be added to or changed according to your personal taste, or whatever happens to be in your kitchen at the time!

SERVES 6

1 x 200g/7 oz tin tuna fish, flaked
2 hard-boiled eggs, sliced
100g/4 oz cooked French beans
350g/¾ lb firm tomatoes, sliced or quartered
1 green pepper, deseeded, cored and sliced
1 crisp lettuce

Wild Rice Salad with Radicchio.

½ cucumber, peeled and either sliced or cut into chunks
150ml/¼ pint garlicky French dressing
Black olives
1 x 45g/1½ oz tin anchovy fillets
Freshly chopped parsley or chives, if available

Line a large salad bowl with the lettuce leaves and sprinkle on a little of the dressing. Arrange the tomato, cucumber, pepper and French beans in layers. On the top put the flaked tuna fish, make a lattice with the drained anchovy fillets and decorate with the hard-boiled egg slices and the whole black olives.

Just before serving, pour on the rest of the French dressing and garnish with the chopped parsley or chives.

DEEP-FRIED MUSHROOMS

INGREDIENTS FOR 2 DOZEN

24 even-sized button mushrooms
1 egg, beaten
50g/2 oz fresh white breadcrumbs
Parsley to garnish
Oil for deep frying

Above: Potato Salad (top), New Potato Salad with Frankfurters (left) and Salad Niçoise (Bottom).

Facing page: Deep-Fried Mushrooms, Deep-Fried Onion Rings, Fried Broccoli and Fried Courgettes.

Remove the stalks from the mushrooms and reserve for another recipe. Dip the mushroom caps in the beaten egg and coat with breadcrumbs. Deep-fry for 1 minute in hot oil (350°F/180°C) until golden brown. Drain on kitchen paper and serve at once, garnished with parsley.

FRIED COURGETTES

450g/1 lb courgettes – small, young ones
Oil for deep frying
1 egg white, stiffly beaten
Seasoned flour

Cut the courgettes into ½ cm/¼ " sticks or slices. Dip them in the seasoned flour and then into the stiffly beaten egg white.

Heat the oil to 350°F/180°C and deep-fry or shallow-fry the courgettes, a batch at a time, until golden brown. Drain and serve at once.

This also works well with broccoli, but cut the vegetable into small florets first.

DEEP-FRIED ONION RINGS

A family favourite with steak or liver

1 large Spanish onion, sliced in 5mm/¼″ rings
Oil for deep frying
1 egg white, stiffly beaten
Seasoned flour

Heat the oil to 350°F/180°C.

Dip the onion rings, one at a time, into the seasoned flour and then into the egg white. Deep-fry them a few at a time in the hot oil until golden, about 1–2 minutes. Drain on kitchen paper and serve at once.

COURGETTES AU GRATIN

SERVES 4

450g/1 lb courgettes
½ teaspoon salt
150ml/¼ pint water
1 egg
150ml/5 fl oz double cream
2 tablespoons Gruyère cheese, grated (Cheddar makes a good alternative)
Freshly ground black pepper
10g/½ oz butter

Preheat oven to 400°F/200°C/Gas Mark 6

Wipe the courgettes, trim the ends and cut into 1cm/½″ slices. Place them in a saucepan with the salt and water. Cover the pan and cook over moderate heat until almost all the water has evaporated.

In a bowl mix together the egg, cream and 1 tablespoon of the cheese. Season with black pepper.

Carefully place the courgettes into a "gratin" dish or shallow oven-proof dish. Pour over the cream mixture and sprinkle with the rest of the cheese. Dot a few flecks of butter on the surface and bake in the oven for about 10 minutes, or until just set and golden-brown.

CHINESE SALAD

Salad is actually not a part of Chinese cuisine, but certain Chinese vegetables mixed together and tossed in a soy sauce dressing make an interesting, crunchy salad.

SERVES 4 – 6

225g/½ lb Chinese leaves
100g/4 oz bean sprouts
100g/4 oz bean shoots, thinly sliced
100g/4 oz water chestnuts, thinly sliced
1 stick celery, thinly sliced
50g/2 oz mushrooms, wiped and thinly sliced

Bunch of radishes
1 tablespoon chopped chives or spring onions
DRESSING

75g/3 oz spring onions – green part only – finely chopped
150ml/¼ pint rice vinegar or white wine vinegar
2 tablespoons soy sauce
200ml/⅓ pint groundnut oil
2 tablespoons sesame seed oil
1 dessertspoon sugar
1 teaspoon salt
½ teaspoon ground ginger

An hour before starting, finely slice the radishes almost through with a knife and put in the refrigerator in a bowl of cold water.

Shred the Chinese leaves and put them into a salad bowl together with the other vegetables. Drain the radishes and add.

Put all the dressing ingredients into a screw-top jar, shake well and, just before serving, pour over the salad and toss well.

STUFFED TOMATOES

This makes a lovely light lunch served with salad or is a good accompaniment for any grilled meats.

SERVES 4

4 large even-sized tomatoes
4 rashers of streaky bacon, de-rinded and chopped
1 large onion, finely chopped
1½ mugs of cooked white rice (approximately 75-100g/3-4 oz long grain rice)
1 pinch of mixed herbs
1 clove crushed garlic (optional)
Salt and freshly milled black pepper
A sprinkling of Parmesan or Cheddar cheese

Preheat oven to 350°F/180°C/Gas Mark 4

First prepare the tomatoes by cutting off and discarding the stalk end, then scoop out the flesh and seeds. Put these in a bowl and set aside. Leave the scooped out tomatoes turned down to drain on kitchen paper whilst you prepare the filling.

In a large frying pan, sauté the chopped bacon, turning occasionally until crisp. If necessary, add a little oil at this stage. Add the finely chopped onion and garlic, if using. Gently cook the onion until translucent but not browned. Add the cooked rice, tomato flesh, mixed herbs and seasoning. Cook over a moderate heat, turning frequently until all the ingredients are heated through.

Facing page: Chinese Salad. Overleaf: Stuffed Tomatoes (left), Courgettes au Gratin (centre) and Stuffed Green Peppers (right).

Carefully fill the tomato shells with the stuffing, using a teaspoon. Don't pack them too tightly or the tomatoes will burst whilst cooking. Sprinkle the top of the stuffed tomatoes with a little Parmesan or Cheddar cheese.

Carefully lift the tomatoes onto a greased baking tray and place in the centre of the oven for about 10 minutes, or until they feel tender when the skin is pierced with a sharp knife. Serve at once.

POTATO SKINS

SERVES 4 AS A STARTER OR SNACK

2 large baking potatoes
300ml/10 fl oz soured cream
2 tablespoons chopped spring onions, or
    chopped chives or de-rinded streaky bacon
    grilled till crisp then crumbled
50g/2 oz grated Cheddar cheese

Bake the potatoes in a hot oven until cooked. Leave to cool slightly. Cut each in half and scoop out the potato with a spoon, leaving enough inside so that the skins keep their shape. Spoon in the soured cream until nearly filled. Sprinkle with the chopped spring onion or chives or bacon. Top with the grated cheese and place under a preheated grill until golden brown.

The left-over potato can be used as creamed potato for the main course or, if firm enough, can be sautéed in butter and oil with garlic and herbs for flavour.

STUFFED GREEN PEPPERS

This is a tasty supper dish that goes well with rice and crusty bread to mop up all the lovely juices.

SERVES 4

4 even-sized green peppers
450g/1 lb minced beef
A little oil
1 medium onion, finely chopped
1 crushed clove of garlic (optional)
½ teaspoon dried mixed herbs
397g/1 x 14 oz tin of Italian tomatoes
1 tablespoon tomato purée
150ml/¼ pint beef stock made with a stock cube
Salt and freshly ground black pepper

Preheat oven to 350°F/180°C/Gas Mark 4

First begin by preparing the peppers. Cut off the stalk end and cut out all the white pith and remove all the seeds. To be sure all the seeds are removed, turn peppers upside down on a work surface and give them a sharp tap. Place the peppers in an oven-proof dish that can hold them without the peppers falling over.

Heat a little oil in a large frying pan, add the chopped onion and garlic and cook gently until translucent but not brown. Then add the beef and turn constantly until it is evenly browned. Add half the tin of tomatoes and ¾ tablespoon of tomato purée together with the mixed herbs and seasoning. Mix well, turn the heat down and cook for a few minutes. Half the amount of stock should be added to the mince at this stage so that the mixture is nice and moist.

Stuff the peppers with the mince mixture and, if there is any left, place it around the peppers in the oven-proof casserole. Then just tip in the rest of the tinned tomatoes mixed with the tomato purée to provide a sauce for the peppers to cook in. Add the rest of the stock to the casserole, cover and cook in the oven for 20 – 25 minutes, or until the peppers are tender when pierced with a sharp point.

POMMES DE TERRE BOULANGÈRE

SERVES 4 – 6

900g/2 lb potatoes, peeled and thinly sliced
1 large onion, finely chopped
450ml/¾ pint hot stock
50g/2 oz butter
Salt and freshly ground black pepper

Preheat oven to 350°F/180°C/Gas Mark 4

Generously butter a wide, shallow baking dish.

Arrange a layer of potatoes in the base of the dish, then a little onion and salt and pepper. Continue until you have used all the ingredients, finishing with a layer of potatoes and seasoning.

Pour in the stock and fleck the surface with dots of butter. Place the dish on the highest shelf of the oven and cook for 45 minutes. The potatoes should be soft when pierced with a sharp knife or skewer and the top should be golden-brown. They can be finished off under a hot grill if necessary.

SPRING VEGETABLE CURRY

A very mild curry but full of delicious vegetables which, of course, can be varied according to availability. This dish reheats well and can be made a day in advance. If you like your vegetables "crunchy" reduce the cooking times.

SERVES 6 – 8

25g/1 oz butter
2 small onions, finely chopped
2 carrots, cut into sticks
2 courgettes, sliced
2 tomatoes, skinned, deseeded and roughly
    chopped
450ml/¾ pint stock (chicken or vegetable)

Spring Vegetable Curry (top), Pommes Dauphinoises (centre left), Pomme de Terre Boulangère (centre right), Potato Skins (bottom left) and Hot Cucumber and Tarragon in a Lemon Sauce (bottom right).

6 new potatoes, scrubbed
½ small cauliflower, cut into florets
50g/2 oz green beans
50g/2 oz mangetout
25g/1 oz beurre manié (10g/½ oz flour and 10g/½ oz butter blended together to form a smooth paste)
Salt and pepper
1 tablespoon chopped parsley
1 tablespoon chopped fresh mint

CURRY

1 medium onion, finely chopped
25g/1 oz butter
10g/½ oz curry powder
1 dessertspoon apricot jam
Juice of ½ lemon

In a large flame-proof casserole or a saucepan, melt the butter and add the onions, carrots, courgettes and tomatoes. Sauté for about 5 minutes over a gentle heat, stirring occasionally. Then add the stock and the new potatoes and simmer for 10-15 minutes. Add the cauliflower and cook until tender – about 5-10 minutes. Add the beurre manié and stir until the liquid thickens before adding the green beans, mangetout, herbs and seasoning. Simmer for 2 more minutes.

Meanwhile, in a small pan, add the butter and chopped onion and cook until the onion softens. Add the curry powder and fry for a further minute. Finally, mix in the jam and lemon juice, bring to the boil and add this sauce to the vegetables. Incorporate well.

POMMES DAUPHINOISE

This dish is particularly good served with steak.

SERVES 4

450g/1 lb potatoes
40g/1½ oz butter
150ml/¼ pint double cream
150ml/¼ pint milk
1 clove of garlic, crushed
Nutmeg
Salt and freshly ground black pepper

Preheat oven to 400°F/200°C/Gas Mark 6

Peel the potatoes and, on a mandoline or with a very sharp knife, slice into very thin, even slices. Wash the potato slices in cold water to get rid of some of the starch, then dry in a clean tea towel. In a well buttered gratin dish or shallow oven-proof dish, arrange a layer of potato slices, a sprinkling of crushed garlic, salt and pepper and then another layer of potato and seasoning until all the ingredients are used.

Mix together the cream and milk and pour over the potatoes. Sprinkle the surface with freshly grated nutmeg and then fleck the butter on top. Bake on a high shelf of the oven for approximately 1 hour, until golden.

HOT CUCUMBER AND TARRAGON IN A LEMON SAUCE

A lovely first course on a summer's day.

SERVES 4–6

2 cucumbers
Juice of half a lemon
50g/2 oz butter
1 teaspoon flour
4 tablespoons milk
1 tablespoon cream
½ dessertspoon chopped tarragon
Salt and pepper

Garnish – few sprigs of tarragon

Peel the cucumbers and cut in quarters lengthways, removing all the seeds. Cut into 2.5cm/1″ segments. Cook in a little salted boiling water, together with a squeeze of lemon juice, for a few minutes until tender. Meanwhile, prepare the sauce by melting 20g/¾ oz of the butter in a saucepan and stirring in the teaspoonful of flour. Add the milk gradually and bring to simmering point, stirring all the time until the sauce is smooth. Remove the pan from the heat and add the rest of the butter bit by bit, stirring again until you have a smooth, buttery sauce. Add the cream, lemon juice and chopped tarragon. Season to taste. When the cucumber is cooked, drain well and toss in the lemon sauce. Garnish with a few sprigs of tarragon.

THREE LETTUCE SALAD

There are so many different varieties of lettuce now available in the shops that salads need never be dull. Choose three that vary in colour, shape and taste e.g. endive, radicchio, oak leaf, Lamb's lettuce, chicory, cos etc. and toss the leaves in your favourite dressing.

CUCUMBER SALAD WITH YOGHURT AND MINT

A cool, refreshing salad originating from the Middle East.

SERVES 4

1 large cucumber (approximately 375g/12 oz)·
1 teaspoon salt
1 teaspoon sugar
1 tablespoon finely chopped fresh mint
150ml/5 fl oz carton plain yoghurt
Black pepper

Peel and cut the cucumber in half lengthways. Remove the seeds and cut into thin slices. Sprinkle on the salt and sugar and leave to stand for about thirty minutes. Drain well and add the mint, yoghurt and black pepper. Chill and use fairly quickly.

WALDORF SALAD

Created at the famous Waldorf Hotel in New York.

SERVES 6

450g/1 lb crisp eating apples (red and green)
2 tablespoons lemon juice
½ head celery, chopped
50g/2 oz walnuts, roughly chopped
1 lettuce
150ml/¼ pint mayonnaise
Salt and pepper

Wash and core the apples (leave on skins) and slice into a bowl. Sprinkle on the lemon juice and toss in a tablespoon of the mayonnaise. Leave to stand for 30 minutes. Add the celery and walnuts and the rest of the mayonnaise. Season to taste and thoroughly mix all ingredients. Line a salad bowl with the lettuce and pile the salad into the middle.

MUSHROOM QUICHE

SERVES 4–6

PASTRY

175g/6 oz plain flour
Pinch of salt
75g/3 oz butter in small pieces
1 small egg
Cold water

Three Lettuce Salad (top), Waldorf Salad (bottom left) and Cucumber Salad with Yoghurt and Mint (bottom right).

FILLING
225g/8 oz mushrooms, wiped clean and sliced
1 medium onion, finely chopped
25-40g/1-1½ oz butter
2 eggs
150ml/5 fl oz double cream
150ml/5 fl oz milk
Pinch dried sage or 2 fresh leaves chopped finely
Pinch dried mixed herbs
Salt and black pepper
50g/2 oz Cheddar cheese, grated (optional)

Preheat oven to 400°F/200°C/Gas Mark 6

In a large mixing bowl, sieve together the flour and salt. Add the butter and rub into the flour until the mixture resembles breadcrumbs. Add the egg and knead lightly to a firm dough, adding a little cold water if necessary. (The pastry making can, of course, be done in a food processor.) Roll out the pastry on a floured board and use it to line a 23cm/9″ flan dish. Chill for at least 30 minutes.

Facing page: Spiced Red Cabbage.

Below: Spinach and Ham Quiche (top), Mushroom Quiche (bottom left) and Fresh Asparagus Quiche (bottom right).

Heat the butter in a saucepan and sauté the chopped onion until soft and transparent. Add the sliced mushrooms and cook them for 2-3 minutes. Arrange the mushroom mixture on the base of the flan case. Whisk the eggs, cream and milk together, add salt, pepper and herbs and pour this over the filling.

Sprinkle the cheese over the top, if liked, place the flan on a baking sheet and put into the preheated oven. Bake for 30-35 minutes, until the filling is set and the pastry crisp and golden brown. Serve at once – the quiche is at its best at this stage, but will reheat fairly well.

SPICED RED CABBAGE

Particularly good with sausages, ham, roast pork, roast turkey and braised beef. This dish reheats well so it can be made in advance. It also freezes well.

SERVES 4 – 6

---

1 medium red cabbage, quartered, cored and shredded finely
450g/1 lb onions, chopped finely
450g/1 lb apples, peeled, cored and finely chopped

3 tablespoons light soft brown sugar
¼ teaspoon ground cinnamon
¼ teaspoon ground cloves
¼ teaspoon ground nutmeg
Salt and black pepper
5 tablespoons wine vinegar (or white wine)
25g/1 oz butter

Preheat oven to 300°F/150°C/Gas Mark 2

In a large casserole, arrange a layer of cabbage, onion and apple. Season with salt and pepper, sprinkle on a third of the sugar and spices. Repeat twice until all ingredients are used. Pour in the wine vinegar and dot the surface with knobs of butter. Place in the preheated oven and cook gently for 2½ – 3 hours, stirring 2 or 3 times during the cooking.

Serve hot.

FRESH ASPARAGUS QUICHE

This dish is worth preparing when asparagus is in season, and is a good way of using the fine-stalked asparagus or "sprue".

PASTRY
175g/6 oz plain flour
Pinch of salt
75g/3 oz butter in small pieces
1 small egg
Cold water

FILLING
350g/¾ lb "sprue" asparagus
 or medium-sized stalks
50g/2 oz Gruyère or Cheddar cheese, grated
2 large eggs
300ml/10 fl oz double cream
Salt and black pepper

Preheat oven to 350°F/180°C/Gas Mark 4

In a large mixing bowl, sieve the flour and salt. Add the pieces of butter and rub into the flour with your fingertips until the mixture resembles breadcrumbs. Add the egg and knead lightly to a firm dough, adding a little cold water if necessary. Roll out on a floured board and line a 20cm/8" round flan tin. Chill for at least 30 minutes. Prick the base with a fork and bake blind for 15 minutes in a preheated oven. Increase heat to 375°F/190°C/Gas Mark 5.

Steam or boil the asparagus for about 5 minutes and then cut into 2.5 cm/1" lengths. Scatter the asparagus over the pastry base and sprinkle on ¾ of the cheese. Beat together the eggs, cream and seasoning and pour over the asparagus. Sprinkle the remaining cheese over the top. (If you have Parmesan this can be substituted on the top for the Gruyère.)

Bake in the centre of the oven for 30 – 40 minutes until just set and golden brown. Serve warm in order to appreciate the flavour of the fresh asparagus.

RATATOUILLE

A Mediterranean stew of peppers, aubergines, tomatoes, courgettes and onions. Excellent served either hot or cold, on its own or as a starter or with grilled meat. An interesting addition to the buffet table.

SERVES 6 – 8

3 large aubergines
3 large courgettes
2 large onions
2 large green peppers
1 large red pepper
1 large tin tomatoes
2 or 3 large cloves garlic
4 tablespoons olive oil
Salt and black pepper
Fresh parsley or basil

Cut the unpeeled aubergines and courgettes into 6mm/¼" thick slices. Put them in a colander, sprinkle with a little salt and leave for an hour to drain. Pat dry. Peel and coarsely chop the onion, crush the garlic and fry gently in the oil for about 5 minutes until the onion becomes transparent. Do not brown. Cut the peppers into strips and add to the frying pan, together with the aubergines. Cook for a further 20 minutes and add the tomatoes and courgettes. Season with salt and pepper and cover the pan with a lid. Simmer for about 45 – 50 minutes, stirring gently occasionally, until the vegetables are tender but still retain their shape. Serve hot or cold, sprinkled with fresh basil or parsley.

SPINACH AND HAM QUICHE

SERVES 4 – 6

PASTRY
175g/6 oz plain flour
Pinch of salt
75g/3 oz butter in small pieces
1 small egg
Cold water

FILLING
225g/8 oz frozen spinach or
 450g/1 lb fresh spinach
1 medium onion, finely chopped
10g/½ oz butter
100g/4 oz ham, chopped
2 eggs

Ratatouille.

150ml/5 fl oz double cream
Salt and pepper
100g/4 oz Cheddar cheese, grated

Preheat oven to 400°F/200°C/Gas Mark 6

In a large mixing bowl, sieve the flour and salt. Add the pieces of butter and rub between your fingers until the mixture resembles breadcrumbs. Add the egg and knead lightly to a firm dough, adding a little cold water if necessary. Roll out on a floured board and use to line a 23cm/9″ flan dish. Chill for at least 30 minutes.

Cook the frozen spinach in boiling salted water until tender, drain and leave to cool. If using fresh spinach, wash it thoroughly and discard any coarse stalks. Cook in a heavy-based saucepan with just a little butter and salt and pepper. Shake the pan from time to time until the spinach is cooked (about 7 – 8 minutes). Then drain and press out any excess moisture and chop it up with a sharp knife. Leave to cool.

Melt the butter in a pan and cook the chopped onion until soft and transparent but not brown.

Beat together the eggs and cream, and mix in the onion, spinach and ham. Season to taste and add half of the grated Cheddar. Pour this mixture into the flan case and sprinkle with the remaining cheese. Bake in a preheated oven until the filling is golden brown and the pastry crisp.

Serve hot with a green salad.

CAULIFLOWER CHEESE

SERVES 4

1 medium-sized cauliflower
40g/1½ oz margarine or butter
40g/1½ oz flour
300ml/½ pint milk
100g/4 oz Cheddar cheese, grated
Salt and pepper

Cook the cauliflower in boiling salted water until just tender (do not over-cook). Drain and put into an oven-proof dish.

While the cauliflower is cooking, melt the margarine or butter in a small saucepan, stir in the flour and cook for one minute. Remove from the heat and stir in the milk gradually. Bring to the boil and continue to cook until it thickens and is completely smooth, stirring all the time. Add most of the cheese and season with salt and freshly ground black pepper. Pour the sauce over the hot cauliflower, sprinkle with the remaining cheese and brown under a hot grill.

Below: the simple ingredients that go to make Cauliflower Cheese.

Facing page: Celery, Swede and Carrot Bake (left) and Leeks in a White Sauce (right) – Calabrese can also be cooked and served in this fashion.

CELERY, SWEDE AND CARROT BAKE

This "medley" of vegetables with its cheese and breadcrumb topping is a meal in itself, but is good with roasts and pies as well.

SERVES 6 – 8

4 carrots, diced
½ swede, diced
1 large onion, finely chopped
4 sticks of celery, finely sliced
½ tin of tomatoes (or 4 tomatoes, skinned, deseeded and chopped)
50g/2 oz breadcrumbs
25g/1 oz Cheddar cheese, grated
Butter or oil for sautéing the vegetables
Salt and black pepper

Preheat oven to 400°F/200°C/Gas Mark 6

Melt 50g/2 oz butter (or equivalent oil) in a large, heavy-based saucepan and add the chopped onion. Fry gently until soft and transparent, add the celery and cook for a further 5 minutes. Add the diced carrots and swede and the tomatoes and sauté them for 15 minutes until just tender. Season to taste with salt and pepper and turn the vegetable mixture into an oven-proof casserole or pie dish. Sprinkle the top with the breadcrumbs and grated cheese. Dot with flecks of butter and put into the preheated oven for 15-20 minutes until the top is golden.

LEEKS IN A WHITE SAUCE

8 medium-sized leeks
1 tablespoon butter
1 tablespoon flour
300ml/½ pint milk or milk and cream
Salt and pepper

Clean the leeks thoroughly after removing the ends and most of the green part. Cook for about 15 – 20 minutes in salted boiling water until tender.

Meanwhile, make the sauce by melting the butter in a small saucepan and adding the flour. Stir for a minute with a wooden spoon. Remove from the heat and add a little of the milk, beating all the time. Return to the heat and gradually add the rest of the milk, stirring all the time until smooth. Bring to the boil and cook for a further minute. Season to taste.

Thoroughly drain the leeks and transfer to a hot serving dish. Pour over the white sauce and serve at once.

The sauce can be varied by adding a little Dijon mustard or grated cheese.

RICE SALAD

SERVES 10

450g/1 lb long-grain rice
1 small can sweetcorn, drained
1 small green pepper, diced
1 small bunch of spring onions, finely chopped
50g/2 oz walnuts, chopped
2 tablespoons parsley, finely chopped
2 tablespoons chives, finely chopped
150ml/¼ pint French dressing

Cook the rice in plenty of boiling, salted water for 12 – 15 minutes until tender. Drain and tip into a salad bowl. Pour over the French dressing whilst the rice is still warm. Leave it to get cold before adding the rest of the ingredients. Cover and keep the salad cool until needed.

FIVE BEAN SALAD

The ingredients shown would be ideal for a large party, so modify the amount if you are only entertaining a few people. Ring the changes with the kind of beans you use – there is such a variety now available. Although they are more expensive, for speed and convenience I use tinned beans but, of course, dried ones would be more economical.

1 x 439g/15 ½ oz tin Borlotti beans
1 x 439g/15 ½ oz tin red kidney beans
1 x 439g/15 ½ oz tin chickpeas
1 x 439g/15 ½ oz tin flageolet beans
1 x 439g/15 ½ oz tin cannellini or white kidney beans

Drain the beans and mix them with a good vinaigrette (with garlic if you like) and maybe a little chopped onion and plenty of chopped fresh herbs.
Refrigerate, covered, until needed.

MUSHROOM AND SOUR CREAM SALAD

SERVES 4

175g/6 oz button mushrooms
150ml/5 fl oz soured cream
1 – 2 cloves garlic, crushed
1 teaspoon lemon juice
Salt and black pepper
2 tablespoons chopped chives
Pinch cayenne pepper

Wipe the mushrooms with kitchen paper to remove any compost (do not wash them) and slice.
Add the garlic, lemon juice, chives and cayenne pepper to the soured cream and season to taste with salt and pepper. Lightly fold the mushrooms into the dressing. Chill before serving.

VEGETABLE PIE WITH CHEESE PASTRY

Vary the filling of this vegetarian pie according to the availability of the vegetables and your individual taste.

SERVES 4 – 6

900g/2 lb mixed vegetables e.g. onions, carrots, celery, cauliflower, mushrooms, leeks
40g/1½ oz butter
300-450ml/½ - ¾ pint stock
1 bay leaf
Salt and black pepper
2 tablespoons fresh chopped herbs or 1 teaspoon dried mixed herbs

CHEESE PASTRY

225g/8 oz plain flour
Pinch of salt
100g/4 oz grated Cheddar cheese
100g/4 oz butter or margarine
Half a beaten egg
1 tablespoon cold water

Preheat oven to 400°F/200°C/Gas Mark 6

Prepare the vegetables and cut into 2.5 cm/1" pieces. Melt the butter in a large pan and add the vegetables. Sauté gently for 3-4 minutes before adding enough stock to just cover the vegetables, bay leaf and salt and pepper. Simmer them for about 10-15 minutes – they should still be crisp. Remove from the heat and strain off the stock and reserve. Put the vegetables into the bottom of a 1 litre/2 pint pie dish. Sprinkle over the herbs and about 300ml/½ pint of the stock and allow to cool.

Meanwhile, sieve the flour and salt into a large bowl. Add the fat that has been cut into 1 cm/½" pieces and rub it lightly into the flour with your fingertips. Continue rubbing until the mixture resembles fine breadcrumbs. Stir in the grated cheese. Make a well in the centre and gradually add the beaten egg and cold water, incorporating it with a knife. A soft but not sticky dough is the required consistency. Turn it out onto a floured board and lightly roll out to just larger than the size of the pie dish. Roll out some trimmings into a strip the width of the rim. Dampen the rim with cold water and press on the strip of pastry all around. Then moisten the pastry rim with cold water before laying the pastry lid on top. Press the two edges firmly together. Make a couple of slits to allow the steam to escape whilst cooking and decorate the top with pastry leaves if desired. Brush with the remaining egg and place in the centre of the oven for approximately 35-40 minutes, until the pastry is golden.

Vegetable Pie with Cheese Pastry.

CARROT SALAD WITH RAISINS AND NUTS

SERVES 4

50g/2 oz raisins or sultanas
450g/1 lb young carrots
50g/2 oz walnuts or peanuts or pecan nuts,
    coarsely chopped
2 tablespoons parsley, finely chopped
1 tablespoon lemon juice
75ml/2½ fl oz French dressing
Salt and black pepper

In a small bowl, place the raisins and pour over boiling water. Leave for a few minutes until the fruit has plumped up. Drain.

Grate the carrots into a larger bowl, add the nuts of your choice, the raisins and the parsley and sprinkle with the lemon juice. Pour in the French dressing and mix well. Season with salt and black pepper if necessary. Serve as soon as possible.

CHEF'S SALAD

A sustaining and easily prepared salad.

225g/8 oz cooked chicken
225g/8 oz cooked ham
225g/8 oz Cheddar or other hard cheese
Lettuce leaves

Simply cut the meat and cheese into easily manageable pieces and arrange attractively on a bed of lettuce. Serve with potato salad and pickles.

FRENCH BEAN AND MUSHROOM SALAD

SERVES 4

450g/1 lb French beans
175g/6 oz button mushrooms, sliced
25g/1 oz butter

FRENCH DRESSING

2 tablespoons wine vinegar
1 tablespoon lemon juice
1 clove garlic, crushed (optional)
1 teaspoon prepared mustard
Salt and black pepper
1 tablespoon fresh mixed chopped herbs e.g.
    Thyme, parsley and chives
180ml/6 fl oz pure olive oil or your favourite salad
    oil

Top and tail the beans and cook in boiling salted water for about 8 minutes, until tender. Drain and then plunge them into cold water and pat dry with a tea towel or kitchen paper. Sauté the mushrooms in the butter for two to three minutes. Allow to cool.

Put all the French dressing ingredients into a screw-topped jar. Shake vigorously until well combined.

Put the beans and mushrooms into a serving dish and pour over enough dressing to coat the vegetables well. Toss gently. Keep any excess dressing in the refrigerator for future use.

CHICKEN AND SPRING VEGETABLE SALAD

SERVES 4

450g/1 lb small new potatoes, cooked
4 cooked chicken breasts
½ a cucumber, peeled
2 red peppers
1 bunch of spring onions, chopped
A handful of fresh herbs, chopped (e.g. tarragon,
    basil, mint, lemon thyme)

DRESSING

150ml/¼ pint mayonnaise
150ml/¼ pint soured cream
Salt and freshly ground black pepper

Cut the potatoes into quarters and cut the chicken into large chunks, discarding any skin or bone. Roughly chop the cucumber. Cut the ends of the peppers and remove the pith and seeds, then roughly chop the flesh. Toss all the ingredients together in a large salad bowl, adding the chopped spring onion and herbs.

Mix together the soured cream, mayonnaise and seasoning and pour over the salad.

WATERCRESS AND ORANGE SALAD

The ingredients of this colourful salad, being such healthy ones, make this dish an excellent one to serve in the winter.

SERVES 4

2 bunches watercress
2 oranges
150ml/¼ pint French dressing

Slice off the ends of the bunches of watercress. Pick over, removing any yellowing leaves or very thick stalks. Rinse well in cold water and store in a plastic bag in the refrigerator until needed.

Watercress and Orange Salad (top left), Chef's Salad (centre right) and Carrot Salad with Raisins and Nuts (bottom left).

Remove the peel and pips from the oranges and cut them into slices and then quarters. Place in an attractive bowl with the watercress. Add the French dressing and toss lightly just before serving.

CHICKEN SALAD WITH MANGETOUT AND PINE NUTS

SERVES 4 – 6

450g/1 lb cooked chicken
225g/8 oz mangetout peas
50g/2 oz pine nuts (walnuts could be used instead)

DRESSING

150ml/5 fl oz plain yoghurt
1 teaspoon lemon juice
75ml/3 fl oz mayonnaise
1 clove garlic, crushed (optional)
¼ teaspoon paprika
2 drops tabasco
Salt and black pepper

Above: Five Bean Salad, Chicken and Spring Vegetable Salad, French Bean and Mushroom Salad, Chicken Salad with Mangetout and Pine Nuts, and Mushroom and Sour Cream Salad.

Facing page: Rice Salad (top), Coleslaw (bottom left) and Tomato Salad (bottom right).

GARNISH

1 tablespoon finely chopped parsley or other fresh herbs

Cut the chicken into bite-sized pieces. Top and tail the mangetout and remove strings. Cook in a small amount of boiling salted water for 1 – 2 minutes only. Drain and plunge them into cold water so they keep their bright green colour. Pat dry. Put into a bowl with the chicken and pine nuts. Mix together all the dressing ingredients until well blended. Pour over the chicken and mangetout and toss gently.

Garnish with chopped herbs.

TOMATO SALAD

The best times of the year to make this salad are summer and autumn, when the tomatoes are sun-ripened and sweet. Experiment with the type of

tomatoes, particularly the fat, Mediterranean ones. Fresh herbs, particularly basil, chives and parsley, are an excellent addition, so too are sliced Spanish onion or chopped spring onions. Sliced hard-boiled egg or tuna fish or anchovies can turn a simple tomato salad into a more substantial dish, accompanied by crusty French bread.

SERVES 4

4 large tomatoes
1 tablespoon chopped herbs
Salt and black pepper
Few slices of onion or chopped spring onions
French dressing

Slice the tomatoes into a dish and top with the herbs and sliced onions. Season to taste and pour on enough French dressing to coat well. Serve at once.

BRUSSELS SPROUTS WITH CHESTNUTS

675g/1½ lbs Brussels sprouts
350g/¾ lb chestnuts
Butter

Make a nick in the chestnuts and boil them in plenty of water for 3 – 4 minutes. Turn off the heat and peel the chestnuts. If they are a little on the hard side, cook them for a little longer without their shells.

Meanwhile, trim the sprouts and cook in boiling salted water for 8 – 10 minutes. They should still be a little crisp. Drain and mix with the chestnuts. Dot with knobs of butter.

COLESLAW

An ideal salad – especially if you own a food processor.

SERVES 6

675g/1½ lb firm white cabbage
1 small onion
225g/½ lb carrots
2 sticks celery
50g/2 oz sultanas
2 tablespoons chopped parsley
Salt and pepper
300ml/½ pint mayonnaise

Shred the cabbage finely, chop the onion and celery finely and grate the carrots. Put all these vegetables into a large bowl and add the sultanas and parsley and season to taste. Pour in the mayonnaise and incorporate the ingredients well.

Red Cabbage, Bacon and Blue Cheese Salad (left), Red Kidney Bean Salad (right) and Beetroot, Onion and Soured Cream Salad (bottom).

RED KIDNEY BEAN SALAD

A quick and easy bean salad.

SERVES 6

2 x 432g/15 ¼ oz cans red kidney beans
1 small onion, finely chopped

DRESSING

110ml/4 fl oz salad oil
2 tablespoons red wine vinegar
1 clove garlic, crushed
1 tablespoon mixed fresh herbs, finely chopped
1 pickled gherkin, finely chopped
Few drops tabasco

Drain the cans of beans and put them into a bowl together with the chopped onion. Put all the dressing ingredients into a screw-topped jar and shake them well. Pour the dressing over the beans and leave for an hour or so before serving.

BEETROOT, ONION AND SOURED CREAM SALAD

SERVES 4 – 6

675g/1 ½ lb cooked beetroot, sliced
1 medium Spanish onion, finely sliced
4 spring onions, chopped
1 x 142ml/5 fl oz carton soured cream
1 teaspoon lemon juice
Salt
Freshly ground black pepper

Mix together the soured cream, lemon juice and salt and pepper.

Arrange the beetroot and onion slices on a serving dish. Pour over soured cream mixture and garnish with the chopped spring onions. Serve at once.

STUFFED AUBERGINES

A tasty supper dish

2 medium-sized aubergines
50g/2 oz bacon, chopped
2 tomatoes
50g/2 oz breadcrumbs
½ onion, grated
Salt and pepper
½ teaspoon made mustard
175g/6 oz Cheddar cheese, grated

Preheat oven to 400°F/200°C/Gas Mark 6

Remove stalks from the aubergines, halve lengthways and remove the flesh, leaving 4 shells. Chop the flesh. Skin and chop the tomatoes, grate the cheese. Mix the flesh with the bacon, tomatoes, breadcrumbs, onion and half the cheese. Incorporate the mustard and season with salt and pepper to taste. Place the aubergines into a greased oven-proof dish, fill the halves with the mixture and sprinkle over the remaining cheese. Cover the dish and bake for 15 minutes. Remove cover and continue to cook for a further 7 – 10 minutes.

RED CABBAGE, BACON AND BLUE CHEESE SALAD

An easily prepared first course. Danish blue cheese is ideal, but for a special occasion try Roquefort.

SERVES 6

Small head of red cabbage, cored and finely sliced into long strips
225g/8 oz bacon, diced
1 tablespoon oil
75g/3 oz blue cheese, crumbled

CROÛTONS

4 slices white bread 1.25 cm/½ " thick and cubed
4 tablespoons oil

VINAIGRETTE DRESSING

200ml/⅓ pint oil
3 tablespoons wine vinegar
1 tablespoon Dijon mustard
Salt
Freshly ground black pepper

Heat 1 tablespoon oil in a frying pan and cook bacon until crisp. Remove and drain on kitchen paper. Add the 4 tablespoons of oil, heat until sizzling, add the cubes of bread and fry until golden brown on all sides. Remove and drain on kitchen paper.

For the vinaigrette, whisk the mustard, salt and pepper and wine vinegar together and very gradually whisk in the oil until the dressing emulsifies (like making mayonnaise).

Put red cabbage into serving bowl or bowls. Mix in the bacon and croûtons. Just before serving, dress with the vinaigrette and decorate with the blue cheese.

GRATIN OF TURNIPS

Young turnips are particularly good for this dish, which transforms an everyday root vegetable.

SERVES 4 – 6

700g/1 ½ lb turnips
25g/1 oz butter
1 egg
Salt and pepper
50g/2 oz Gruyère or Cheddar cheese, grated
4 tablespoons Parmesan cheese

Preheat oven to 325°F/160°C/Gas Mark 3

Brussels Sprouts with Chestnuts (top), Gratin of Turnips (centre left) and Stuffed Aubergines (bottom).

Grease a shallow oven-proof dish with half of the butter. Peel the turnips and slice finely. Whisk together the egg and double cream. Layer a quarter of the turnip slices in the bottom of the dish. Season well with salt and freshly-ground black pepper. Pour over a quarter of the egg and cream mixture and sprinkle on a quarter of the cheese. Repeat until all the ingredients are used up. Dot the final layer with the remainder of the butter. Cover the dish with a lid or piece of foil and bake in the preheated oven for approximately one hour. Remove cover and bake for a further 30 minutes until the top is golden brown and the turnips are tender.

Pasta Recipes

SMOKED SALMON ROMA

This quick dish has a fresh, light tasting sauce, perfect for summer eating. A simple green salad goes well.

100g/4 oz smoked salmon, cut into strips
2 courgettes, cut into sticks
1 small onion, chopped
A little butter and oil for frying
225g/8 oz fine ribbon pasta (linguine)
250ml/8 fl oz single cream mixed with two
    tablespoons of soured cream and left to set for
    a couple of hours
Fresh dill
Salt and black pepper
Lemon and dill to decorate

Fry the onion in a little butter and oil until soft. Add the courgettes and sauté for a few minutes. Do not overcook, they should remain crisp. Add the chopped dill. Add the cream mixture and gently heat through. Season to taste. Fold in the salmon strips. Keep warm.

Cook the pasta as directed on packet, drain. Put the pasta in an oval dish and pour the sauce into the centre. Decorate with lemon wedges and dill scattered over.

TORTELLINI WITH MUSHROOMS AND BACON

This is an excellent supper dish. The tortellini are stuffed with various fillings. I think the pork ones go well here. Flat leaved parsley could be substituted for coriander leaves.

225g/8 oz packet of tortellini, dried or fresh
175g/6 oz streaky bacon rashers, chopped
1 small chopped onion
225g/½ lb small button mushrooms
3 teaspoons cornflour
150ml/¼ pint milk
300ml/½ pint single cream
2 teaspoons ground coriander
Salt and pepper
Chopped coriander leaves

Sauté the bacon gently until the fat runs out. Add onions and cook 5 minutes until soft. Add cornflour, cook 2 minutes, add milk and bring gently to boil. Add mushrooms and cook a further

2 minutes. Add coriander. Add the cream, and warm through. Season. Cook tortellini, then fold into sauce.

Serve with coriander leaves scattered over.

CHICKEN AND AVOCADO WITH GREEN PEPPERCORNS SERVED WITH TAGLIATELLE

A rich, luxurious sauce this, not for weight-watchers.....

2 large chicken breasts, boned
100g/¼ lb button mushrooms, sliced
4 spring onions, chopped
1 red pepper, sliced
1 avocado, cut into cubes
1 clove garlic
1 chicken stock cube
2 egg yolks
300ml/½ pint double cream
2 teaspoons crushed green peppercorns
225g/8 oz green tagliatelle
2 teaspoons French mustard
1 teaspoon cornflour
Salt and black pepper
3 tablespoons dry vermouth
Toasted sesame seeds
Chopped parsley to garnish

Cut the chicken pieces into strips across the grain and leave to marinate for a few hours in the dry vermouth. Sauté the red pepper, crushed garlic and spring onions (reserve a few green tops for decoration) in a little butter and oil. Add green peppercorns. Add chicken and vermouth and cook for a few minutes. Add stock cube dissolved in 150ml/¼ pint hot water and simmer 5 minutes or until chicken loses its pink colour. Add mushrooms.

Tortellini with Mushrooms and Bacon (top), Chicken and Avocado with Green Peppercorns served with Tagliatelle (centre left) and Smoked Salmon Roma (bottom).

Mix together the cream, mustard, cornflour, egg yolks and seasoning, then add to pan. Heat until simmering.

Meanwhile, cook pasta according to directions, and toss in butter and sesame seeds.

Arrange pasta on serving dish and pour chicken mixture over. Scatter with chopped parsley and reserved onion tops.

TAGLIATELLE IN CREAM AND HAM

This is a lovely dish served with garlic bread and a green salad.

SERVES 4

275-350g/10-12 oz fresh tagliatelle or fettucine
300ml/10 fl oz double cream
100g/4 oz Parma ham or smoked Westphalian
    ham
50g/2 oz butter
2 tablespoons Parmesan cheese
Salt and freshly ground black pepper
Freshly grated nutmeg

Bring a large saucepan of salted water to the boil and add the pasta. Stir with a fork until the water comes back to the boil. Cook fresh pasta for about 3 minutes or until tender. Meanwhile, snip the ham into strips with kitchen scissors.

When the pasta is cooked, drain it well. Whilst the pasta is draining, start melting the butter in the saucepan, add the drained pasta, ham, Parmesan and seasoning and gently toss the pasta with a spoon and fork until the ingredients are well mixed. Then add the cream and a little freshly grated nutmeg. Turn pasta out onto a hot serving dish and serve at once.

LAYERED PASTA SALAD

This is an excellent salad for a busy weekend – it can be prepared the night before and only needs a nutty wholemeal loaf to accompany. Add the dressing at the last minute if you don't want it to trickle through.

Crisp lettuce leaves i.e. Webb or Cos
225g/½ lb cooked ham, sliced in strips
175g/6 oz diced Cheddar cheese
100g/4 oz tubed pasta or spirals
1 red onion, thinly sliced and mixed with 4 sliced
    radishes
225g/8 oz packet frozen peas
Chopped parsley to decorate

DRESSING

150ml/5 fl oz mayonnaise
150ml/5 fl oz soured cream
1 tablespoon Dijon or whole grain mustard

Cook pasta according to instructions and freshen under cold water. Leave to cool.

Cook frozen peas, drain and cool.

In a large glass bowl place the torn lettuce leaves. Follow with a layer of the ham, then cheese, half the onion mixture, the pasta, another layer of onion mix, then lastly the peas.

Combine the dressing ingredients and spread over the salad. Decorate with chopped parsley.

LASAGNE

This dish can also be made with lasagne verdi (green spinach lasagne). It is an ideal supper or party dish as it can be made well in advance and popped in the oven at the last moment to emerge golden and bubbling and extremely appetizing.

SERVES 6

225g/½ lb lasagne

RAGÙ SAUCE

2 tablespoons olive oil
50g/2 oz bacon, finely chopped
1 clove garlic, peeled and crushed
1 onion, finely chopped
1 carrot, finely chopped
450g/1 lb minced beef
75g/3 oz chicken livers, finely chopped
1 x 397g/14 oz tin tomatoes
2 tablespoons tomato purée
150ml/5 fl oz wine
1 teaspoon dried basil
Salt and black pepper

BÉCHAMEL SAUCE

600ml/1 pint milk
1 bay leaf
Thyme
½ small onion
¼ teaspoon grated nutmeg
50g/2 oz plain flour
Salt and black pepper
150ml/5 fl oz double or single cream

To finish: 50-75g/2-3 oz grated Parmesan cheese

Preheat oven to 375°F/190°C/Gas Mark 5

In a large, heavy-based pan, heat the olive oil and fry the bacon, onion and garlic for 3 or 4 minutes. Add the carrot followed by the minced beef and chopped chicken livers and brown them, stirring all the time. Add the tinned tomatoes, tomato purée, wine, basil and seasoning. Bring to the boil, then reduce the heat and simmer this Bolognese ragù for

Layered Pasta Salad.

114

20 minutes covered and 20 minutes uncovered. The final sauce should not be too runny. Check the seasoning and add more if necessary.

To make the Béchamel sauce, put the milk, bay leaf, thyme, onion and nutmeg into a saucepan and bring slowly to the boil. Remove from the heat, cover and leave the milk to infuse for 15 minutes. Then melt the butter in a heavy-based saucepan, stir in the flour and cook for a couple of minutes over gentle heat, stirring continuously. Strain the milk and gradually add it to the roux (butter and flour), stirring all the time until a smooth sauce is achieved. Bring the sauce to the boil and then simmer for 2-3 minutes (any lumps that might result can be worked out with a balloon whisk). Season to taste and stir in the cream.

Cook the lasagne in a large pan of boiling salted water (with a little oil added) for about 10 minutes if dried or 3 minutes if fresh pasta is used. Drop the sheets into the water one at a time (do not overcook them) and transfer them to a bowl of cold water to prevent them sticking together.

To assemble the pasta, grease a shallow square or rectangular oven-proof dish and put a layer of the meat sauce (about a quarter) in the base, followed by a quarter of the Béchamel sauce and a layer of the pasta on the top. Repeat this process until all the

ingredients are used up, finishing with a layer of Béchamel sauce. Sprinkle the grated Parmesan liberally over the top.

Bake in the centre of a preheated oven until golden and bubbling – about 30 minutes.

Serve with a crisp green salad.

TOMATO SAUCE

A tasty sauce for pasta, pizzas, barbecues or for serving with other vegetables. Freezes well.

1kg/2 lb fresh tomatoes, skinned and chopped, or 1 x 800g/1 lb 12 oz tin peeled tomatoes
1 large onion, chopped finely
Clove garlic, crushed
1 tablespoon tomato purée
1 dessertspoon tomato ketchup
150ml/5 fl oz dry white or red wine
½ teaspoon sugar
Oregano and basil (fresh basil is particularly good if available)
Salt and freshly ground black pepper
1 tablespoon each of butter and oil

Heat the oil and butter together in a saucepan, add the onion and garlic and fry until soft. Add the tomatoes, wine, tomato purée and ketchup and cook over a medium heat for 30 – 40 minutes (less if using fresh tomatoes), stirring occasionally to break down large pieces of tomato. Turn down heat, add salt and pepper and herbs to taste. Simmer for a further ten minutes.

Facing page: Lasagne (top), Tagliatelle in Cream and Ham (centre right) and Pasta with Tomato Sauce (bottom).

Below: ingredients for Pesto Sauce.

PESTO SAUCE

Fresh basil has a wonderful fragrance, a reminder of sunny Italian days.

50g/2 oz chopped basil leaves
1 clove of garlic, chopped
1 tablespoon pine nuts
50g/2 oz Parmesan cheese, grated
4 tablespoons olive oil
Salt to taste

Crush the garlic and pine nuts using a mortar and pestle and add basil. Stir in the cheese and add the oil until a thick paste results. Add salt.
    Serve over cooked ribbon noodles.

Sweet and Savoury Pancakes

PANCAKES

Like most people, I always remember to make pancakes on Shrove Tuesday but tend to forget about them at other times of the year. They of course make an excellent medium for savoury and sweet fillings and keep well for up to 3 days in the refrigerator or in the freezer for up to a month – longer than that and they tend to become brittle, unless filled with a sauce.

MAKES 18 PANCAKES

BASIC BATTER

100g/4 oz plain flour
Good pinch of salt
Scant 300ml/½ pint milk
3 eggs
2 tablespoons melted butter or oil

For frying: 75g/3 oz clarified butter or oil

Sift the flour with the pinch of salt into a mixing bowl, make a well in the centre and add half the milk. Whisk until smooth and then whisk in the eggs. Do not overbeat. Add the melted butter or oil and half of the remaining milk. Allow to stand for at least half an hour (it can be left overnight in the refrigerator if necessary).

Just before using, stir in the remainder of the milk so that the pancake batter has the consistency of thin cream. Grease your crêpe pan or frying pan lightly with clarified butter or oil and, when very hot and slightly smoking, drop a couple of tablespoons of batter into the pan (this will vary according to the size of the pan) and roll it around until it evenly coats the base. Cook over fairly high heat until the pancake is brown on the underside and either toss or turn it over with a spatula. Quickly brown the other side. Turn out onto a wire rack or a clean tea towel. Regrease the pan if necessary and repeat until all the batter has been used. Stack and keep warm in the oven or allow to cool, separate the pancakes with greaseproof paper and store in a plastic bag in the fridge or freezer until needed.

Crêpes Suzette.

CRÊPES SUZETTE

A classic way of serving pancakes or crêpes. Try to fry your crêpes as thinly as possible for this dish.

SERVES 4 (Allow about 4 crêpes per person)

ORANGE BUTTER

50g/2 oz butter
50g/2 oz sugar
Grated rind of 1 orange
1 – 2 tablespoons Grand Marnier or Curaçao

TO FLAME

25-40g/1-1½ oz butter
2 tablespoons brandy
2 tablespoons Grand Marnier or Curaçao

Cream together the butter, sugar and grated orange rind until light and fluffy. Add the orange liqueur and spread a little of this orange butter on one side of each crêpe.

In a small saucepan, put the brandy and orange liqueur ready to flame the crêpes at the last moment.

Melt the butter in a large frying pan, add a crêpe, orange butter side down, and cook very quickly for half a minute. Fold in half and half again into the traditional triangular shape and put to one side of the pan. Repeat until all the crêpes are cooked.

Heat the liqueur in the small saucepan, set it alight and pour it over the crêpes. Serve at once.

MUSHROOM AND HAM PANCAKES

MAKES 12 PANCAKES

25-40g/1-1½ oz butter
1 tablespoon finely chopped onion
100g/4 oz chopped bacon or ham
100g/4 oz mushrooms, sliced
1 tablespoon finely chopped parsley
Salt and pepper
150ml/¼ pint béchamel sauce
1 egg yolk

Make up the pancakes and keep warm. In a small pan, melt the butter and add the onion and bacon or ham. Cook over a low heat until soft but not brown. Stir continually. Add the mushrooms, parsley and seasoning. Continue to cook for a further five minutes.

Make up the béchamel sauce, season it well and beat in the egg yolk. Stir in the mushroom mixture and put a spoonful of this on each pancake. Either just fold each one over or roll like a cigar. Arrange on a hot serving dish, sprinkle with a little more chopped parsley if liked and serve at once.

SEAFOOD PANCAKES

Excellent as a starter, main course or supper dish. Vary the fish used according to taste and season.

SERVES 4 AS A MAIN COURSE.

BASIC PANCAKE BATTER

100g/4 oz plain flour
Pinch of salt
Scant 300ml/½ pint milk
3 eggs
2 tablespoons melted butter or oil

FISH STOCK

Fish bones from the whitefish used
1 onion
1 carrot
1 bay leaf
Few whole black peppercorns
300ml/½ pint dry white wine
600ml/1 pint cold water

SEAFOOD FILLING

225g/8 oz whitefish – sole, lemon sole, plaice etc – cut into strips
100g/4 oz scallops
100g/4 oz white crab meat
100g/4 oz cooked, peeled prawns
50g/2 oz mussels, shelled (optional)
Juice of ½ lemon
Salt and black pepper
1 tablespoon parsley, finely chopped

VELOUTÉ SAUCE

75g/3 oz butter
75g/3 oz plain flour
300ml/½ pint milk
Approx. 300ml/½ pint fish stock
Salt and black pepper

LIAISON

150ml/¼ pint double cream
2 egg yolks

Preheat oven to 350°F/180°C/Gas Mark 4

Prepare pancakes in the usual way and keep them warm.

Fish Stock In a large saucepan bring all the ingredients to the boil and simmer for about 20 minutes. Poach the whitefish and scallops in the stock for 1-2 minutes (no longer or the scallops will

become rubbery). Drain with a slotted spoon and reserve.

Velouté Sauce Melt the butter in a heavy-based saucepan and, when bubbling, add the flour. Stir over medium heat for 1-2 minutes, remove from the heat and add a little of the strained fish stock. Beat well until smooth. Add the milk and bring gradually to the boil, stirring all the time. Add the lemon juice. Season to taste. A thick pouring consistency is needed so add more fish stock until this is achieved.

Add the fish to half of the velouté sauce (if scallops are very large, halve or quarter them) and the chopped parsley. Adjust seasoning if necessary. Add a generous tablespoonful of this mixture to each pancake, roll up and place in a greased, shallow baking dish.

Meanwhile, whisk together the egg yolks and cream and stir into the remaining sauce. Reheat very gently, stirring all the time. Do not boil. Adjust seasoning and pour over the pancakes. Bake in a moderate oven for 20 – 30 minutes.

SPINACH AND CHEESE PANCAKES

This dish freezes very well and can just be popped into a pre-heated oven for a tasty supper.

SERVES 4 – 6

12 Pancakes

FILLING

450g-675g/1-1½ lbs fresh spinach
3-4 tablespoons of milk or 1 tablespoon cream
50-75g/2-3 oz butter
50g/2 oz mushrooms, sliced
50g/2 oz grated cheese

SAUCE

40g/1½ oz butter
40g/1½ oz flour
600ml/1 pint milk
Salt and freshly ground black pepper
75-100g/3-4 oz grated Cheddar cheese

Preheat oven to 350°F/180°C/Gas Mark 4

Make pancakes as described in previous recipe and set aside.

Meanwhile, prepare the filling. Strip the leaves of the spinach off the stalks and wash thoroughly. Place the spinach in a large saucepan without adding any more water. Sprinkle with salt and cook until tender. Drain thoroughly and squeeze out any excess water. Chop finely, mixing in 1-1½ oz of the butter. Melt the rest of the butter in a small pan and add the mushrooms. Sauté for a few minutes until lightly cooked. Add this to the spinach with the grated cheese and cream or milk. Mix well together.

Make a sauce with the butter, flour and milk by placing all the ingredients in a medium-sized saucepan and placing over a medium heat. Stir well continuously with a balloon whisk to avoid any

lumps. When the mixture starts to thicken, turn the heat down, continuing to beat for about 1 minute until the sauce is cooked. Add the cheese and season. Mix well.

Add a few tablespoons of the sauce to the spinach and mix well. Divide the spinach amongst the pancakes and roll them up. Arrange the pancakes in a shallow oven-proof dish, pour over the rest of the sauce, sprinkle over some more grated Cheddar cheese and bake in the oven for about 30 minutes until browned and bubbling.

ITALIAN PANCAKES

Fill pancakes with stiffly-whipped double cream flavoured with brandy or your favourite liqueur.

Roll them up and chill for at least 1 hour.

Just before serving, sprinkle on crumbled ratafia or amaretti biscuits and a measure of brandy or other liqueur.

Seafood Pancakes, Spinach and Cheese Pancakes and Mushroom and Ham Pancakes.

CRÊPES WITH BLACK CHERRIES AND FLAKED ALMONDS

Fill thin pancakes with stoned black cherries flavoured with a little kirsch.

Roll up like cigars and sprinkle with toasted flaked almonds.

Serve warm or cold with cream

APPLE PANCAKE LAYER WITH APRICOT SAUCE

This is an effective way of presenting pancakes, enhanced by a delicious apricot sauce.

SERVES 4 – 6

8 pancakes
675g/1½ lb apples
25g/1 oz butter
1 tablespoon apricot jam
1 tablespoon lemon juice
1 tablespoon demerara sugar

SAUCE

225g/8 oz apricot jam
300ml/½ pint water
Juice and rind of 1 lemon
2 teaspoons cornflour

Preheat oven to 375°F/190°C/Gas Mark 5

Peel, core and thinly slice the apples and sprinkle with the tablespoon of lemon juice. Melt the butter in a medium-sized saucepan. Add the jam and sugar and stir over a low heat until a smooth sauce, then add the apple slices. Coat them with the sauce, cover the pan and cook very gently until the apple is just tender and the slices still intact. Stir occasionally to prevent the mixture from sticking. Allow to cool slightly before layering up the pancakes with this mixture on an oven-proof plate or dish. Finish with a layer of apples on the top.

To make the sauce, boil the jam, lemon rind and water together in a small saucepan, stirring all the time until smooth. In a cup, mix the lemon juice and cornflour together to a smooth paste. Add to the jam sauce and mix well, cook for a further minute. Pour the sauce over the top of the layered pancakes and then transfer them to a hot oven and cook for 10 minutes. Serve hot or warm with cream.

CRÊPES WITH PINEAPPLE AND KIRSCH

Soak chopped fresh or drained tinned pineapple in kirsch for 1 hour or more. Reserve some of the pineapple for decoration, add the rest to crème patissière and use to fill the pancakes.

Facing page: (clockwise from top right) Apple Pancake Layer with Apricot Sauce; Crêpes with Nectarines and Orange Liqueur; Crêpes with Pineapple and Kirsch; Italian Pancakes, and Crêpes with Black Cherries and Flaked Almonds.

Above: Pancakes with Bananas and Rum.

CRÊPES WITH NECTARINES AND ORANGE LIQUEUR

Soak chopped fresh nectarines or peaches in orange liqueur for 1 hour or more. Reserve some of the fruit for decoration, add the rest to crème patissière and use to fill the pancakes.

PANCAKES WITH BANANAS AND RUM

SERVES 4

4 bananas
50g/2 oz butter
2 tablespoons demerara sugar
2 tablespoons brown rum

Peel and slice the bananas and fry gently in a pan with the butter until they just start to turn golden. Sprinkle with demerara sugar, add the brown rum and set it alight. Let the flames burn for a few seconds before arranging the bananas on warm pancakes with a little of the sauce. Serve warm with cream.

Ices and Cold Puddings

FRESH FRUIT FLAN FILLINGS

If time is short the flans can be filled with whipped double cream. Otherwise a variety of fillings can be used. The classic one is crème patissière, but try one of the following:

FOR 1 x 23cm/9″ FLAN CASE

225g/8 oz cream cheese
75g/3 oz caster sugar
3 tablespoons double cream
Grated rind of ½ lemon
1 tablespoon orange juice

Simply mix all the ingredients together until smooth. Fill the flan case with the cream cheese mixture and top with raspberries, strawberries, redcurrants, blueberries or seedless grapes etc, or combine 2 or 3 of these fruits in the same flan.

Glaze with a little raspberry jam warmed through with a little lemon juice or, if using grapes, apricot jam.

CRÈME PÂTISSIÈRE

Makes about 300 ml/½ pint. A good alternative to cream, with a delicious flavour. Can be made in advance and kept in the fridge for 2-3 days.

300ml/½ pint milk
500g/2 oz caster sugar
2 level tablespoons cornflour
3 egg yolks
10g/½ oz butter
Few drops vanilla essence or a vanilla pod

Pour the milk into a saucepan with the vanilla pod. Bring to the boil and leave to infuse. Whisk together the egg yolks, sugar and cornflour until thick and creamy. Add vanilla essence at this stage if you do not have a vanilla pod. Remove pod from milk and slowly pour liquid over the egg yolk mixture, stirring continually. Rinse out saucepan and return the mixture to it. Stir vigorously over a low heat until it becomes thick. Transfer to a bowl and beat in the butter. Allow to cool. Cover with cling film until needed. The crème patissière can be flavoured with a little liqueur or lightened by the addition of whipped cream.

TRANCHE DES FRUITS

A spectacular dessert to make when summer fruits are cheap and plentiful.

400g/14 oz puff pastry
Assorted fruit e.g. 2 kiwi, 2 peaches, 100g/¼ lb cherries, small punnet strawberries, 100g/¼ lb grapes
3 tablespoons jam (apricot is good as it does not mask the colour of the fruit, but if all red fruit are used, try raspberry)
1 tablespoon lemon juice
Egg for glazing

Preheat oven to 425°F/220°C/Gas Mark 7

Roll out the pastry into a large rectangle approximately 8mm/⅓″ thick. With a sharp knife, cut off strips from all sides 2.5cm/1″ wide. Transfer the rectangle to a dampened baking sheet and, with cold water, moisten the edges. Lay the strips along the edges (make sure the strips are trimmed evenly) and press down lightly so both surfaces stick. Prick the base with a fork, leaving the edging strips plain. Flute or crimp the edges with a knife or finger and thumb. Glaze with a little beaten egg. Place the "tranche" into a hot oven, baking it blind for 15 – 20 minutes, until risen and golden. Remove from the oven and cool on a wire rack.

To fill: Slice the peaches and kiwi fruit. Stone or pip the cherries and grapes and leave the strawberries whole. Place the fruit carefully in rows according to size or colour. Meanwhile, put the jam into a small saucepan together with the lemon juice and bring to the boil, stirring continually. Allow to cool but not to reset. (If it is too thick, add a little boiling water.) Using a pastry brush, liberally coat the fruit with the jam glaze.

Do not make this dessert too long in advance – leave it as late as possible, not more than 1 – 3 hours before serving.

As an alternative, fill the base with 300ml/½ pint of crème patissière or whipped double cream followed by the fruit on top.

A rich pâte sablée, or pâte brisée (sweet, shortcrust pastry – see recipes on page 164) and a variety of fillings makes a delicious base for numerous fruits such as redcurrants (facing page), blueberries and figs (overleaf bottom) and grapes and kiwi fruit (following page). Overleaf top: Tranche des Fruits.

Above: Lime Mousse (top left), Pineapple Surprise (top right) Lemon Syllabub (centre) and Heavenly Pie (bottom).

PINEAPPLE SURPRISE

For some years pineapples have been relatively cheap and plentiful in the shops. This recipe is a good way of using the small ones.

Allow 1 half pineapple per person. Scoop out the flesh and cut into chunks. Put a large spoonful of your favourite sorbet (lemon is nice) or ice cream in the base of each half and pile on a mixture of fresh fruit. Strawberries, black grapes and the pineapple itself look particularly colourful.

Sprinkle on a little kirsch (optional) and serve at once.

LIME MOUSSE

This is a tangy alternative to a lemon mousse and ideal after a rich main course.

SERVES 4

3 eggs
100g/4 oz caster sugar
Juice and rind of 4 limes
1 level tablespoon of powdered gelatine
150g/¼ pint double cream
Green food colouring (optional)

Sprinkle the gelatine over 2 tablespoons of water in a small pan and leave to soak for 5 minutes. Separate the eggs, putting the yolks into a large bowl and the whites into another. Finely grate the rind from the limes and add to the egg yolks together with the caster sugar. Squeeze the juice from the fruit and add to the soaked gelatine. Place the saucepan over a low heat, stirring continuously until the gelatine has dissolved. Do not allow the gelatine to boil.

Whisk the egg yolks, rind and sugar until pale and creamy. Slowly pour in the dissolved gelatine, whisking all the time. Continue to whisk until the mixture has cooled and is starting to thicken. Lightly beat the double cream and fold gently into the mixture. At this stage add green food colouring, if liked. Whisk egg whites until stiff and fold into the egg and lime mixture with a metal spoon. Pour into individual dishes, tall stemmed glasses or into one large serving dish. Chill for at least two hours.

HEAVENLY PIE

SERVES 6

350g/12 oz caster sugar
¼ teaspoon cream of tartar
4 eggs, size 2, separated
3 tablespoons lemon juice
1 tablespoon grated lemon rind
⅛ teaspoon salt
300ml/½ pint whipped cream
150ml/¼ pint whipped cream, optional for
    decoration

Preheat oven to 250°F/120°C/Gas Mark ½
Well grease a 23 – 25 cm/9″ – 10″ pie plate

Sieve together 225g/8 oz of the sugar and the cream of tartar. Beat egg whites until stiff but not dry until they form peaks. Slowly add the sugar mixture and pile into the well-greased pie plate. Hollow out the centre and do not spread the mixture out too close to the rim. Bake on the centre shelf of the oven for one hour. Turn off the heat and leave for a further hour with the oven door closed. Do not be tempted to peep at this stage.

Filling In a basin, beat the egg yolks and the remaining 100g/4 oz of caster sugar, stir in the lemon juice, rind and salt. Cook over a pan of boiling water until thick (a few minutes). Allow to cool and combine with the whipped cream. Fill the meringue shell with this lemon mixture and decorate with lemon slices or chocolate curls and additional piped whipped cream.

This is an excellent dessert for the freezer.

GINGER ICE CREAM

A short-cut way of producing a delicious ice cream.

1 litre/1¾ pints home-made or good commercial
    vanilla ice cream
2 tablespoons stem ginger, finely chopped
1 teaspoon ground ginger
1 tablespoon syrup from the stem ginger jar
    (optional)

Allow the vanilla ice cream to soften a little and simply mix-in the ginger ingredients until they are well incorporated. Freeze until firm. One hour before serving, remove the ice cream from the freezer to the refrigerator.

RHUBARB AND GINGER FOOL

This dessert is delicious served with almond tuile biscuits.

SERVES 4

900g/2 lb rhubarb, coarsely chopped
50-75g/2-3 oz demerara sugar
1 teaspoon ground ginger
300ml/10 fl oz double cream

Simmer the rhubarb until tender with the sugar and a little water. Cool slightly, then rub through a sieve or purée in a blender. Mix in the ginger. Pour into a large bowl and allow to cool completely.

Whip the double cream until it is stiff, and fold gently into the rhubarb purée using a metal spoon. Pour into a pretty glass dish and chill until required.

GINGER AND ADVOCAAT CREAM

A very rich dessert – a little goes a long way.

SERVES 6

6 tablespoons Advocaat liqueur
3 tablespoons ginger jam
450ml/¾ pint double cream, stiffly whipped
4 pieces of preserved stem ginger
2 tablespoons syrup from the ginger jar (optional)

In a blender, liquidise together the Advocaat and ginger jam and fold into the stiffly whipped cream. Slice the preserved ginger thinly, reserving some for decoration, and stir into the cream. Spoon the mixture into glasses, decorate with the ginger and drizzle a little syrup over each one. Chill before serving.

LEMON SYLLABUB

SERVES 6

1 lemon
45 – 60ml/1½ – 2 fl oz brandy
150ml/¼ pint sweet white wine
300ml/½ pint double cream
75g/3 oz caster sugar
Lemon rind to garnish

Pare lemon rind thinly. In a small bowl, squeeze the juice of the lemon and add enough brandy to make

Rhubarb and Ginger Fool (left), Ginger and Advocaat Cream (centre) and Ginger Ice Cream (right).

up to 75ml/2½ fl oz. Add the rind and leave for at least six hours and then strain and stir in the caster sugar until dissolved. At this stage add the wine. Meanwhile, in another bowl, whip the cream until it holds it shape. Whisking continuously, gradually pour the lemon juice, brandy and wine into the cream – it should form soft peaks. Transfer into glasses and chill for several hours. Cut the lemon rind into thin strips, blanch for 2 – 3 minutes in boiling water, cool and use to decorate the syllabub.

CHOCOLATE ROULADE

SERVES 8 – 10

5 eggs, separated
225g/8 oz caster sugar
175g/6 oz plain chocolate
2 tablespoons water

FILLING

300ml/½ pint double cream flavoured with a
   liqueur or vanilla essence, lightly whipped

Preheat oven to 350°F/180°C/Gas Mark 4

Line a shallow Swiss roll tin with oiled greaseproof paper.

Separate the eggs and beat the yolks into the sugar until the mixture is pale yellow. Melt the chocolate with the 2 tablespoons of water in a pan over gentle heat, or melt in a microwave on defrost for 6 minutes. Beat the melted chocolate into the egg yolk and sugar mixture. Whip the egg whites until very firm and cut and fold into the chocolate mixture.

Pour the mixture into the Swiss roll tin and place in the oven. Bake the roulade for 20 minutes.

Remove the roulade from the oven and cool slightly. Cover the roulade with a clean tea cloth wrung out in cold water, this is to prevent a hard crust forming. Place the roulade in the refrigerator and leave for 12 – 24 hours.

Lay a piece of greaseproof paper on a flat surface and dust with icing sugar. Tip out the roulade upside down on to the prepared paper and remove the oiled greaseproof paper. Cover the roulade with the whipped cream and roll it up like a Swiss roll. Dust with a little extra icing sugar. Keep in the refrigerator until ready to serve.

This roulade freezes very well and thaws in just a few hours.

VANILLA AND FRESH FRUIT ROULADE

SERVES 8 – 10

5 eggs, separated
225g/8 oz caster sugar
A few drops vanilla essence
2 tablespoons honey

FILLING

300ml/10 fl oz double cream
Fresh fruits in season

Preheat oven to 350°F/180°C/Gas Mark 4

Line a shallow Swiss roll tin with oiled greaseproof paper.

Beat the egg yolks with the sugar until pale yellow and thick. Beat in the vanilla essence and honey.

Whip the egg whites until very stiff and fold into the egg yolk mixture. Pour into the prepared tin and bake in the oven for 20 minutes or until the mixture is firm to the touch.

Remove the roulade from the oven and allow to cool for a few minutes, then cover with a clean, damp tea towel and place in the refrigerator.

Meanwhile, whip the cream until it is slightly stiff. Then prepare a fruit that is in season. In the summer strawberries, raspberries or peaches are ideal, whereas in the winter, thinly sliced kiwi fruit or mango are lovely with this roulade.

Turn the roulade out upside down onto clean greaseproof paper sprinkled with soft brown or granulated sugar. Remove the oiled greaseproof paper carefully. Cover the roulade with the whipped cream and cover the cream sparingly with the fruit of your choice. Roll up the roulade and decorate along the top and around the edges with pieces of fruit to make an attractive dessert.

PRALINE ROULADE

SERVES 8 – 10

5 eggs, separated
100g/4 oz caster sugar
50g/2 oz ground almonds
½ teaspoon vanilla essence

FILLING

300ml/10 fl oz double cream
75g/3 oz whole almonds
300g/11 oz caster sugar

Preheat oven to 350°F/180°C/Gas Mark 4

Have ready a shallow Swiss roll tin lined with oiled greaseproof paper.

Beat egg yolks into sugar until pale yellow in colour, then beat in ground almonds and almond essence. Whip egg whites until very stiff and fold into egg yolk mixture. Pour the roulade mixture into the prepared tin and bake for 20 minutes. Allow to cool for a few minutes then cover with a clean, damp tea towel and place in the refrigerator.

Meanwhile, put the almonds and sugar in a small, heavy-based pan and place over gentle heat, shaking

Vanilla and Fresh Fruit Roulade (left), Chocolate Roulade (centre) and Praline Roulade (right).

the pan occasionally until the sugar has melted. Continue cooking until the sugar has turned a rich golden brown. Turn the mixture out onto a lightly-oiled baking tray. Leave until cold, then crush or grind the praline. Sprinkle half of the praline onto a clean piece of greaseproof paper. Turn the roulade out upside down and remove the greaseproof paper. Whip the double cream until stiff and cover the roulade. Sprinkle the praline over the cream, reserving a small amount.

Roll up the roulade and use the reserved praline to sprinkle and press onto the surface of the roulade.

This roulade is delicious served with a fresh fruit salad.

JELLY ORANGES

A quick and easy sweet for children.

125g/4½ oz orange jelly
6 medium oranges
150ml/5 fl oz double cream
    or thick natural yoghurt (Greek is nice)

Make up the jelly according to the instructions on the packet. Leave to cool. Meanwhile, slice off a "lid" from each of the oranges and reserve. With a sharp knife, scoop out the flesh from each orange and chop it roughly. If the oranges do not stand up by themselves, cut a thin slice from the base, still leaving the skin intact. When the jelly is cold but not set, add the orange flesh and spoon into the orange skins. Leave to set.

Just before serving, put a spoonful of whipped cream or yoghurt on the top of each orange and finish each one off with a "lid".

ORANGE CUSTARD TART

PASTRY

225g/8 oz plain flour
100g/4 oz margarine
Pinch of salt
2 tablespoons cold water

FILLING

1 orange
4 eggs
300ml/½ pint milk
100g/4 oz caster sugar

To decorate: 2 – 3 oranges

Preheat oven to 375°F/190°C/Gas Mark 5

Pastry: Sieve the flour and salt together into a mixing bowl. Add the fat in small pieces and rub into the flour with your fingertips until the mixture resembles fine breadcrumbs. Mix to a stiff dough with cold water. Roll out to fit a 20cm/8″ flan ring or pie dish.

Filling: Grate the rind of the orange, squeeze the juice and add to the eggs, milk and sugar. Beat well and pour into the pastry case. Bake for about 40 minutes in a preheated oven until golden. Leave to cool.

Meanwhile, peel carefully the oranges for decoration. Slice them and arrange the slices on top of the tart.

Facing page: Jelly Oranges (top centre), Orange Custard Tart (bottom left) and Almond Orange Gateau (right).

Below: Raspberry Sherry Trifle.

RASPBERRY SHERRY TRIFLE

A traditional family favourite.

SERVES 6 – 8

6 – 8 trifle sponge cakes
Raspberry jam
4 tablespoons medium sherry
1 tin raspberries
   or 225g – 350g/8 – 12 oz frozen raspberries
600ml/1 pint custard
300ml/½ pint double cream
Flaked almonds or ratafias for decoration

Split the sponge cakes, spread with raspberry jam, sandwich together again and arrange in the base of a glass bowl. Drain the tin of raspberries and use a little of the juice to sprinkle over the sponge cakes, together with the sherry. If frozen raspberries are used, thaw fruit.

Make the custard and, when cool, pour over the trifle base. Leave until completely cold. Whip the

cream until it forms soft peaks and spread over the custard. Just before serving, decorate with flaked toasted almonds, ratafias, cherries or angelica, or anything suitable you may find in your cupboard.

ALMOND ORANGE GATEAU

A mouthwatering cake, rich enough to serve as a dessert.

175g/6 oz butter
175g/6 oz caster sugar
6 eggs
100g/4 oz self-raising flour
175g/6 oz ground almonds

FILLING
298g/10½ oz tin mandarin oranges, drained
50g/2 oz icing sugar
150ml/5 fl oz double cream
5g/¼ oz gelatine
1 tablespoon hot water
Apricot jam
1 orange
Toasted sliced almonds

2 x 18cm/7″ round cake tins (greased and floured)
Preheat oven to 375°F/190°C/Gas Mark 5

In a bowl, cream together the butter and sugar, gradually beat in the eggs and fold in the flour and ground almonds.

Pour into the cake tins and bake for 30 – 35 minutes until cooked. Turn out onto cake racks to cool.

For the filling, purée the mandarin oranges and icing sugar. Lightly whip the cream and fold into the fruit mixture. Dissolve the gelatine in 1 tablespoon hot water and add. Put the filling into one of the cleaned cake tins that has been dampened, and refrigerate until it sets (about 2 hours).

Remove from the tin and set between the 2 sponge layers. Brush apricot jam across the top of the cake and decorate with sliced almonds and oranges.

PINEAPPLE LAYERED CREAM

SERVES 4

300ml/½ pint double cream
450ml/15 fl oz natural yoghurt
100g/4 oz muscavado or demerara sugar
376g/13¼ oz tin crushed pineapple (drained)

Whip the cream to soft peaks and fold in yoghurt.

Place drained pineapple in the base of 4 individual glasses or a large serving dish. Put cream mixture on top. Sprinkle sugar over and leave for several hours.

CHILLED CHOCOLATE LAYER PUDDING

SERVES 4

2 rounded tablespoons of drinking chocolate
1 level dessertspoon coffee powder
100g/4 oz fresh white breadcrumbs
100g/4 oz demerara sugar
150ml/5 fl oz single cream
150ml/5 fl oz double cream
Chocolate chips for decoration

Mix together chocolate and coffee powders, crumbs and sugar. Whisk cream until thick and forms peaks.

In a glass serving dish, layer the chocolate/coffee mixture and the cream, finishing with a cream layer. Chill for several hours. Decorate with chocolate chips.

COFFEE MERINGUE CAKE

Not for weightwatchers this gooey confection!

SERVES 6 – 8

MERINGUES
4 egg whites
225g/8 oz caster sugar

FILLING
100g/4 oz granulated sugar
6 tablespoons water
4 egg yolks
275g/10 oz unsalted butter
1 – 2 tablespoons instant coffee
    dissolved in 1 tablespoon hot water

TO DECORATE
100g/4 oz finely chopped nuts (walnuts
    or almonds)
2 tablespoons icing sugar

Preheat oven to 250°F/120°C/Gas Mark ½

Draw a 23cm/9″ circle on each of 3 pieces of greaseproof paper or Bakewell paper. Place the paper on 3 baking sheets. Lightly oil the greaseproof paper. Whisk the egg whites until stiff, then whisk in half the sugar until stiff and glossy. Fold the remaining sugar in gently with a metal spoon. Spread the mixture evenly over the 3 circles and bake in a preheated oven for 1½-2 hours.

Leave the meringues to cool before peeling off the paper.

Pineapple Layered Cream (top left), Chilled Chocolate Layer Pudding (top right) and Coffee Meringue Cake (bottom).

To make the buttercream filling, firstly dissolve the sugar in the water in a pan over gentle heat, then boil steadily until the mixture forms a "thread". To test, take a little on a teaspoon, allow to cool slightly and it should pull to a fine thread when pressed between thumb and forefinger. Pour this syrup, while still hot, onto the egg yolks and whisk until a thick mousse is formed.

Meanwhile, in another bowl, cream the butter until soft and beat in the egg and sugar mousse a little at a time. Add the coffee. Allow to cool. Use this cream to sandwich the meringue rounds together, leaving enough to spread over the top and sides. Press the chopped nuts on top and around the sides of the cake.

Cut strips of greaseproof paper about 2 ½ cm/1″ wide and lay across the top of the cake, leaving equal spaces between the strips. Dust the top with icing sugar and then carefully remove the paper, leaving an attractive and professional looking finish to this rich dessert.

VANILLA FLOATING ISLANDS

SERVES 6

CUSTARD

450ml/¾ pint milk
4 egg yolks
50g/2 oz caster sugar
1 level tablespoon cornflour
Few drops vanilla essence

MERINGUE ISLANDS

4 egg whites
150g/5 oz caster sugar
2 tablespoons crushed praline

Heat the milk in a saucepan until almost boiling. In a mixing bowl, mix together the egg yolks, sugar and cornflour. Slowly add the hot milk and stir well. Strain the mixture back into the saucepan and set over a low heat. Stir until the custard thickens but do not allow the mixture to boil. Turn the custard into a clean bowl and add a few drops of vanilla essence. Stir the mixture, to prevent a skin forming, until it is cold. Cover with cling film.

In a medium-sized mixing bowl, whisk the egg whites until stiff. Add the sugar, a spoonful at a time, beating well after each addition.

Fill a frying pan with water and bring to simmering point. With a tablespoon, scoop out mounds of meringue mixture and drop gently into the water, using another tablespoon to help remove the mixture from the first spoon. Only cook four or five at a time.

Vanilla, Chocolate and Coffee Floating Islands.

Poach the meringues gently for 3 or 4 minutes, then scoop from the water with a draining spoon and place on kitchen paper to drain. Continue poaching all the meringue mixture in the same way.

Place the custard in a large serving dish and gently pile the poached meringues on top. Chill until ready to serve then sprinkle with crushed praline.

VARIATIONS

Chocolate Floating Islands For the custard, continue as before, but flavour the custard with one tablespoon of cocoa powder dissolved in a little hot water until it makes a smooth paste. Omit the vanilla essence. Add the chocolate mixture to the custard, beating well.

When the dish is assembled, sprinkle with cocoa powder until the dish is finely covered.

Coffee Floating Islands For the custard, continue as before, but flavour the custard with a level tablespoon of coffee granules mixed to a smooth paste with a little hot water. Add this to taste to the custard, beating well. Omit the vanilla essence.

When the dish is assembled, sprinkle with finely grated nutmeg until the dish is finely covered.

VANILLA ICE CREAM

A rich, custard-based ice cream

MAKES 852ml/1½ PINTS

300ml/10 fl oz milk
1 vanilla pod or a few drops vanilla essence
4 egg yolks
100g/4 oz caster sugar
300ml/10 fl oz whipping or double cream

Turn freezer to its lowest setting before you begin

Slit open the vanilla pod and add to the milk in a small saucepan. Bring to the boil, turn off the heat and leave to infuse for 20 minutes. Remove the vanilla pod. If vanilla essence is used, the infusion is not necessary. Whisk the egg yolks together with the sugar and gradually stir in the strained milk. Return to the saucepan and cook very gently over low heat, stirring constantly, for about 3 or 4 minutes until the custard thickens and coats the back of a wooden spoon. Leave to cool and fold in the stiffly whipped cream. Spoon into a shallow container and freeze until the sides begin to harden. Turn into a bowl and whisk. Return to the freezer to set hard.

Transfer from the freezer to the refrigerator an hour before serving.

Fresh fruit ice creams.

MANGO ICE CREAM

900ml/1½ pints vanilla ice cream
    (custard based – see recipe)
2 ripe mangoes
2 teaspoons lemon or lime juice

Turn freezer to its lowest setting before you begin

Peel the mangoes and remove the stones. Liquidize the flesh with the lemon or lime juice to a smooth purée. Combine with the custard ice cream and turn out into a freezing tray. Freeze for 3 – 4 hours until the ice cream has frozen to a depth of about 2cm/¾ " around the sides. Turn out into a bowl and beat until smooth. Return it to the freezing tray and freeze until firm.

Transfer the ice cream from the freezer to the refrigerator an hour before serving.

CHERRY ICE CREAM

225g/8 oz cherries
150ml/5 fl oz water
50g/2 oz sugar
Juice of ½ a lemon
2 tablespoons cherry brandy or kirsch
Basic vanilla ice cream

Stone and halve the cherries and poach gently in the previously dissolved water and sugar. Strain and cool. Add the alcohol and stir mixture into the basic ice cream. Freeze.

BLACKCURRANT ICE CREAM

This has both a delicious taste and colour, and the same recipe can apply to redcurrants and raspberries.

SERVES 6 – 8

450g/1 lb blackcurrants
175g/6 oz caster sugar
150ml/5 fl oz water
300ml/½ pint double cream, lightly whipped

Wash the blackcurrants and, without stripping them off their stalks, push them through a nylon sieve into a mixing bowl, extracting as much pulp as possible. Discard skins, pips and stalks. In a small saucepan, dissolve the sugar in the water and boil for 3 more minutes. Pour the liquid over the fruit pulp. Allow to cool slightly and fold in the whipped cream. Transfer to a polythene box or ice tray and freeze until the ice cream is just beginning to set. Remove from freezer or refrigerator, turn into a bowl and beat thoroughly. Return ice cream to its container and freeze until firm.

Remove from freezer one hour before serving.

Above: Coeur à la Crème.

Facing page: A pastry base from Lemon Tart recipe (page 164), filled with Crème Pâtissière and topped with fresh cherries makes a delicious summer dish.

COEUR À LA CRÈME

An irresistible dessert that looks extremely pretty when the traditional heart-shaped moulds are used. However, small ramekins are also effective. Try using the curd cheese mixture as a flan filling with red summer fruits piled on top and glazed.

SERVES 6

450g/1 lb curd cheese
100g/4 oz caster sugar
Grated rind of a lemon
3 large ripe peaches
Juice of ½ lemon
2 tablespoons orange liqueur
4 tablespoons dry white wine

To decorate: 6 ripe strawberries

Simply combine the curd cheese, sugar and lemon rind together (this can be done in a food processor). Press the mixture into six small moulds. Chill for

4 – 6 hours. Meanwhile, skin, halve and stone the peaches. Liquidize the flesh and mix in the lemon juice, orange liqueur and dry white wine.

When you are ready to serve, turn out the moulds onto flat plates and spoon a little peach purée around each one. Partly slice each strawberry and fan them out to decorate each plate.

Many different fruits could be used with the coeur à la crème – try blueberries as a dramatic contrast, or raspberries.

PASSION FRUIT ICE CREAM

This most fragrant of fruits makes a delicious ice cream.

SERVES 6 – 8

6 – 8 passion fruit
225g/8 oz sugar
250ml/8 fl oz water
300ml/10 fl oz double cream, whipped

Turn freezer down to lowest setting.

Scoop out the pulp from the passion fruit into a basin. Simmer together the sugar and water for 3 minutes and pour onto the fruit. Leave to cool

slightly before sieving. Discard the black seeds. Pour this bright orange juice into a shallow container and freeze until the edges are firm and the middle mushy. Beat well and fold in the whipped cream. Freeze.

Transfer from the freezer to the refrigerator for an hour before serving.

REDCURRANT AND RASPBERRY ICE CREAM

SERVES 6 – 8

225g/8 oz raspberries
225g/8 oz redcurrants
175g/6 oz sugar
150ml/¼ pint water
300ml/½ pint double cream

Simply sieve the raspberries and redcurrants into a mixing bowl. There is no need to remove the stalks from the redcurrants. When all the pulp has been extracted discard the skins, pips and stalks.

In a saucepan, put the sugar and water and bring gently to the boil, stirring until the sugar has dissolved, then boil for 3 minutes. Remove from the heat and add the fruit purée. Stir well. Allow to cool. Whip the cream until floppy, not stiff, and fold this into the fruit mixture. Turn out into a polythene box and freeze for 3 – 4 hours until it starts to go mushy. Remove from the freezer, turn it out into a bowl and beat thoroughly. Pour the ice cream back into the box, cover and freeze. An hour before serving, transfer from the freezer to the refrigerator.

MELON WITH RASPBERRIES

Choose ripe Ogen or Galia melons and simply halve them, remove the seeds and fill the cavities with fresh raspberries. Sprinkle on a little liqueur such as framboise or a little port.

FRESH FRUIT SALAD

Any combination of fresh fruit makes a welcome dessert for weight watchers, or at the end of a rich meal.

Instead of making a sugar syrup to provide the liquid, use fresh orange juice or even an exotic fruit juice like passion fruit.

If you have the time, take the pips out of grapes – your guests will appreciate the effort.

Bananas, apples and pears benefit from lemon juice being squeezed over them to stop them discolouring. For health reasons and for colour, keep the skin on apples and pears. A handful of strawberries or a sliced kiwi fruit adds impact.

A green fruit salad using melon, grapes, apples, pears, kiwi fruit is a little out of the ordinary. A red fruit salad using summer fruits – strawberries, cherries, raspberries, redcurrants etc looks good.

CRÈME BRÛLÉE

This dessert is very rich and particularly good served with fresh pineapple, fruit compôte or fresh fruit salad. It is a good dinner party dessert as it must be made the day before required.

SERVES 6 – 8

4 egg yolks
50g/2 oz caster sugar
1 level teaspoon cornflour
300ml/½ pint double cream
300ml/½ pint single cream
Vanilla essence – a few drops
6 x 7.5 cm/3″ ramekins or 1 x 1 litre/1¾ pt
    soufflé dish

Blend together the egg yolks, cornflour, caster sugar and vanilla essence in a bowl. Meanwhile, heat the cream until it reaches boiling point and pour it into the bowl with the other ingredients, stirring all the time with a wooden spoon. Mix well and return to the saucepan on a gentle heat. Stir continually until the cream has thickened. This will take a few minutes. If the cream overheats, remove from the heat and beat until it becomes smooth. Divide the mixture between the six ramekins or pour into the soufflé dish. Leave to cool. Cover with cling film and refrigerate overnight.

For the Caramel

METHOD 1
75g/3 oz granulated sugar
3 tablespoons water

Place the sugar and water in a pan over a low heat until the sugar dissolves. Boil until a golden brown colour. Pour this caramel over the cream and chill until required.

METHOD 2

Sprinkle the top of the chilled cream with granulated sugar. Place under a very hot preheated grill until the sugar melts and turns golden. Do not allow to burn. Return the crème brûlée to the refrigerator until needed.

Facing page: Melon with Raspberries (top), Fresh Fruit Salad (centre left) and Crème Brulée (bottom).

Overleaf: Summer Pudding (left) and Easy Raspberry Mousse (right).

EASY RASPBERRY MOUSSE

Cream is still an expensive ingredient, so just for a change use evaporated milk, especially when the consumers are to be children!

SERVES 4

175g/6 oz evaporated milk
375g/13 oz can of raspberries
1 packet raspberry jelly
1 egg white (optional, but increases volume)

Chill the can of evaporated milk for at least an hour in the refrigerator. Drain the liquid from the tin of raspberries into a measuring jug and make up to 300ml/½ pint with water. Use this liquid to make the jelly, following the packet instructions. Leave to cool until just on setting point.

Whisk the egg white until stiff. Whisk the evaporated milk until thick and frothy. Whisk the jelly and add the evaporated milk. Continue whisking for a couple more minutes. Fold in the beaten egg white and the raspberries. Turn into a mould and leave to set.

CHOCOLATE CREAM PIE

SERVES 6

BISCUIT CRUST

225g/8 oz digestive or gingernut biscuits
150g/5 oz butter

FILLING

300ml/½ pint milk
25g/1 oz caster sugar
25g/1 oz plain flour
1½ level teaspoons cornflour
2 eggs, beaten
25g/1 oz unsalted butter
100g/4 oz plain dark chocolate, grated
2 teaspoons brandy
Icing sugar
150ml/¼ pint double cream
Additional grated chocolate for decoration

Biscuit Crust Crush the biscuits, a few at a time, in a grinder or in a plastic bag with a rolling pin. Put into a mixing bowl. Melt the butter gently in a small saucepan over a low heat and add to the biscuit crumbs. Mix well together and turn into a 18–20cm/7–8″ shallow flan or pie dish. With your fingers or the back of a spoon, press the crumb mixture over the base and up the sides of the dish. Chill for at least two hours.
Filling In a saucepan, gently heat the milk. Meanwhile, blend together the sugar, flour and beaten eggs in a bowl. Stir in the hot milk and return this mixture to the saucepan. Cook over a low heat, stirring continuously until it thickens and is just coming to the boil. Remove the pan from the heat and add the chocolate, butter and brandy. Stir until these ingredients have been well incorporated, and

allow to cool. Turn this mixture into the biscuit crust and dust with icing sugar to prevent a skin forming. Refrigerate.

Just before serving, whip the cream until it forms soft peaks. Spread over the filling. Decorate with grated chocolate.

SUMMER PUDDING

This dessert must be prepared at least 24 hours before it is needed and is an excellent way of using up a glut of soft summer fruits. Most soft fruits can be used, but raspberries and redcurrants should predominate, both for taste and final colour.

SERVES 6

900g/2 lb mixed soft fruit (i.e. raspberries, redcurrants, blackcurrants, cherries, strawberries)
8 slices day-old white bread with crusts removed
100g/4 oz caster sugar (more or less can be used according to taste)

Prepare and wash fruit and place in a heavy-based saucepan together with the caster sugar. Cook over a low heat until the sugar dissolves and the juices start to run.

Line the base and sides of a greased 850ml/1½ pint pudding basin with some of the slices of bread, overlapping the slices slightly so any gaps are filled. Pack in the fruit and enough juice to stain the bread. Cover with the remaining slices, pour on a little more juice and retain the rest. Cover the basin with a saucer or plate which rests on the pudding itself. Add a 450g/1 lb weight or heavy tin or jar, in order to compress the pudding. Leave to stand overnight in the refrigerator or a cool place. To turn out, loosen the sides with a palette knife and invert onto a serving plate.

Serve with double cream or, if obtainable, clotted cream.

CHOCOLATE PROFITEROLES

SERVES 4–6 MAKES APPROXIMATELY 18 PROFITEROLES

CHOUX PASTRY

65g/2½ oz strong plain flour
50g/2 oz butter, cut into small pieces
¼ level teaspoon salt
2 eggs, well beaten (size 2–3)
150ml/5 fl oz cold water

Chocolate Profiteroles (top), Chocolate Mousse (centre) and Chocolate Cream Pie (bottom).

FILLING AND SAUCE

300ml/½ pint double cream
225g/8 oz plain chocolate
3 tablespoons cold water

Preheat oven to 400°F/200°C/Gas Mark 6

Sift the flour and salt together onto a piece of greaseproof paper. Put the butter and water together in a medium-sized saucepan over medium heat. Once the butter has melted and the mixture is almost boiling, remove from the heat and immediately tip in the sifted flour all in one go. Beat vigorously with a wooden spoon until a smooth ball of paste forms that leaves the pan sides clean. Return to the heat to dry out the mixture slightly (about half a minute). Remove from the heat and gradually beat in the egg until the mixture becomes less solid but resembles a stiff paste. It is now ready to be cooked.

Grease a couple of baking sheets and either with 2 spoons or with a large piping tube make small, round shapes.

Cook in a moderately hot oven for 10 minutes and then increase the heat to 425°F/220°C/Gas Mark 7 and cook for another 15 – 20 minutes until light golden. Remove and, with the handle of a teaspoon, pierce the side of each choux bun to allow the steam to escape. Return to the oven for a further 2 minutes to make even crispier.

Cool on a wire tray and store in an air-tight container. Fill not more than an hour or two before serving.

To fill Whip the double cream until fairly stiff and fill each profiterole, using a teaspoon. Melt the chocolate and water together in a basin over a saucepan of simmering water. Pour this chocolate sauce over the profiteroles and serve at once.

Crème Pâtissière (see recipe) can be used as an alternative filling for the choux buns.

REDCURRANT GRIESTORTE

SERVES 6

3 large eggs, separated
125g/5 oz caster sugar
Grated rind and juice of 1 lemon
50g/2 oz fine semolina
1 level tablespoon ground almonds
150ml/5 fl oz double cream
1 tablespoon milk
100g/4 oz redcurrants
Icing sugar
Small amount of caster sugar and flour
1 20 x 30cm/8 x 12" Swiss roll tin

Preheat oven to 350°F/180°C/Gas Mark 4

Line the Swiss roll tin with non-stick paper to extend the sides. Butter the paper and sprinkle with a little caster sugar and a dusting of flour.

In a bowl, whisk egg yolks with sugar until thick and creamy. Whisk in lemon juice. Combine ground almonds, semolina and lemon rind and stir carefully into the mixture. Whisk egg whites till stiff, then fold egg yolk mixture gently through the egg whites. Turn into the Swiss roll tin. Cook for about 30 minutes till risen and pale golden brown. Turn out carefully onto a sheet of non-stick paper dusted with caster sugar. Trim edges if necessary. Roll up loosely with paper inside. Cool on a wire rack.

Whisk together cream and milk until fairly stiff. Unroll the cake, spread with cream and sprinkle with redcurrants, reserving some for decoration. (One or two small sprays look effective on top.) Roll up, dust with icing sugar. Decorate.

Griestorte freezes well.

PINEAPPLE UPSIDE-DOWN CAKE

SERVES 6

2 large eggs
100g/4 oz butter or margarine
75g/3 oz self-raising flour
25g/1 oz ground almonds
2 tablespoons milk
½ teaspoon vanilla essence
Few drops almond essence

TOPPING

Small tin pineapple rings
25g/1 oz butter
25g/1 oz demerara sugar
25 – 50g/1 – 2 oz glacé cherries

Preheat oven to 375°F/190°C/Gas Mark 5

Cut pineapple rings in half and leave to drain, conserving juice to make a sweet sauce if liked. Halve the cherries. Cream butter and sugar till light and fluffy. Beat eggs lightly and gradually add to the creamed mixture together with the essences. Sieve flour, stir in ground almonds and fold into mixture, adding the milk to make a soft batter consistency.

Prepare a 20 cm/8" square tin or 18 cm/7" round cake tin by melting 25g/1 oz butter in the base. Grease the sides. Sprinkle demerara sugar over the melted butter. Arrange pineapple halves on the sugared base and decorate with cherries. Carefully spread the mixture on top of the fruit. Bake in a preheated oven for 45 minutes. Remove. Loosen sides with a knife and turn onto a warmed dish. Serve either with a sauce made from the pineapple juice thickened with a dessertspoon of cornflour and boiled for 2 – 3 minutes and sweetened to taste, or custard or cream.

Top: Pineapple Upside-Down Cake – may be served hot or cold. Bottom: Redcurrant Griestorte.

BAKED STUFFED PEACHES

SERVES 6

6 yellow peaches
75g/3 oz amaretti or ratafia biscuits
1 egg yolk
2 tablespoons of sugar
25g/1 oz butter
12 almonds

Preheat oven to 350°F/180°C/Gas Mark 4

Cut the peaches in half, take out the stones and some of the pulp to make a fairly deep hollow. Crush the biscuits and add the pulp, egg yolk, sugar and butter. Combine well and stuff the peaches with this mixture. Put an almond on each. Place in a buttered, shallow, fireproof dish and bake in the oven for 30 – 40 minutes. Serve hot with cream.

PEACH MELBA

This classic dessert was created by Escoffier for Dame Nellie Melba, the famous Australian opera singer.

SERVES 4

2 large, ripe peaches
2 teaspoons brown sugar
225g/8 oz raspberries
50 – 75g/2 – 3 oz icing sugar
Vanilla ice cream

Plunge the peaches into a bowl of boiling water for 1 minute. Remove and peel. Halve the fruit, sprinkle with brown sugar and put under a medium hot grill for a few minutes until tender. Alternatively, poach the peaches in a sugar syrup, until tender.

Rub the raspberries through a sieve and sweeten the resulting purée with the icing sugar.

Assemble this dessert by putting a scoop of vanilla ice cream at the bottom of each glass, cover with a peach half and top with the raspberry purée.

FRESH PEACH AND HAZELNUT MERINGUE

SERVES 6 – 8

3 large egg whites
175g/6 oz caster sugar
75g/3 oz ground hazelnuts
300ml/½ pint double cream
Few whole roasted hazelnuts
4 large firm ripe peaches

Preheat oven to 350°F/180°C/Gas Mark 4.
Grease and line the bases of 2 x 18 cm/7″ sandwich tins with greaseproof or silicone paper. Lightly oil the paper.

Whisk the egg whites until stiff and then add the sugar, a tablespoon at a time, still whisking. With a metal spoon, gently fold in the ground hazelnuts. Divide the mixture between the two tins, levelling it out. Bake in the centre of the preheated oven for 20 – 30 minutes. Allow the tins to cool before turning the meringues out onto a wire rack. Take off the base papers.

Whip the cream and to half of it add the chopped flesh of two of the peaches. Use this mixture to sandwich the meringues together. Decorate the top with the rest of the cream (piped if desired), the carefully cut slices of the other peaches and the whole hazelnuts.

MILLE FEUILLES WITH BLACK CHERRIES AND APRICOTS

A variety of fruit could be used to fill the mille feuilles. In summer raspberries, strawberries and cherries are plentiful but in winter, when suitable fruit are scarce and expensive, try tinned or frozen fruit. They work very well for this dessert.

225g/8 oz puff pastry
450ml/¾ pint double cream, stiffly whipped
3 tablespoons raspberry or strawberry jam
12 – 18 apricot halves
225g/½ lb cherries, stoned and halved

Preheat oven to 450°F/230°C/Gas Mark 8

Roll out the pastry until it is one large thin rectangle approximately 25x30cm/10x12″ in size. Prick the pastry well and place on a large baking sheet that has been dampened with cold water. This creates a steamy atmosphere and helps make the pastry rise. Place on the shelf above centre in the preheated oven and bake until golden (7 – 10 minutes). Remove from the oven, trim off any rough edges and cut the pastry into 3 equal pieces, lengthways. Turn each piece over and return to the oven for another 3 or 4 minutes until they brown and become crisp. Remove and cool on a wire rack.

To assemble Spread 2 layers with jam and sandwich the 3 layers together with half the whipped cream and most of the fruit. Pipe the rest of the cream along the sides and the top and decorate with remaining fruit.

Fresh Peach and Hazelnut Meringue (top), Peach Melba (bottom left) and Baked Stuffed Peaches (bottom right).

SUMMER FRUIT JELLY WITH PORT

This is an exotic jelly for "grown-ups" to remind them of their nursery days! However, you will find this a favourite with children and for them you can always substitute water for the port!

SERVES 8

450g/1lb blackcurrants
100g/4 oz caster sugar
225g/8 oz black cherries, stoned weight
225g/8 oz raspberries
225g/8 oz strawberries
8 teaspoons powdered gelatine
110ml/4 fl oz hot water
150ml/¼ pint port

TO DECORATE

A few extra strawberries and unstoned cherries

Put the blackcurrants and 150ml/¼ pint cold water into a large saucepan and bring to the boil. Reduce heat and simmer, covered, for about 10 minutes. Remove from the heat and rub the fruit through a nylon sieve. Put the resulting purée into a measuring jug, add 150ml/¼ pint port and enough cold water to make 1 pint of liquid. Return the liquid to the pan and add the sugar. Stir over low heat until the sugar has dissolved and then bring to the boil. Add the fruit and remove from the heat.

Meanwhile, pour the hot water into a small bowl and sprinkle on the gelatine. Leave to soften and then place the bowl in a pan of simmering water and stir until the gelatine has dissolved. Do not allow to boil. Stir this into the fruit mixture and then pour the whole jelly into a 1.4 litre/2½ pint mould which has been rinsed out in cold water. Leave to set. This jelly can be made well in advance.

Turn out the jelly onto a dish or glass stand and decorate with the extra fruit.

Serve with whipped cream or crème fraiche.

CHOCOLATE MOUSSE

A favourite dessert with people of all ages, simple to make and can be prepared well in advance.

SERVES 4

100g/4 oz plain chocolate (Meunière if you
    can buy it)
15g/½ oz butter
4 eggs

Break the chocolate into small pieces in a basin and set the basin in a saucepan half-filled with hot water over a low heat. Stir occasionally. When melted, add the butter and blend well.

Summer Fruit Jelly with Port.

Separate the eggs, adding the yolks only to the chocolate mixture. Stir well and remove the basin from the heat.

Whisk the egg whites until stiff and, using a metal spoon, gently fold them into the chocolate mixture. Pour into individual glasses or one large bowl. Chill for several hours. Decorate, if liked, with swirls of whipped double cream or, using a skewer, make several holes in the mousse and pour over a little brandy, Grand Marnier or Tia Maria just before serving.

GOOSEBERRY FOOL

A very pretty dessert and delicious served with tuile biscuits.

450g/1 lb gooseberries, topped and tailed
2 tablespoons water
100g/4 oz caster sugar
1 egg white
300ml/½ pint double cream

Wash the gooseberries and place in a pan with the water. Bring to the boil and simmer for about 10 minutes, until the fruit is soft. Fold in the sugar, stir and then remove the pan from the heat. When the sugar is dissolved, rub the gooseberry mixture through a sieve. Leave the purée to cool.

Whisk together the egg white and cream until thick and gently fold into the gooseberry purée. Spoon into individual glasses or a serving dish and chill.

APRICOT CREAM WITH BRANDIED GRAPES

SERVES 6

225g/½ lb dried apricots
300ml/10 fl oz milk
2 egg yolks
2½ tablespoons caster sugar
Cinnamon stick
300ml/10 fl oz double cream
15g/½ oz gelatine
20 black grapes
100g/4 oz black and white grapes
2 tablespoons brandy
1 ring mould

Soak the apricots in cold water for at least an hour. Drain and reserve 120ml/4 fl oz of the water. Lightly whip the cream. Macerate the 100g/4 oz black and white grapes in the brandy. Put the apricots, cinnamon stick and water in a saucepan. Cook gently until the apricots are soft, remove the cinnamon stick and purée the fruit.

Beat the egg yolks in the sugar until pale and creamy. Bring the milk to the boil and pour over the yolk mixture. Soften the gelatine with 2 table-

spoons water and stir into the custard. Allow the mixture to cool and, when thickened, add the apricot purée and 20 black grapes. Fold in the whipped cream and place in the mould which has been rinsed out with iced water. Chill for at least one hour.

Unmould the cream and decorate with the grapes that have been soaked in brandy.

ALMOND AND APRICOT MERINGUE CAKE

The addition of toasted flaked almonds to the meringue turns this into a mouth-watering dessert.

SERVES 8

BASE

225g/8 oz caster sugar
100g/4 oz toasted flaked almonds
4 egg whites

FILLING

100g/4 oz dried apricots, soaked overnight in a little water
1 tablespoon rum or brandy
300ml/½ pint double cream, stiffly whipped
50g/2 oz toasted flaked almonds

DECORATION

Icing sugar to dust
Whipped cream (optional)
Grated plain chocolate (optional)

Preheat oven to 325°F/160°C/Gas Mark 3

In a bowl, mix together the caster sugar and almonds. In another bowl, whisk the egg whites to form stiff peaks and beat in 1 tablespoon of the sugar and almond mixture. With a metal spoon, fold in the remainder.

Oil 2 baking sheets and line with silicone paper. Oil the surface of the paper. Spread the meringue into 2 x 18cm/7″ circles. Bake in the centre of the oven for 40 minutes. Turn out onto wire trays to cool and strip off the base papers.

Meanwhile, cook the soaked apricots gently with a little sugar for 10–15 minutes until tender. The apricot mixture should be fairly stiff. Leave to get absolutely cold. Add the rum or brandy and fold in the whipped cream and toasted almonds.

Sandwich the 2 meringue circles together with the apricot cream. Dust the top with icing sugar or

Almond and Apricot Meringue Cake (top), Gooseberry Fool (centre left – served with French Tuiles Biscuits – recipe page 193), Mille Feuilles with Black Cherries and Apricots (centre right) and Apricot Cream with Brandied Grapes (bottom).

pipe with whipped cream and sprinkle with more flaked almonds or grated chocolate.

This meringue freezes well, but open freeze for 3 – 4 hours and then pack in a rigid container. Allow to thaw for about 5 hours at room temperature.

CRUNCHY CHOCOLATE MERINGUE CAKE

A mouthwatering dessert. The chopped hazelnuts give the meringue a crunchy texture.

SERVES 10

MERINGUE

6 egg whites
350g/12 oz caster sugar
100g/4 oz finely chopped hazelnuts

CHOCOLATE SAUCE

275g/10 oz plain chocolate
350ml/12 oz double cream

Preheat oven to 350°F/180°C/Gas Mark 4
Line 3 x 20cm/8″ sandwich tins with bakewell paper

In a large bowl, whisk egg whites until stiff then gradually mix in sugar until mixture is glossy. Fold in chopped hazelnuts, saving a few for decoration. Divide the mixture between the 3 tins and bake in the oven for 30 – 35 minutes, until the meringue is crisp on the top. To ensure the layers cook at the same rate, move tins around during baking.

After baking, leave meringues in tins for one minute, then turn out carefully and peel away paper. The meringue should be crispy on top and soft underneath.

Chocolate Sauce Reserve a couple of squares for decoration. Place chocolate in a heavy-based pan and add 160ml/6 fl oz of cream. Heat gently until chocolate has melted completely. Leave until cold.

Whip remaining cream. Place one meringue on a plate, spread half of the chocolate sauce over it and smother the sauce with the whipped cream. Cover with the second meringue and repeat. Place last meringue on top and decorate with remaining nuts and grated chocolate.

STRAWBERRY LAYERED GATEAU

A delicious confection, comprising a sponge made with double cream sandwiched between meringue and filled with whipped cream and crushed strawberries. Raspberries, loganberries or blackberries could also be used.

SERVES 10

SPONGE MIXTURE

50g/2 oz butter
100g/4 oz caster sugar
4 egg yolks
1 teaspoon vanilla essence
75g/3 oz plain flour
25g/1 oz cornflour
2 level teaspoons baking powder
6 tablespoons double cream

MERINGUE MIXTURE

4 egg whites
225g/8 oz caster sugar
4 drops vanilla essence

FILLING

1 punnet fresh strawberries
450ml/¾ pint double cream

Preheat oven to 300°F/150°C/Gas Mark 2

An electric mixer is a great asset for this recipe

Place all the ingredients for the sponge in a basin and beat until smooth. Divide the mixture between 2 x 23cm/9″ sandwich tins.

Meringue Beat egg whites until stiff and gradually blend in the sugar and vanilla essence. Divide the meringue and spread over the sponge mixture. Bake in the centre of a preheated oven for 45 minutes. Allow to cool in the tins.

Filling Crush strawberries and mix with whipped cream. Remove sponge-meringue layers from the tins and sandwich together with the filling.

HONEYED APPLE MOUSSE

SERVES 6

1.35kg/3 lb dessert apples
40g/1½ oz butter
Grated rind of 1 lemon
3 tablespoons honey
10g/½ oz gelatine
75ml/2½ fl oz water
300ml/½ pint double cream
100g/4 oz granulated sugar
450ml/¾ pint water
Shelled walnuts to decorate

Peel, core and grate all but two apples. Put 10g/½ oz of the butter into a medium-sized saucepan with the grated apple and cook gently until the juice starts to run; increase the heat and cook to a pulp. Add the lemon rind and cook a little longer until a purée. Take the pan off the heat and add the honey.

Meanwhile, dissolve the gelatine in 75ml/2½ fl oz water (this can be done in a bowl which is

Strawberry Layered Gateau (top left), Crunchy Chocolate Meringue Cake (top right) and Honeyed Apple Mousse (bottom).

Above: Mango and Date Fruit Salad (top) and Caramelized Oranges (bottom).

Facing page: Chocolate Pears (top), Pears in Red Wine (bottom left) and Baked Pears in Cider (bottom right).

standing in a pan of simmering water, but do not allow the gelatine to boil). When clear, add the gelatine to the apple purée. Allow to cool. Lightly whip the cream and fold gently into the mixture. Turn into a 23cm/9″ shallow mould that has been oiled and leave to set.

Peel, quarter and core the remaining two apples.

Make a sugar syrup by dissolving the sugar gently in 450ml/¾ pint water. Boil for a couple of minutes and add the apple quarters. Reduce the heat and poach for 7 minutes. Leave to cool in the syrup with the lid on – this will make the apples translucent. Drain the apples and use the sugar syrup to caramelize the walnuts. Put the rest of the butter into the syrup and boil until reduced to a caramel. Remove from the heat and drop 9 or 10 regular-shaped walnuts into the mixture – lift out when coated and place on a baking sheet to cool. When ready to serve, turn the mousse out onto a plate and decorate with the poached apples and walnuts.

CARAMELIZED ORANGES

SERVES 4

8 large seedless oranges (navel are best)
225g/8 oz granulated sugar
150ml/¼ pint cold water
150ml/¼ pint warm water

Put the sugar and cold water in a pan and dissolve the sugar over a very gentle heat. Do not stir the sugar or the caramel will crystallize. Once all the sugar has melted, bring to the boil and cook steadily until the caramel is a rich brown colour. Dip the base of the pan into lukewarm water to prevent further cooking, then quickly add the warm water to the pan. Replace the pan on the heat to dissolve the caramel in the water, then pour the liquid caramel into a bowl to cool.

Pare the rind from 1 orange using a potato peeler, cut into thin strips and cook for 1 minute in boiling water, then drain.

Cut the rind, pith and first membrane from the oranges, leaving the flesh exposed. Do this over a bowl to avoid losing the juice. Cut the oranges across in even slices and arrange in a deep glass dish. Pour the caramel on top and sprinkle over the cooked orange strips. Chill well before serving.

PEARS IN RED WINE

SERVES 6

6 firm pears with stalks
100g/4 oz sugar
450ml/¾ pint red wine (nothing too grand or too
    sweet – Beaujolais or Côtes du Rhone would be
    ideal)
5cm/2″ piece of cinnamon stick
Strip of lemon rind
Juice of 1 lemon

Choose a saucepan that will just hold the pears
when put in upright. Into the pan put the wine,
sugar, cinnamon stick, lemon rind and juice. Heat
gently until the sugar is dissolved and then bring to
the boil. Boil for 5 minutes. Allow to cool slightly.
Carefully peel the pears and take out the core from
the base so that the stalks remain intact. If
necessary, take a thin slice off the bottom of the
pears so that they will stand upright.

Put the fruit into the saucepan containing the
syrup. If not completely immersed add a little
water. Cover with a lid and simmer for 30 – 40
minutes until the pears are tender (the time will
vary according to the variety and ripeness of the
fruit).

CHOCOLATE PEARS

*An impressive party dessert that can be prepared
the day before.*

SERVES 4

4 ripe pears
10g/½ oz shelled walnuts, finely chopped
10g/½ oz glacé cherries, finely chopped
100g/4 oz plain chocolate
4 dessertspoons cold black coffee
25g/1 oz unsalted butter
1 – 2 dessertspoons rum or brandy (optional)
2 eggs
Angelica to garnish

Peel the pears and cut out the cores from the base,
leaving the stalks intact. Cut a thin slice from the
base of each pear so that it will stand upright. Mix
together the chopped walnuts and glacé cherries
and, with a small teaspoon, press some of this
mixture into each pear cavity. Stand the pears in a
serving dish.

Melt the chocolate with the coffee in a bowl over
a pan of hot water, stirring occasionally. Remove
the bowl from the heat and stir in the butter and the
rum or brandy. Separate the eggs, beat the yolks one

at a time and add them to the chocolate mixture. Whisk the egg whites until they are stiff and, with a metal spoon, fold them gently into the chocolate mixture.

Spoon the mixture over the pears, coating them evenly.

Cut the angelica into leaves, put a slit in either side of the pear stalks and insert these leaves. Refrigerate the pears until required.

Serve with whipped cream.

BAKED PEARS IN CIDER

The cider turns the pears a wonderful golden colour.

SERVES 6

6 pears (they can be hard ones)
100g/4 oz sugar
300ml/½ pint sweet cider
300ml/½ pint water
Rind of ½ a lemon

Preheat oven to 300°F/150°C/Gas Mark 2

Peel the pears thinly, leaving on the stalks, and stand them upright in a deep casserole. Sprinkle them with sugar and pour over the cider and water, mixed. Add the lemon rind. Cover with a lid or double tinfoil and cook in a moderately cool oven until they are tender. This may take 4 – 5 hours.

When cooked, leave to cool, then remove the fruit to a serving dish. Strain the liquid and boil it in a small saucepan until reduced by half to a thick syrup. Allow to cool before pouring over the pears. Chill well. Serve with whipped cream.

CONTINENTAL GATEAU

An easy dessert that can be prepared a day or two in advance, or frozen for future use. It is very rich, and so goes a long way!

SERVES 8

2 packets sponge fingers (20 per packet)
100g/4 oz caster sugar
100g/4 oz butter
1 egg yolk
150ml/¼ pint milk
½ cup medium sherry
100g/4 oz ground almonds
3 teaspoons coffee essence
Chopped nuts to decorate

In a basin, cream together the butter and sugar until light and fluffy and gradually beat in the egg yolk and half the milk. Stir in ground almonds and coffee essence. Onto a shallow plate, pour the remaining milk and sherry. Dip the sponge fingers separately into this liquid and arrange a layer (approximately 7)

on a long, flat dish. Cover with a layer of the egg and sugar mixture. Repeat. Completely cover gateau with remaining mixture. Mask sides with chopped nuts and decorate. Leave for several hours before serving.

STRIPY MANGO DELIGHT

A quick and easy dessert enhanced by the stunning colour of the fruit.

SERVES 6

4 large, ripe, fresh or tinned mangoes
1 tablespoon lemon juice
Icing sugar
450ml/¾ pint double cream, lightly whipped, or Greek yoghurt

Peel the mangoes, chop the flesh roughly and process in a blender until a smooth purée. Stir in the lemon juice and icing sugar to taste. The quantity will depend on the fruit and individual preference.

Then, in a large glass bowl or individual glasses, layer the mango purée and the whipped cream or yoghurt, swirling the mango into the cream in the final layer. Chill.

MANGO AND DATE FRUIT SALAD

SERVES 4

3 ripe mangoes
12 dates
2 tablespoons white wine

Slice the mango flesh away from the stone in even slices. Cut the dates in half and remove the stones.

Place the mango flesh and the stoned dates in a pretty glass dish and sprinkle on the white wine. Cover with cling film and chill until required.

This fruit salad goes particularly well with a crème brûlée or vanilla ice cream.

LEMON SOUFFLÉ

A popular dessert for many years.

SERVES 6 – 8

6 level teaspoons gelatine
4 tablespoons hot water
4 large eggs
100g/4 oz caster sugar
Grated rind and juice of 2 lemons
300ml/½ pint double cream

DECORATION

150ml/¼ pint double cream, whipped.
Chopped nuts

Stripy Mango Delight (top), Lemon Souffle (bottom left) and Continental Gateau (bottom right).

Prepare a 600ml/1 pint soufflé dish by fixing a collar of greaseproof paper around the rim to come approximately 7.5 cm/3″ above the edge. Fasten with string or sticky tape. Sprinkle the gelatine onto the hot water and stir until dissolved. If necessary, place the bowl in a pan of simmering water but do not allow the gelatine to boil. Whisk egg yolks, sugar, rind and juice together until thick and pale. Stir in the gelatine. Leave until it begins to set.

Meanwhile, whip the cream until a trail just holds its shape on the surface. Whisk the egg whites until they hold their shape as peaks. Fold the lemon mixture into the cream and then gently fold in the whites. Pour into the soufflé dish and refrigerate. Just before serving, peel off the paper collar and decorate the soufflé with swirls of double cream. Press chopped toasted nuts around the sides.

Hot Puddings

REDCURRANT AND RASPBERRY CRUMBLE

SERVES 4 – 6

225g/8 oz redcurrants
225g/8 oz raspberries
75g/3 oz caster sugar

CRUMBLE TOPPING

225g/8 oz plain flour (or wholewheat flour)
100g/4 oz soft brown or demerara sugar
75g/3 oz butter in small pieces

Preheat oven to 350°F/180°C/Gas Mark 4

Strip the redcurrants from their stalks, hull the raspberries if necessary and combine the two fruits. Place in the bottom of a pie dish and sprinkle with the caster sugar.

For the crumble topping, put the flour in a large mixing bowl together with the pieces of butter. Rub together with your fingertips until the mixture resembles fine breadcrumbs (this can be done in a food processor). Add the sugar and mix thoroughly before spooning over the fruit. Press down lightly with a fork. Bake on a high shelf for 40 – 45 minutes until just starting to turn brown.

Serve with cream, custard or ice cream.

APRICOT AND SOURED CREAM FLAN

SERVES 6

PÂTE BRISÉE (sweet shortcrust pastry)

200g/7 oz flour
85g/3½ oz butter
½ teaspoon salt
1 tablespoon sugar
3 tablespoons water

FILLING

450g/1 lb ripe apricots, halved and stoned
300ml/10 fl oz soured cream
40g/1½ oz caster sugar
Few drops almond essence

TOPPING

50g/2 oz demerara sugar
50g/2 oz blanched flaked almonds
10g/½ oz butter

Preheat oven to 400°F/200°C/Gas Mark 6

For the pastry, place the flour in a bowl and add the butter. With a knife, cut the butter into very small pieces. Make a well in the flour and butter mixture, add the salt and sugar and pour in the water, a little at a time, mixing together with a wooden spoon. Form the pastry into a ball with your hands – it should be workable without being too soft. Roll the pastry in flour and leave to rest for 30 minutes. On a floured board, shape the pastry with the palm of your hand into a large round. Fold this into four and roll out into the required size with a rolling pin. Transfer carefully to a flan tin, 20-25cm/8 – 10″. Trim by running the rolling pin across the edges of the tin. Glaze with beaten egg. Bake blind in a moderately hot oven for 15 – 20 minutes. Remove.

To make the filling, beat the soured cream, caster sugar, egg yolks and almond essence together in a bowl. Arrange the apricot halves in the flan case and pour over the cream mixture. Return the flan case to the oven for a further 20 minutes.

Meanwhile, combine the demerara sugar and almonds and sprinkle on top of the flan and dot with butter. Bake for another 20 minutes until the apricots are tender. Serve warm.

LEMON TART

A rich pâte sablée complements the tangy filling of this tart.

PASTRY (Pâte Sablée)

150g/5 oz plain flour
50g/2 oz icing sugar
A pinch of salt
100g/4 oz butter
1 egg yolk
Few drops vanilla essence

Facing page: Redcurrant and Raspberry Crumble.

Overleaf: Apricot and Soured Cream Flan (top), Lemon Tart (centre right) and Plum and Cognac Cream Tart (bottom left).

FILLING

Finely grated rind and juice of 2 large lemons
3 large eggs
175g/6 oz caster sugar
150ml/¼ pint double cream

Preheat oven to 350°F/180°C/Gas Mark 4

Into a food processor, sift the flour, icing sugar and salt. Add the butter cut up into large dice. Process until the mixture resembles fine breadcrumbs. Stop and add the egg yolk and vanilla essence. Process until the pastry forms a ball around the blade. Do not process any longer. Chill the pastry for 30 minutes.

Roll out the pastry thinly on a floured board and line a 20cm/8″ flan tin. Bake blind in a preheated oven for about 15 minutes. Remove and reduce heat to 300°F/150°C/Gas Mark 2.

To make the filling, whisk together all the ingredients lightly and pour into the pastry case. Return it to the cooled oven for another 15 minutes, or until the filling has just set.

Serve warm.

MARMALADE BREAD AND BUTTER PUDDING

A variation on the traditional pudding.

SERVES 4 – 6

12 slices white bread
Butter
Marmalade
50g/2 oz sultanas
50g/2 oz caster sugar
450ml/¾ pint milk
75ml/2½ fl oz double cream
3 large eggs
Grated nutmeg

Preheat oven to 325°F/160°C/Gas Mark 3

Spread the bread with butter and marmalade, leaving enough buttered bread only for the top layer. Arrange some of the marmalade bread in a buttered oven-proof dish. Sprinkle with some of the sultanas and sugar. Repeat.

The final layer should be the buttered bread only. Sprinkle this top layer with sugar. Whisk the eggs and then incorporate the milk and cream. Pour over the bread and sprinkle over some grated nutmeg. Bake in a warm oven for 45 – 60 minutes, until the pudding is set and the top is crisp and golden.

Serve warm.

RHUBARB CRUMBLE

SERVES 4 – 6

675g/1½ lb rhubarb
50g/2 oz sugar

TOPPING

175g/6 oz plain flour
75g/3 oz margarine
75g/3 oz brown sugar

Preheat oven to 350°F/180°C/Gas Mark 4

Base Wash rhubarb and cut into 2.5 – 5cm/1 – 2″ pieces and place in a greased 1.1 litre/2 pint ovenproof dish together with the 50g/2 oz sugar.

Topping Rub together the flour and margarine until they resemble fine breadcrumbs. Add the brown sugar and put this mixture on top of the fruit. Bake for 30 – 40 minutes.

Serve with custard or ice cream.

SUTHERLAND APPLE PUDDING

SERVES 6

100g/4 oz butter
100g/4 oz sugar
225g/8 oz self-raising flour, sifted
1 egg
¼ teaspoon salt
50g/2 oz sultanas
2 dessertspoons brown sugar
½ teaspoon ground cinnamon
450g/1 lb cooking apples

Preheat oven to 350°F/180°C/Gas Mark 4

Melt the butter and mix with the sugar. Add the egg and beat lightly. Gradually add the sifted flour and salt. Grease a shallow pudding dish and spread two-thirds of this mixture over the bottom of the dish.

Peel, core and slice the apples thinly and place over the mixture together with the sultanas. Sprinkle

Rhubarb Crumble (top left), Marmalade Bread and Butter Pudding (top right) and Sutherland Apple Pudding (bottom).

the brown sugar and cinnamon over the top. Place the remaining pudding mixture in spoonfuls on top of the apples. Bake in the centre of the oven for 40 – 45 minutes.

Serve hot or cold.

DEEP-FRIED APPLE PUFFS

MAKES ABOUT 12

450g/1 lb puff pastry
675g/1½ lb cooking apples
40g/1½ oz granulated sugar (more if liked)
Squeeze of lemon juice
Oil for deep frying
Caster sugar for dusting

Peel and core the apples and cook them with the sugar and lemon juice until a purée.

Roll out the pastry thinly and cut out circles approximately 7.5cm/3″ in diameter. Put a teaspoon of apple purée on one half of each circle. Dampen the edges with cold water, fold over pastry and seal edges tightly. Heat oil and deep-fry the apple puffs until golden brown.

Drain on kitchen paper and serve at once, dusted with sugar.

PLUM AND COGNAC CREAM TART

The colour of the plums contrast well with the yellowy custard and the cognac makes it a little bit special.

SERVES 6

PÂTE BRISÉE
200g/7 oz flour
85g/3½ oz butter
½ teaspoon salt
1 tablespoon sugar
3 tablespoons cold water

FILLING
6 – 8 ripe dessert plums, halved and stoned
1 egg
40g/1½ oz caster sugar
25g/1 oz flour
150ml/5 fl oz double cream
1 – 2 tablespoons cognac
1 tablespoon vanilla sugar or demerara sugar.

Preheat oven to 400°F/200°C/Gas Mark 6

Make up the pastry as for the Apricot and Soured Cream Flan. Roll out and line a 20cm/8″ flan tin and bake the flan blind for 15 minutes. Remove from the oven. Arrange the plum halves in the pastry case and return the flan to the oven for 15 minutes to partly cook the fruit.

Meanwhile, in a bowl, whisk together the egg

and sugar until thick, add the flour and beat until smooth. Add the cream and cognac and mix well. Spoon the custard over the plums, sprinkle with vanilla sugar or demerara sugar and return the tart to the oven. Bake for another 20 minutes until the custard is set. Serve warm or cold.

CHURROS

These are a speciality of Spain, which are sold in bags from stalls in the street. They are great fun to cook for a small group of children.

SERVES 4

50g/2 oz butter, cut into small pieces
150ml/5 fl oz cold water
60g/2½ oz strong plain flour, sieved
2 eggs, well beaten
Oil for deep frying
100g/4 oz caster sugar mixed with 1 teaspoon
    ground cinnamon

Put the butter and water in a heavy-based saucepan and bring gently to the boil. "Shoot" the flour in all at once and stir vigorously until all the flour is incorporated and the mixture leaves the sides of the pan. Cool slightly before beating in the eggs gradually until a glossy paste is formed.

In a deep-fryer or large saucepan with a basket, heat the oil to 350°F/180°C. Spoon some of the mixture into a piping bag with a 1cm/½″ nozzle.

When the oil is hot enough, pipe approximately 15cm/6″ lengths of choux paste into the pan and fry quickly until golden (about 3-4 minutes). Lovely wiggly shapes will evolve. Do not try to fry too many at once. Remove from the oil, drain and sprinkle with the sugar and cinnamon mixture. Serve at once while fresh and warm.

JAM SANDWICH FRITTERS

A teatime treat for the children.

2 slices white or wholemeal bread per person
Butter for spreading
Red jam
1 egg
150ml/¼ pint milk
4 tablespoons cooking oil
25g/1 oz butter
25g/1 oz caster sugar

Remove the crusts from the bread. Spread with butter and sandwich together with jam. Cut into quarters. Heat the cooking oil and 25g/1 oz butter in a frying pan.

In a bowl, beat together the egg and milk and, using a fork, dip the sandwiches into the mixture. Fry gently until both sides are lightly browned. Serve immediately on a hot dish, sprinkling each sandwich with a little caster sugar.

Left: Fruit Fritters. Right: (clockwise from top) Churros, Deep-Fried Apple Puffs and Jam Sandwich Fritters.

followed by a layer of stewed apple. Drain the peaches and cover the apple with them. Pour over the brandy. Roll out the other half of the pastry, dampen the edge and cover the tart, pressing it firmly around the edge. Trim the edge. Make 2 or 3 cuts on the top to allow the steam to escape. Brush with milk.

Bake for approximately 25 minutes. Dust with a little icing sugar just before serving.

MINCEMEAT, PEACH AND APPLE FLAN

SERVES 6

225g/8 oz flan pastry
75-100g/3-4 oz stewed apple and mincemeat
425g/14½ oz tin peach slices
2 tablespoons brandy (optional)

Preheat oven to 375°F/190°C/Gas Mark 5

To make the pastry, sift 225g/8 oz plain flour with a pinch of salt into a basin with 25-50g/1-2 oz icing sugar. Cut 150g/5 oz butter into small pieces and add to the sifted mixture. Rub in the butter until it resembles fine breadcrumbs. Mix with one beaten egg and a little cold water until a soft, pliable consistency. Knead lightly until smooth and chill for 1 hour.

Roll out half the pastry and line a 20 cm/8″ flan dish. Spread a layer of mincemeat on the base,

FRUIT FRITTERS

Bananas, apples and pineapples lend themselves well to being deep-fried in a light, fluffy batter.

BASIC BATTER for 6 – 8 people

100g/4 oz plain flour
Pinch of salt
25g/1oz sugar
2 eggs, separated
200ml/⅓ pint milk
1 tablespoon melted butter or oil

Apples, cored and cut into rings
    about 1cm/½″ thick
Pineapple rings – 1cm/½″ thick
Bananas, quartered (halved and slit lengthways)
Oil or fat for deep frying

171

Sieve the flour and salt into a basin. Add the sugar. Make a well in the centre and put in the beaten egg yolks and half of the milk. Stir until it forms a smooth paste. Add the rest of the milk until a thick batter forms. Leave to stand for at least 1 hour. Just before using, whisk the egg whites until stiff and fold into the batter together with the melted butter or oil.

Heat the deep fat or oil until almost smoking hot. Test by dropping in a cube of bread. If it rises to the surface and turns golden in 30 seconds the oil is ready to cook the fritters.

Dip the pieces of fruit in the batter, a few at a time, allowing the excess batter to drip off, and deep-fry for 3 – 4 minutes until crisp and golden. Drain on kitchen paper and keep warm in a moderate oven(350°F/180°C/Gas Mark 4) while cooking the rest of the fruit.

Sprinkle with caster sugar and serve.

FRENCH APPLE FLAN

SERVES 6

PASTRY CASE

75g/3 oz plain flour
75g/3 oz self-raising flour
50g/2 oz butter
50g/2 oz margarine
25g/1 oz sifted icing sugar
Cold water (about 2 – 3 tablespoons)

FILLING

4 tablespoons apricot jam
2 tablespoons water
Juice of one small lemon
575g/1¼ lb Bramley apples
1 tablespoon caster sugar

Preheat oven to 400°F/200°C/Gas Mark 6

Place flours in a bowl then rub in fats until the mixture resembles fine breadcrumbs. Stir in the icing sugar. Mix to a firm but pliable dough with cold water.

Alternatively, sieve the flours into the bowl of a food processor, adding the fats in small pieces. Process for 5 seconds. Add the icing sugar and process for 2 seconds. Then, with the motor on, add cold water until all the ingredients form a dough.

Knead the dough lightly on a floured surface. Roll the pastry out and use to line a 23 – 24cm/9 – 9½″ loose-bottomed French fluted flan tin.

Boil together the jam and water for 2 – 3 minutes, stirring constantly. Sieve the glaze into a cup to cool.

Mincemeat, Peach and Apple Flan (top), Apple Dumplings (bottom left) and French Apple Flan (bottom right).

Squeeze the lemon juice into a bowl. Peel, core and thinly slice the apples straight into the lemon juice. Arrange the apple slices neatly in the pastry case. Sprinkle with the sugar.

Place the flan on a baking sheet and cook in the preheated oven for approximately 35 minutes. Whilst still hot, brush the flan with the apricot glaze.

Serve warm with thick cream.

CHOCOLATE PUDDING

SERVES 4

50g/2 oz butter
100g/4 oz caster sugar
250g/9 oz self-raising flour
1 teaspoon baking powder
¼ teaspoon salt
1 egg, beaten
300ml/½ pint milk
50g/2 oz cooking chocolate
1 teaspoon vanilla essence

Beat the butter and sugar to a cream in a mixing bowl. Sieve the flour, baking powder and salt together and beat the egg and milk together. Add the sieved flour mixture to the creamed butter and sugar alternately with the beaten egg and milk. Melt the chocolate, add to it the vanilla essence and beat this into the flour mixture.

Steam in a well-buttered pudding basin covered with greaseproof paper and foil for 2 hours. During cooking, top up the level of water (which should reach halfway up the basin) with boiling water if necessary.

Serve with a hot sauce – either chocolate or cocoa added to a sweet, white sauce – or custard.

TREACLE TART

An old-fashioned favourite. Good served with custard or cream.

SERVES 4 – 6

225g/8 oz shortcrust pastry
8 tablespoons golden syrup
2 tablespoons lemon juice
50g/2 oz fresh white breadcrumbs

Preheat oven to 375°F/190°C/Gas Mark 5

Roll out the pastry and line a 20cm/8″ shallow pie plate. Reserve any trimmings.

In a small pan, warm the syrup and lemon juice, add the breadcrumbs and pour over pastry base. Roll out the pastry trimmings and cut into thin strips. Use these to make a lattice pattern over the syrup filling. Dampen the ends of the strips and press them lightly onto the edge of the tart.

Bake in the centre of the oven for 25 – 30 minutes, until the pastry is cooked and the filling golden and firm.

Syrup Sponge Pudding

SERVES 4 – 6

175g/6 oz self-raising flour
1 level teaspoon baking powder
¼ teaspoon salt
100g/4 oz margarine or butter
100g/4 oz caster sugar
2 eggs (large)
2 tablespoons milk
3 tablespoons golden syrup

Sieve together the flour, baking powder and salt.

Facing page: Chocolate Sponge Pudding (top), Steamed Sultana Pudding (centre right) and Syrup Sponge Pudding (bottom).

Above: Treacle Tart.

In a large bowl, cream the margarine or butter with the caster sugar until light and fluffy. In a small bowl, beat the eggs and milk together.

Add the sieved flour to the creamed fat and sugar, folding in lightly with a metal spoon and adding a little of the liquid at a time to make a smooth batter.

Grease a 1.1 litre/2 pint pudding basin and put the syrup at the bottom. Spoon in the mixture, cover with greased greaseproof paper, then foil, pleating the latter under the rim of the basin to secure.

Have ready a saucepan of boiling water, to reach halfway up the basin. Steam gently for 1½ – 2 hours or pressure-cook according to instructions. Add more boiling water during cooking when necessary to maintain the level. Loosen sides of pudding with a knife and turn out onto a hot dish. Serve with custard or cream or more melted syrup.

Bakewell Tart.

SPOTTED DICK

One of Britain's most traditional puddings!

FOR 4 – 6 PEOPLE

225g/½ lb self-raising flour
¼ teaspoon salt
75g/3 oz shredded suet
75g/3 oz sugar
100-175g/4-6 oz currants (pre-washed)
150ml/¼ pint milk (or milk and water mixed)
Caster sugar for dusting

In a bowl, sieve the flour and salt together and stir in the sugar, suet and currants. Mix to a soft consistency with the liquid. Shape on a floured board into a roll. Have ready a large saucepan of boiling water and a floured cloth. Wrap the suet pastry in a well-greased piece of greaseproof paper, then in the cloth, tying both ends with string but leaving enough room for the pudding to expand during cooking.

Lower the pudding into the boiling water and allow to simmer gently for 1½ hours – top up with more boiling water if necessary, but do not let the water go off the simmer.

Unwrap carefully and serve in slices with a sprinkling of sugar and a white sauce or vanilla custard.

APPLE DUMPLINGS

An old fashioned method of using apples; cheap and ideal for a winter pudding.

SERVES 4

4 even-sized apples
50g/2 oz brown sugar
50g/2 oz dried fruit
50g/2 oz butter
450g/1 lb shortcrust pastry
Beaten egg or milk to glaze

Preheat oven to 375°F/190°C/Gas Mark 5

Peel and core each apple and fill the cavities with the sugar, fruit and dabs of butter. Cut the pastry into 4 even-sized pieces and roll out each piece thinly. Place an apple on each square of pastry. Draw up the points and press them together on the top as well as the edges. Cut off any surplus pastry, which can then be re-rolled and used to make decorative leaves. Put the dumplings, smooth side up, onto a greased baking sheet. Brush with beaten egg or milk. Bake for 30–60 minutes according to size. Test with a skewer to see if the apple is cooked. Serve with custard or ice cream.

STEAMED SULTANA PUDDING

SERVES 4

100g/4 oz butter or margarine
100g/4 oz caster sugar
175g/6 oz self-raising flour
100g/4 oz sultanas
Pinch of salt
2 eggs beaten together with 2 tablespoons milk

Cream together the fat and sugar until soft and fluffy. Sieve together the flour and salt and add the sultanas. Add to the fat and sugar mixture alternately with the beaten egg and milk.

Spoon into a well-buttered 1.1 litre/2 pint pudding basin. Cover with greased greaseproof paper and foil, tucking the edges securely around the rim.

Steam for 1½ hours in a pan of boiling water, with the water coming halfway up the sides of the basin. Top up with extra boiling water during cooking if necessary.

Loosen the sides of the pudding with a knife and turn out onto a hot dish. Serve with custard or a jam sauce.

BAKEWELL TART

SERVES 8

175g/6 oz shortcrust pastry
100g/4 oz butter
100g/4 oz caster sugar
2 large eggs
75g/3 oz ground almonds
75g/3 oz crumbs (from trifle sponges, madeira cake or fresh white bread)
1 tablespoon milk
Grated rind and juice of half a lemon
½ teaspoon baking powder
½ teaspoon vanilla essence
Few drops almond essence
2 tablespoons raspberry jam or lemon curd

Preheat oven to 400°F/200°C/Gas Mark 6

Line a 900ml/1½ pint greased, shallow pie dish with shortcrust pastry rolled thinly. Save trimmings for decoration. Spread jam or lemon curd over the pastry. Cream butter and sugar together, add flavourings, beat in eggs and fold in crumbs and ground almonds mixed. Add the baking powder and milk. Pour this mixture over the jam. Decorate the top with pastry strips.

Bake at 400°F/200°C/Gas Mark 6 for 15 minutes. Turn oven down to 350°F/180°C/Gas Mark 4 and bake for a further 20–25 minutes until the tart is golden brown and firm to the touch.

CHOCOLATE SPONGE PUDDING

SERVES 4–6

210g/7½ oz self-raising flour
10g/½ oz cocoa
¼ teaspoon salt
75g/3 oz butter or margarine
75g/3 oz sugar
1 egg, beaten
4 tablespoons milk
½ teaspoon vanilla essence

Sieve the flour, cocoa and salt into a mixing bowl. Add the butter or margarine cut into small pieces. Rub the fat lightly into the sieved flour with your fingertips until the mixture resembles fine breadcrumbs. Add the sugar, then the beaten egg, milk and vanilla essence. Beat until smooth. Turn into a 900ml/1½ pint buttered pudding basin, cover with greaseproof paper and foil and steam for 1½ hours. Top up the level of the water (which should be halfway up the outside of the basin) with boiling water if necessary.

When it is cooked, loosen the sides of the pudding with a knife and turn out onto a hot dish. Serve with a hot chocolate sauce or a white, sweet sauce or custard.

Cakes and Biscuits

STRAWBERRY CREAM HORNS

450g/1 lb puff pastry
1 egg
Icing sugar
150ml/¼ pint double cream
Small punnet strawberries

Preheat oven to 400°F/200°C/Gas Mark 6

Roll out pastry into a strip 50 x 30cm/20″ x 12″. Brush with beaten egg and cut lengthways into strips 1cm/½″ wide. Dampen horn tins and wind pastry around, slightly overlapping. Bake on a dampened baking sheet for about 10 minutes until golden. Allow the pastry to cool for a couple of minutes before easing horn tins away. Cool on a wire tray.

Wash and hull strawberries and add to stiffly-whipped double cream. Fill the cream horns and dust with a little sieved icing sugar.

CURD TARTLETS

MAKES ABOUT 18

100g/4oz shortcrust pastry
40g/1½ oz margarine
225g/8 oz curd cheese
50g/2 oz caster sugar
50g/2 oz currants
1 egg
Pinch cinnamon
Pinch nutmeg

Preheat oven 425°F/220°C/Gas Mark 7

Roll out pastry and line patty tins. Melt the margarine and mix in all the other ingredients. Spoon the filling into the pastry cases.

Bake in a hot oven for 15 – 20 minutes. Allow to cool in the tins for ten minutes and then remove to a wire rack.

Dainty Chocolate Eclairs and Florentines (top) and Strawberry Cream Horns, Curd Tartlets, Viennese Fingers and Cinnamon Squares (bottom).

FLORENTINES

100g/4 oz syrup
100g/4 oz butter
40g/1½ oz plain flour
40g/1½ oz sultanas
50g/2 oz glacé cherries
50g/2 oz flaked almonds
1 teaspoon lemon juice
175g/6 oz plain chocolate

Preheat oven to 375°F/190°C/Gas Mark 5

In a small saucepan, melt together the syrup and butter. Sieve in the flour and add the sultanas, cherries, almonds and lemon juice. Combine well. Cool the mixture a little and then spoon heaped dessertspoonfuls (use a teaspoon if you want dainty biscuits) onto a greased baking sheet. Leave room between each spoonful for the mixture to spread. Bake in the preheated oven until golden – about 12 minutes. Leave to cool for about 7 minutes then transfer the Florentines to a cooling rack.

Melt the chocolate in a small bowl placed in a saucepan of simmering water. Spread on the undersides of the biscuits and draw the prongs of a fork across the chocolate to create the traditional finish. Store in an air-tight tin.

VIENNESE FINGERS

An old-fashioned biscuit with an up-to-date taste!

225g/8 oz butter
50g/2 oz icing sugar
175g/6 oz plain flour
50g/2 oz cornflour
Few drops vanilla essence
175g/6 oz plain chocolate

Preheat oven to 350°F/180°C/Gas Mark 4

In a bowl, cream together the butter and sugar, add the cornflour, plain flour and vanilla essence. Beat thoroughly. Place the mixture into a piping bag with a star nozzle (medium size). Pipe in rows onto a baking sheet lined with silicone paper, each biscuit about 7.5 cm/3″ long. Bake for 15 minutes until a light golden colour. Cool on a wire rack. Place chocolate in a small bowl in a saucepan of simmering water until melted.

Dip one end of each biscuit into the melted chocolate.

CINNAMON SQUARES

225g/8 oz butter
100g/4 oz caster sugar
225g/8 oz flour
100g/4 oz semolina
1 teaspoon ground cinnamon
1 egg, beaten
75g/3 oz flaked almonds
25g/1 oz granulated sugar

Preheat oven to 350°F/180°C/Gas Mark 4

In a bowl, cream the butter and caster sugar until light and fluffy. Sieve together the flour, semolina and ground cinnamon and fold gently into the butter/sugar mixture. Press into an 29 x 18 cm/11½ x 7″ greased Swiss roll tin. Prick lightly with a fork, brush with the beaten egg and sprinkle on the flaked almonds and, finally, the granulated sugar. Bake in the preheated oven for about 20 minutes. Remove and mark into squares whilst still warm in the tin. When cool, remove with a palette knife.

BARM BRACK

Barm Brack is a delicious fruit loaf eaten all the year round in Ireland but especially popular at Hallowe'en when, by tradition, a ring is hidden in the loaf and the one who finds it will be the next to wed.

450g/1 lb flour
½ teaspoon cinnamon
½ teaspoon salt
¼ teaspoon grated nutmeg
50g/2 oz softened butter
75g/3 oz caster sugar
300ml/½ pint tepid milk
15g/¾ oz fresh yeast
1 egg (size 2)
225g/½ lb sultanas
175g/6 oz currants
50g/2 oz cut mixed peel
1 tablespoon honey

Preheat oven to 400°F/200°C/Gas Mark 6

Add salt and spices to the flour and sift into a large mixing bowl. Rub in the butter – this can be done in an electric mixer or food processor at low speed. Add one teaspoon of the sugar and one teaspoon of the milk to the yeast and mix well. Add the remainder of the sugar to the flour mixture and incorporate well. Lightly beat the egg, add the milk and pour this onto the yeast mixture. Add this to the flour and sugar and beat well, either by hand or using the dough hook of your electric mixer, until the batter becomes stiff and elastic. Fold in the mixed fruit and cover the bowl with a lightly greased polythene bag. Leave the dough in a warm place to rise for 1–2 hours. Divide the mixture between 2 greased loaf tins 21 x 11 cm/8½″ x 4½″ or two 17cm/7″ cake tins. Cover again and allow to rise for a further 30 minutes. Bake for one hour in the centre of the preheated oven. Dissolve the honey in two tablespoons of hot water and brush over the brack. Return it to the oven for five more minutes with the heat turned off. Turn out onto a wire rack to cool. Slice and butter.

SODA BREAD

Excellent at teatime with butter and home-made strawberry jam. Also good with prawns, smoked salmon or fish patés.

225g/½ lb plain white flour
1 level teaspoon salt
1 level teaspoon sugar
1 level teaspoon cream of tartar
1 heaped teaspoon bicarbonate of soda
450g/1 lb plain wholemeal flour
475ml/16 fl oz sour milk or fresh milk mixed with
    1 tablespoon yoghurt

Preheat oven to 400°F/200°C/Gas Mark 6

Add salt, sugar, cream of tartar and bicarbonate of soda to the plain white flour. Sift into a large mixing bowl. Add wholemeal flour and combine thoroughly with a round-ended knife, using a lifting action to aerate the mixture. Make a well in the centre, add the milk and work until the dough leaves the sides of the bowl clean. Knead by hand into a ball and place on a greased baking tray. Gently flatten the loaf and mark the top with a deep cross. Brush the top with a little milk and place in the oven for 40 minutes. Remove, turn the loaf upside down and return to the oven for a further five minutes. The loaf is cooked if it sounds hollow when tapped on the base. Wrap it in a slightly dampened cloth and stand on its side to cool. Cut into wedges and butter generously.

GINGERBREAD

450g/1 lb plain flour
1 level teaspoon salt
1 level tablespoon ground ginger
1 level tablespoon baking powder
1 level teaspoon bicarbonate of soda
225g/8 oz demerara sugar
175g/6 oz butter
175g/6 oz treacle
175g/6 oz golden syrup
300ml/½ pint milk
1 egg, beaten

Preheat oven to 325°F/160°C/Gas Mark 3

Grease and line a 23cm/9″ square cake tin. Sift the flour, salt, ginger, baking powder and bicarbonate of soda into a large mixing bowl. In a saucepan, warm together the sugar, butter, treacle and syrup until melted, but do not allow it to boil. Mix in the milk and beaten egg. Make a well in the centre of the dry ingredients and quickly pour in the liquid and mix thoroughly. Pour the mixture into the tin and bake in the oven for 1½ hours or until the gingerbread is firm to the touch.

Turn out to cool on a wire rack. This gingerbread keeps well in an airtight tin, if you can keep it that long!

CRUMPETS

Wonderful for afternoon tea on a cold winter's day.

MAKES ABOUT 12

225g/8 oz strong plain flour
1 teaspoon salt
1 tablespoon dried yeast
1 teaspoon caster sugar
275ml/½ pint milk
55ml/2 fl oz water

Crumpet rings are available in specialist kitchen shops, but egg rings will do as well.

Heat milk and water together in a small saucepan until hand hot. Transfer to a jug and stir in the sugar and dried yeast. Leave in a warm place until it develops a frothy head. Meanwhile, sift the flour and salt into a mixing bowl, make a hollow in the centre and, when ready, pour in the yeast mixture. Incorporate ingredients with a wooden spoon, beating to a smooth batter. Cover bowl with a tea towel and leave to stand for 45 minutes.

Grease a heavy, based frying pan and the insides of the egg or crumpet rings.

When the pan is hot, spoon a tablespoon of batter into each ring. After about 5 minutes the traditional holes will appear. Lift off rings and turn the crumpets over carefully. Cook for a further minute. Repeat this process until all the batter is used up.

Serve warm with plenty of butter and homemade jam.

If kept longer, toast to reheat.

LIGHT FRUIT CAKE

This cake is very quick and easy to make and is a delicious addition to any tea table.

350g/12 oz self-raising flour
225g/8 oz margarine or butter, cut into small
    cubes
100g/4 oz caster sugar
350g/12 oz mixed fruit
2 eggs, beaten, and enough milk to make up to
    235ml/7½ fl oz

Preheat oven to 300°F/150°C/Gas Mark 2

Grease and line an 18cm/7″ inch cake tin.

Sift the flour into a large bowl and add the fat. Rub in the fat until the mixture resembles breadcrumbs. Stir in the sugar and mixed fruit. Make a well in the centre of the dry ingredients and slowly add the eggs and milk beaten together. Mix together until everything is thoroughly incorporated. Tip the cake mixture into the prepared tin and make a slight well in the centre.

Bake in the centre of the oven for about 2 hours, or until a skewer inserted in the cake comes out clean. Remove from the oven and leave in the tin for 5 minutes to cool, then turn out onto a wire rack to cool completely

SCOTCH PANCAKES (DROP SCONES)

MAKES ABOUT 24

225g/8 oz plain flour
2 level teaspoons cream of tartar
1 level teaspoon bicarbonate of soda
½ level teaspoon salt
25g/1 oz caster sugar
2 teaspoons golden syrup
1 egg, beaten
Scant ⅓ pint milk
Lard for cooking

Set a griddle, heavy-based frying pan or hot plate over heat. Meanwhile, sift together the flour, cream of tartar, bicarbonate of soda and the salt into a bowl. Stir in the sugar. Make a well in the centre and gradually add the milk, beaten egg and syrup until a smooth pouring batter is formed (it must not be too thin).

Grease the cooking surface lightly with a little lard and, when a slight haze appears, pour on dessertspoons of the batter, a few at a time, leaving plenty of space between the pancakes. When bubbles appear on the surface and the undersides are brown, flip them over with a palette knife. Cook for a further few moments. Serve at once with butter and jam.

Scotch pancakes also freeze very well and can be reheated in a hot oven, under a grill or in a toaster.

DAINTY CHOCOLATE ÉCLAIRS

MAKES ABOUT 12

CHOUX PASTRY

50g/2 oz butter
150ml/¼ pint water
75g/3 oz plain flour
2 eggs

Preheat oven to 400°F/200°C/Gas Mark 6

Place the butter and water in a medium-sized saucepan. Sieve the flour onto a piece of greaseproof paper.

Bring the butter and water gently to the boil, stirring occasionally. Turn off the heat and tip the flour all at once into the liquid. Beat the mixture vigorously with a wooden spoon until it forms a smooth ball of paste. Allow to cool slightly before beating in the eggs, one at a time.

Place the mixture into a piping bag with a 9mm/⅜″ plain nozzle and pipe 5cm/2″ long éclairs onto a dampened baking sheet.

Bake in a preheated oven for about 20 minutes until risen and golden. Slit each éclair down one side to allow the steam to escape. Cool on a wire rack.

When cold, fill with whipped cream (about 300ml/½ pint) and dip the tops in melted chocolate or chocolate glacé icing.

CHOCOLATE FUDGE CAKE

MAKES ONE 18cm/7″ SANDWICH CAKE

100g/4 oz self-raising flour
1 level teaspoon baking powder
100g/4 oz soft margarine
100g/4 oz caster sugar
A drop of vanilla essence
1 heaped tablespoon cocoa powder
2 tablespoons boiling water
2 eggs

CHOCOLATE FROSTING

75g/3 oz icing sugar
25g/1 oz cocoa powder
40g/1½ oz butter
2 tablespoons water
50g/2 oz caster sugar

Preheat oven to 350°F/180°C/Gas Mark 4

Sift the flour and baking powder into a large mixing bowl. Add the margarine and sugar. Combine the cocoa powder and boiling water in a small bowl and mix until smooth. Add the paste to the mixing bowl with the eggs and mix well with a wooden spoon. Beat well for about a minute to get a smooth batter. Divide the mixture equally between two greased 18cm/7″ sponge cake tins. Spread the mixture level and bake in the centre of the oven for 25 minutes. Turn out cakes and allow to cool on wire rack while preparing the frosting.

Chocolate Frosting Sift the cocoa powder and icing sugar into a mixing bowl. Measure the butter, water and sugar into a small saucepan. Set over a low heat and stir until the sugar has dissolved and the butter has melted. Bring to the boil then pour at once into the centre of the sifted ingredients. Beat with a wooden spoon to make a smooth icing. At this stage the icing is very soft. It can be used as a smooth coating, in which case the mixture should be stirred gently until thick enough to coat the back of a spoon. Sandwich the cake layers with a little of the icing and

pour the rest over the cake. Spread evenly over the top and sides with a palette knife and leave to set.

For a textured frosting, continue to stir the icing occasionally until thick enough to leave a trail. Spread a little between the cake layers and cover the cake with the rest. Decorate by roughing-up with the tip of a table knife.

VICTORIA SANDWICH CAKE

A favourite for afternoon tea.

100g/4 oz butter or margarine
100g/4 oz caster sugar
2 large eggs
Few drops vanilla essence
100g/4 oz self-raising flour, sifted

TO FINISH

Jam, whipped cream, sifted icing sugar

Preheat oven to 350°F/180°C/Gas Mark 4

Grease two 18cm/7″ straight-sided sandwich tins and line the bases with buttered greaseproof paper.

In a medium-sized mixing bowl, cream together the butter and sugar until light and fluffy. Beat in the eggs one at a time and the vanilla essence. With a metal spoon, gently fold in the sifted flour. When it is all incorporated, divide the mixture equally between the two tins, levelling off the surface. Bake on the centre shelf in the preheated oven for about 25 minutes. Test by pushing your finger gently onto the sponge, it should feel springy and leave no impression. Leave to cool for a minute and turn out onto wire cooling racks. Carefully peel off the greaseproof paper.

When cold, sandwich together with jam and whipped cream and dust the top with sifted icing sugar.

STRAWBERRY JAM

1.8kg/4 lb strawberries
1.8kg/4 lb sugar

Place the hulled strawberries and sugar in a bowl in layers and leave for 12 hours. Put into a pan and bring to the boil. Boil for 5 minutes then return the

Previous page: (clockwise from top right) Victoria Sandwich Cake, Soda Bread, Crumpets, Gingerbread, Light Fruit Cake, Scotch Pancakes, and Barm Brack (centre).

Facing page: Chocolate Fudge Cake (top), and individual fruit flans (bottom), made using a pâté brisée base from the Apricot and Soured Cream Flan recipe (page 164).

mixture to a clean bowl. Leave overnight, then return to the pan. Boil the jam until it reaches setting point.

To check for setting point, spoon a little of the jam onto a saucer and allow it to cool, then push it with your finger – if the skin on the jam wrinkles it is set. If not, boil the jam for a further 4 – 5 minutes and test again. Repeat until a set is reached.

Cool the jam for 15 minutes, stir well and pour into hot jars. Cover and seal in the usual way.

SCONES

MAKES ABOUT 8

225g/8 oz self-raising flour (sifted)
10g/½ oz butter at room temperature
1½ tablespoons caster sugar
Pinch of salt
150ml/¼ pint milk

Preheat oven to 425°F/220°C/Gas Mark 7

Sift the flour into a bowl and rub in the butter using your fingertips. Then stir in the sugar and salt. Take a knife and mix in the milk very slowly. With floured hands, knead the mixture to a soft dough, adding more milk if the mixture seems too dry. Turn the dough out onto a floured board and roll out thickly (not less than 2cm/¾″) using a lightly floured rolling pin. Cut out the scones with a 4 or 5cm/1½″ or 2″ pastry cutter. Place the scones on a greased baking tray. Re-knead any left over dough, re-roll and cut until all the dough has been used up. Dust the scones with a little extra flour, or glaze with a little milk or beaten egg.

Bake near the top of the oven for 12 – 15 minutes. Cool on a wire rack and serve warm split open with butter or, for a real treat, with clotted cream and home-made jam.

STRAWBERRY SHORTCAKE

SERVES 4 – 6

175g/6 oz plus 1 teaspoon butter, softened
225g/8 oz plain flour
50g/2oz icing sugar
1 egg yolk
300ml/½ pint double cream
450g/1 lb strawberries, hulled and washed
2 tablespoons caster sugar

Preheat oven to 375°F/190°C/Gas Mark 5

Using the teaspooon of butter, lightly grease two baking sheets.

Sift the flour and icing sugar into a medium-sized mixing bowl. Cut the remaining butter into small pieces and add it to the mixture. Using your hands, mix the flour and butter together to make a smooth dough.

With a knife, stir in the egg yolk and two tablespoons of the cream. Mix well and form the dough into a small ball. This can also be done in a food processor. Cover the dough with greaseproof paper and chill for thirty minutes. Divide the dough into two equal parts and, on a floured surface, roll each piece into a 9″ circle. Bake in the preheated oven for 40 – 45 minutes until light golden brown. Mark out 8 – 12 wedges and allow to cool slightly before removing from the baking sheet. Leave on a wire rack until cold.

For the 4 layers shown in the photograph simply double up on the quantities.

Using the strawberries and whipped double cream, assemble the shortcake.

CHOCOLATE CRUNCH BISCUITS

225g/8 oz rich tea biscuits
100g/4 oz butter
40g/1½ oz cocoa
50g/2 oz caster sugar
1 tablespoon golden syrup
225g/8 oz cooking chocolate

Place butter, cocoa, sugar and syrup in a heavy-based saucepan and melt slowly. Crush the biscuits in a polythene bag with a rolling pin, but not too finely, and add to the mixture. Press this firmly into a greased tin or dish. Melt the chocolate and pour over the top. Leave in the fridge to set and cut into pieces.

STRAWBERRY CHEESECAKE

BASE
100g/4 oz digestive biscuits
50g/2 oz butter or margarine

2 eggs
3 tablespoons caster sugar
300ml/½ pint milk
3 tablespoons gelatine
4 tablespoons hot water
225g/½ lb Philadelphia cream cheese or
    equivalent
300ml/½ pint double or whipping cream
450g/1 lb strawberries
Quick Gel glaze – optional

Melt the butter or margarine in a small saucepan. Crush the biscuits and add to the pan. Mix well and transfer to an 18cm/7″ loose-based cake tin. Press down evenly.

Strawberry Shortcake (top), Scones (bottom left) and Strawberry Cheesecake (bottom right).

Separate the egg yolks and whites and put the yolks into a basin with the sugar and milk and stand the basin in a pan of gently-simmering water. Whisk the contents of the basin until thick and fluffy.

Soak the gelatine in 4 tablespoons of hot water until dissolved and add to the warm egg mixture. Allow the mixture to cool. When it starts to thicken whisk in the cream cheese and then stir in the lightly-whipped cream. To finish, fold in gently the beaten egg whites. Pour over the crumb base and refrigerate for at least 3 hours.

Decorate with the strawberries and, if liked, a commercial fruit glaze.

CHERRY BITES

175g/6 oz margarine
150g/5 oz caster sugar
1 egg, beaten
275g/10 oz self-raising flour
1 teaspoon vanilla essence
50g/2 oz porridge oats
A few glacé cherries

Preheat oven to 350°F/180°C/Gas Mark 4

In a bowl, beat the margarine until creamy. Mix in the sugar, beaten egg, flour and vanilla essence until well blended and smooth. Divide into walnut-sized pieces. Roll into balls and coat with the porridge oats. Place onto a greased baking tray, flatten slightly and top each one with a piece of glacé cherry.

Bake for 15 – 20 minutes. Remove and cool on a wire rack.

CHOCOLATE FUDGE

A quick and easy recipe.

MAKES 700G/1½ LBS

450g/1 lb granulated sugar
6 tablespoons milk
25g/1 oz butter
175g/6 oz plain chocolate, roughly chopped

Place the sugar and milk in a heavy-based saucepan and stir until a paste. Add the butter and chocolate and stir on a gentle heat until the chocolate has melted. Slightly raise the heat and allow mixture to boil for 5 minutes. Remove from the heat, beat well and pour into a 20cm/8″ square tin that has been well buttered.

Leave until cool and nearly set before cutting into squares.

Sour Cream Cake for Coffee.

SOUR CREAM CAKE FOR COFFEE

An extremely moreish cake from across the Atlantic. More or less cinnamon can be added as preferred. It freezes well.

100g/4 oz butter
200g/7 oz sugar
2 eggs
150ml/5 fl oz carton sour cream
1 teaspoon baking soda
175g/6 oz plain flour
1½ teaspoons baking powder
1 teaspoon vanilla essence

TOPPING

50g/2 oz demerara sugar
2 tablespoons chopped mixed nuts
2 teaspoons cinnamon

Preheat oven to 350°F/180°C/Gas Mark 4

Grease a 23cm/9″ ring mould.

In a large bowl, cream together the butter and sugar until light and fluffy. Add the eggs and soured cream mixed with the baking soda. Blend well. Sieve together the flour and baking powder and fold in gently. Add the vanilla.

Mix topping ingredients together. Pour half the cake mixture into the tin and sprinkle with half the topping. Pour in the remaining mixture and sprinkle with the rest of the topping. Bake for 40 minutes or until risen. Serve warm at coffee time.

KATE'S CARROT CAKE

A lemon or orange glacé icing and marzipan carrots give the finishing touches to this delicious, moist cake.

2 eggs
100g/4 oz dark brown sugar
90ml/3 fl oz oil (sunflower or groundnut)
175g/6 oz carrots, finely grated
100g/4 oz wholemeal self-raising flour
1 teaspoon ground cinnamon
½ teaspoon allspice
50g/2 oz desiccated coconut
2 teaspoons grated orange rind
100g/4 oz walnuts, chopped

LEMON OR ORANGE GLACÉ ICING

100g/4 oz icing sugar
Zest of ½ orange and 4 teaspoons orange juice or lemon zest and juice

Preheat oven to 375°F/190°C/Gas Mark 5

Grease and line the base of an 1 c /7″ cake tin.

In a large bowl, beat together the eggs and sugar until creamy, and very slowly whisk in the oil. Gently fold in the grated carrots and the rest of the ingredients until well mixed. Pour into the cake tin and bake in a preheated oven for 25-30 minutes, until firm to the touch. Cool on a wire rack.

Lemon or Orange Glacé Icing Sift the icing sugar into a bowl, add the zest and orange or lemon juice and mix well. Spread the icing over the cake and coat evenly with a wet palette knife. Decorate with tiny carrots modelled from coloured marzipan.

CUSTARD CREAM BISCUITS

MAKES 40

175g/6 oz margarine
50g/2 oz icing sugar
175g/6 oz plain flour
50g/2 oz custard powder

Preheat oven to 375°F/190°C/Gas Mark 5

In a bowl, cream together the margarine and icing sugar. Add the flour and custard powder and mix well. Divide into small balls and place about 2.5cm/1″ apart on a greased baking tray. Gently squash the top of each ball with a fork. Bake for about 15 – 20 minutes until lightly browned. Remove to a wire rack to cool.

If desired, sandwich the biscuits together with some butter icing or whipped cream, matching up biscuits of roughly the same size.

PETITS FOURS

Petits fours can take many forms, including tiny shapes of Genoise sponge covered with marzipan and coloured fondant icing (see Pink Fondant Cakes), or fruits dipped in chocolate or caramel-ised fruits. Marzipan itself can be coloured and modelled to represent fruits with stunning effect. Little tuile biscuits are simple to make (see recipe). With a little practice you will be able to make a professional plateful of your own petits fours.

CHOCOLATE-DIPPED FRUITS

Melt plain chocolate in a bowl set in a pan of sim-mering water. Half dip fresh strawberries, pine-apple segments, or satsuma or mandarin segments into the chocolate and lay them on non-stick baking paper to set. Try also dipping nuts – especially Brazil nuts – or orange and lemon peel.

MARZIPAN-STUFFED DATES

Remove the stone from each date and replace with marzipan. Serve like this or coated in chocolate.

Kate's Carrot Cake (bottom), Pound Cake (centre), Coffee Ring Cake (top right), Frangipane Tarts (centre right), Petits Fours (bottom right) and Custard Cream Biscuits, Orange Biscuits, Chocolate Crunch Bicuits and Cherry Bites (left).

GLAZED FRESH FRUITS

Orange segments, grapes, strawberries, cherries etc. can be dipped in a syrup made of 225g/8 oz sugar and 75ml/2½ fl oz water. Dissolve the sugar gently in the water and then bring to the boil. Cover and cook without stirring for about 3 minutes. Remove the pan from the heat and dip the fruits into the syrup, a few at a time. Lift them out with a fork. Place on a wire rack or on non-stick baking paper until set.

ALMOND PETITS FOURS

MAKES 24 – 30 CAKES

Rice paper
2 egg whites
100g/4 oz ground almonds
50g/2 oz caster sugar
¼ teaspoon almond essence
Glacé cherries
Angelica
Split blanched almonds

Preheat oven to 350°F/180°C/Gas Mark 4

Line 2 or 3 baking sheets with the rice paper. In a large bowl, whisk the egg whites until stiff and lightly fold in the ground almonds and sugar together with the almond essence.

Transfer this mixture to an icing bag with a large rose nozzle and pipe shapes – rosettes and S shapes are traditional – onto the baking sheets. Decorate with the cherries, angelica or almonds.

Bake on the centre shelf of the preheated oven, for 15 – 29 minutes until golden.

ORANGE BISCUITS

MAKES 20 BISCUITS

100g/4 oz butter
100g/4 oz sugar
1 egg yolk
225g/8 oz sifted self-raising flour·
2 teaspoons finely grated orange rind

Preheat oven to 350°F/180°C/Gas Mark 4

Cream butter until light and fluffy. Stir in the sugar and beat until the mixture is smooth. Add the egg yolk. Mix well before folding in the flour and orange rind. Form the mixture into a ball with your hands and knead it lightly. Cover and chill in the refrigerator for 10 minutes. Remove the dough and place it on a lightly-floured board. Roll out until 5mm/¼" thick. Cut the dough in circles with a 5cm/2" pastry cutter. Place on a greased baking sheet and bake for 12-15 minutes until the biscuits are golden brown.

Remove from the oven and cool on a wire rack. The biscuits will keep well in an airtight tin.

POUND CAKE

This recipe was given to a friend by a Zulu chef working at a stud farm in Pietermaritzburg, South Africa. It was served with sherry, or as a dessert with whipped cream. In fact, my friend ate it with just a smear of butter and found it delicious.

450g/1 lb caster sugar
450g/1 lb unsalted butter
10 eggs, size 3, separated
2 tablespoons sherry
1 teaspoon vanilla essence
450g/1 lb self-raising flour, sieved

Preheat oven to 350°F/180°C/Gas Mark 4

This quantity should be baked in a 25.5cm/10" square tin. Half the above quantity will be sufficient for a 20cm/8" tin.

Grease and flour the cake tin.

In a large mixing bowl, beat the sugar into the butter until creamy. Add the egg yolks only, together with the sherry and vanilla essence. Incorporate well. Fold in the sifted flour with a metal spoon.

In another bowl, whisk the egg whites until stiff (this is probably best done in 2 batches) and fork them lightly into the cake mixture. Transfer the mixture to the cake tin and bake in the centre of the oven for approximately 1½ hours.

FLAPJACKS

MAKES ABOUT 16

100g/4 oz butter or margarine
60g/2½ oz sugar
1 tablespoon golden syrup
150g/5 oz rolled or porridge oats

Preheat oven to 350°F/180°C/Gas Mark 4

Heat butter, sugar and syrup in a small saucepan over a low heat until the sugar dissolves. Add the oats and mix well. Turn out into a greased baking tin 18 x 33 cm/17" x 13" and bake in the oven for 25 – 30 minutes until golden brown. Cut into fingers while still warm and turn out when cold.

COFFEE RING CAKE

3 large eggs
100g/4 oz caster sugar
75g/3 oz self-raising flour, sieved
1 tablespoon very strong, hot coffee liquid

COFFEE ICING

225g/8 oz icing sugar, sieved
1½ tablespoons strong coffee liquid

Preheat oven to 350°F/180°C/Gas Mark 4

Grease a ring tin (the above mixture is sufficient for one round 20cm/8″ tin, 7.5cm/3″ deep).

Whisk the eggs and sugar together very hard (at least 5 minutes with electric whisk) until thick. Add the coffee and gently fold in the sieved flour. Pour into the prepared ring tin and bake in the centre of the preheated oven for 30–35 minutes until well risen, firm to the touch and just shrinking from the sides of the tin.

Cool before turning out.

Coffee Icing In a small pan, mix together the icing sugar and coffee with a wooden spoon and heat very gently until smooth. Pour over the coffee ring cake.

FRANGIPANE TARTS

These old-fashioned tarts are still a firm favourite.

MAKES 12

100g/4 oz rich shortcrust pastry
Red jam
50g/2 oz butter
50g/2 oz caster sugar
1 egg
4 drops vanilla essence
50g/2 oz ground almonds
1 level teaspoon plain flour
Flaked almonds

Preheat oven to 375°F/190°C/Gas Mark 5

Roll out the pastry and line the tartlet tins. Spoon a blob of jam into each one. Set aside.

To make the filling, cream the butter and sugar together until light and fluffy. Stir in the lightly-beaten egg and vanilla essence. Add the ground almonds and flour and mix until all ingredients are incorporated. Place a rounded teaspoon of the mixture into each pastry case. Sprinkle flaked almonds on the top and bake for 15–20 minutes.

FRENCH TUILES BISCUITS

These biscuits retain their flavour better if kept in the freezer in a rigid container rather than in a biscuit tin. Allow an hour at room temperature to thaw.

60g/2½ oz butter
50g/2 oz caster sugar
40g/1½ oz plain flour
40g/1½ oz flaked almonds

Preheat oven to 180°C/350°F/Gas Mark 4

Cream together butter and sugar until pale, and then stir in the flour and almonds. Divide the mixture into marble-sized balls and place them on well-greased baking sheets about 7.5cm/3 inches apart. Flatten the balls with a dampened fork

before placing them in the oven for 8–10 minutes until a pale golden brown. Remove from the oven and leave to cool for a few seconds before lifting the bisuits carefully with a palette knife and placing them on an oiled rolling pin to harden. This gives the biscuits the traditional french 'tile' shape.

These biscuits are delicious served with fruit fools, mousses and ice cream.

CURD CHEESECAKE

This type of cooked cheesecake dates back to the 13th century when soft cheeses were frequently used for filling sweet tarts.

SERVES 8

100g/4 oz shortcrust pastry
450g/1 lb curd cheese
4 eggs, separated
175g/6 oz caster sugar
150ml/5 fl oz single cream
Juice and rind of 1 lemon
1 tablespoon cornflour
50g/2 oz sultanas

Preheat oven to 375°F/190°C/Gas Mark 5

Line the base of a 23 cm/9″ loose-bottomed cake tin with the shortcrust pastry and bake blind for ten minutes. Remove. Turn heat down to 325°F/160°C/Gas Mark 3.

In a large bowl, beat together the egg yolks with the sugar, add the cream, lemon juice and rind and the cornflour. Stir in the curd cheese and sultanas. Whisk the egg whites until stiff and fold into the cheese mixture. Pour onto the pastry base and cook in the middle of the oven for 1 hour, until brown on top and firm to the touch. Carefully remove from tin when cold.

MACAROONS

MAKES ABOUT 24 BISCUITS

100g/4 oz ground almonds
150g/6 oz caster sugar
2 egg whites
1 level tablespoon cornflour
¼ teaspoon vanilla essence
12 blanched almonds
2 teaspoons water

Preheat oven to 375°F/190°C/Gas Mark 5
Line 2 or 3 baking sheets with rice paper or silicone paper

Mix together the ground almonds and sugar and add the unbeaten egg whites, apart from 1 tablespoonful which is to be kept for glazing. Beat well with a wooden spoon and stir in the cornflour, vanilla essence and the water. Pipe or spoon the

mixture onto the baking sheets in large, round buttons. Split the almonds and top each macaroon with a half. Brush lightly with the remaining egg white.

Bake in the centre of a preheated oven until lightly browned and slightly risen, about 15 minutes. Cool on a wire rack. If rice paper has been used, cut around each macaroon. If silicone paper is used, simply peel off the back of the biscuits.

BRANDY SNAPS

Ideal for afternoon tea or as a dinner party dessert.

MAKES ABOUT 16 BISCUITS

50g/2 oz butter
50g/2 oz caster sugar
2 level tablespoons golden syrup
50g/2 oz plain flour
½ level teaspoon ground ginger
1 teaspoon brandy
Finely grated rind of ½ lemon

Clockwise from top right: Chocolate Fruit and Nut Cookies, Scottish Shortbread, Macaroons, Lemon Biscuits, Flapjacks and Brandy Snaps.

To fill: 180ml/6 fl oz double cream

Preheat oven to 350°F/180°C/Gas Mark 4
Grease 2 baking sheets and butter wooden spoon handles

In a saucepan, melt the butter, sugar and golden syrup over a low heat (when measuring syrup, wet tablespoon and dip in flour – the syrup will roll off easily). Stir until blended. Sift flour and ginger and add to the melted ingredients together with the brandy and lemon rind. Leave to cool for 2 minutes and then drop teaspoons of the mixture onto the baking sheets at about 10cm/4″ intervals. Bake a few at a time towards the top of the preheated oven for 7–10 minutes until golden brown and bubbling, with a lacy texture.

Remove from the baking sheets with a palette knife and loosely roll each brandy snap around a wooden spoon handle. Leave until set and then take off gently and cool on a wire rack. These biscuits will keep well for up to one week in an airtight container.

Just prior to serving, pipe or spoon whipped double cream into both ends.

SCOTTISH SHORTBREAD

MAKES 12 WEDGES

100g/4 oz plain flour
50g/2 oz rice flour – this gives a good crisp
    texture
100g/4 oz butter
50g/2 oz caster sugar

Preheat oven to 325°F/160°C/Gas Mark 3

In a bowl, cream together the butter and sugar and add the sifted flours. Using your fingers, lightly mix in all the ingredients until they change from a crumbly texture to a shortbread dough. Roll or press out the dough with your fingers – 0.5cm/¼″ thick – into a tin or shortbread mould. Prick the surface with a fork. Bake for about 45 – 50 minutes until pale golden. Remove. Mark out into wedges or fingers depending on tin or mould shape and allow to cool in the tin or mould. Store in an airtight tin.

LEMON BISCUITS

MAKES 30 BISCUITS

225g/8 oz self-raising flour
Pinch of salt
175g/6 oz butter
100g/4 oz caster sugar
1 level teaspoon finely grated lemon rind
Beaten egg to mix

Preheat oven to 350°F/180°C/Gas Mark 4

Sift flour and salt into a bowl then rub in the butter until it resembles fine breadcrumbs. Add the sugar and lemon rind and mix to a dough with beaten egg. Turn onto a floured work surface and knead the dough gently until smooth. Wrap in cling film and chill for 15 minutes.

Roll the dough out thinly and cut as many rounds as possible with a 5cm/2″ biscuit cutter. Re-knead and re-roll scraps if necessary. Place biscuits on a buttered baking tray and prick with a fork.

Bake in the oven for about 12 – 15 minutes until light golden. Leave to cool on wire racks then store in an airtight tin.

CHOCOLATE FRUIT AND NUT COOKIES

MAKES ABOUT 36

175g/6 oz plain flour
¼ teaspoon baking powder
100g/4 oz butter
175g/6 oz demerara sugar
1 egg, beaten
Few drops vanilla essence
75g/3 oz plain chocolate, coarsely chopped
50g/2 oz almonds, chopped
50g/2 oz walnuts, chopped
50g/2 oz mixed dried fruit

Preheat oven to 350°F/180°C/Gas Mark 4

Sift together the flour and baking powder. In a bowl, cream together the butter and sugar until pale and add the beaten egg and vanilla essence. With a metal spoon, gradually fold in the flour, followed by the chocolate, nuts and fruit. Place generous teaspoons of the mixture onto greased baking sheets, leaving enough space between for the biscuits to spread. Bake in a moderately hot oven for 15 – 20 minutes until golden brown and firm to the touch. Slide off the baking sheets onto wire cooling racks.

A Leisurely Breakfast

SATSUMA MARMALADE

MAKES APPROXIMATELY 5 lb

900g/2 lb satsumas
3 lemons
1.35kg/3 lb sugar
600ml/1 pint water

EITHER simmer the fruit whole in a preserving pan or heavy gauge saucepan until soft *OR* pressure cook in 1 pint of water for 15 minutes.

Cut up the fruit, discarding any pips (this can be done in a food processor, especially if you prefer a less chunky marmalade). Return the fruit to the pan, add the sugar and cook over a medium heat, stirring, until the sugar has dissolved, then boil steadily for 25 minutes. The marmalade is ready when a teaspoonful put onto a cold plate wrinkles when tested with your little finger.

Pot and cover the marmalade in the usual way i.e. in clean, dry jars that have been in a moderately hot oven for 5 minutes. Pour in the marmalade whilst still very hot. Use cellophane discs and elastic bands or proper lids.

A good way of sealing jams and marmalades is to use paraffin wax. This can be obtained from the chemist. Melt the paraffin wax and pour a little onto the jam to form an airtight lid. On opening, take off the wax, wash and save for re-use.

KEDGEREE

Worth the trouble to provide a nourishing breakfast.

SERVES 4 – 6

450g/1 lb smoked haddock fillets
175g/6 oz cooked long-grain rice
50g/2 oz butter
2 hard-boiled eggs, shelled and chopped
2 level tablespoons parsley
⅛ level teaspoon each of nutmeg and cayenne
   pepper
¼ level teaspoon salt
150ml/¼ pint single cream

Preheat oven to 350°F/180°C/Gas Mark 4

Gently poach the haddock in a little water for 7 – 10 minutes until tender. Drain, skin and flake the fish. Combine with the rest of the ingredients and bake

in a greased, oven-proof dish, covered, for about 30 minutes, forking it through occasionally. Pile onto a warm serving dish and garnish with a little more chopped parsley.

SEVILLE MARMALADE

MAKES APPROXIMATELY 4KG/9 LBS

1.35kg/3 lb Seville oranges
Water
2.7kg/6 lb sugar

EITHER – put Sevilles in a pan with 2.84 litres/5 pints of water and simmer gently until soft
OR – pressure-cook Sevilles for 15 minutes in 1.7 litres/3 pints of water.

Chop fruit, flesh and skin, discarding any pips.

Return chopped fruit to pan with 1.14 litres/2 pints of the cooking liquid, bring to the boil and add the sugar. Stir until dissolved and boil steadily for 15 minutes.

To Pot – follow instructions for Satsuma Marmalade.

Seville and Lemon Marmalade can also be made using the following ingredients: 900g/2 lbs Seville oranges, 450g/1 lb lemons, and cooked following the method used above.

PORRIDGE

Although instant porridge is a good standby, if time allows why not try the real thing. In Scotland, porridge is traditionally served with cream and salt, but brown sugar is nice!

SERVES 4

Easier to make than might be imagined, home-made marmalades are the ideal accompaniment to a leisurely breakfast.

150g/5 oz medium rolled oatmeal
1.2 litres/2 pints water
¼ teaspoon salt

In a large saucepan bring the water to the boil and, when bubbling, tip in the oatmeal, stirring constantly. When the water comes back to the boil, reduce the heat, cover the pan and simmer gently for 10 minutes. Stir in the salt, re-cover and continue cooking for another 10 minutes.

MUESLI

Muesli, which originated in Switzerland, makes an ideal, healthy breakfast or daytime snack. Experiment with a variety of whole cereal grains, fresh and dried fruits and serve with milk, yoghurt, fromage frais or blanc or even fresh orange juice.

MAKES APPROXIMATELY 1.125kg/2 ½ lb

225g/8 oz rolled or porridge oats
100g/4 oz whole wheat flakes
100g/4 oz whole rye flakes
100g/4 oz barley flakes
10g/½ oz bran
50g/2 oz dried apricots, chopped
50g/2 oz dried apple rings, chopped
25g/1 oz hazelnuts
25g/1 oz walnuts
225g/8 oz sultanas
175g/6 oz raisins
75g/3 oz brown sugar (optional)

Incorporate all the ingredients well and store in an airtight container.

CORNED BEEF HASH

A tasty breakfast or lunch-time dish. Especially good when topped with a poached egg.

SERVES 4

225g/8 oz corned beef, flaked
50g/2 oz lean streaky bacon, chopped
1 small onion, finely chopped
350g/12 oz mashed potato
2 level tablespoons finely chopped parsley
25g/1 oz dripping or lard
Salt
Freshly ground black pepper

Heat fat in a frying pan and add the bacon and onion. Cook for a few minutes until the onion becomes transparent. In a mixing bowl, combine the corned beef, bacon, onion, potato, seasoning and parsley. Reheat the fat in the pan and add the mixture, pressing it well down. Cook over a moderate heat until the underside is well-browned. Invert onto a warmed serving dish.

GRILLED KIPPERS WITH SCRAMBLED EGG

A substantial breakfast course.

Allow one pair of kippers and one egg scrambled per person.

Grill the kippers under a high heat for two or three minutes each side.

Meanwhile, beat the eggs lightly and cook for a couple of minutes in a saucepan with a knob of butter, a dash of milk and some black pepper, stirring continuously until they are creamy, but still moist.

Left to right: Muesli, breakfast platter with Corned Beef Hash, Kedgeree, Porridge and Grilled Kippers with Scrambled Egg.

Picnics and Barbecues

PISSALADIÈRE

Delicious for a picnic or informal lunch

SERVES 6

FILLING

450g/1 lb ripe tomatoes
1 medium onion
10g/½ oz butter
Pinch of mixed herbs
2 tablespoons tomato purée
2 eggs
100g/4 oz grated cheese
Freshly ground black pepper
Salt
1 x 50g/2 oz tin anchovy fillets
Black olives

PASTRY

100g/4 oz self-raising flour
50g/2 oz butter and white cooking fat, mixed
Cold water

Preheat oven to 375°F/190°C/Gas Mark 5

Make the pastry and roll out to line a 20cm/8" greased quiche tin or porcelain flan dish.

Plunge the tomatoes into boiling water for a few seconds, remove and take off the skins. Halve the tomatoes and remove seeds and cores. Chop the remaining flesh. Peel and finely chop the onion. Melt the butter in a large saucepan and add the tomatoes, onion, herbs and tomato purée. Cover and cook gently for 30 minutes until the mixture is reduced to a nice rich pulp. Take off the heat and allow to cool for a minute or so and then beat in the eggs, cheese and seasoning. Pour this mixture into the prepared flan case, decorate with a lattice of anchovy fillets and dot with halved, stoned black olives. Bake above the centre of the oven for 40 minutes until risen. (Always place a porcelain/china dish on a preheated baking tray to conduct the heat and ensure that the underneath of the pastry is well cooked.)

A tempting picnic, featuring: Pissaladière, Walnut and Banana Loaf, Picnic Chicken Drumsticks, Parsley Scotch Eggs, Piperade, Split French Loaf and Cornish Pasties.

WALNUT AND BANANA LOAF

This cake is very quick and easy.

75g/3 oz soft margarine
100g/4 oz caster sugar
1 large egg, beaten
Grated rind of 1 orange
Grated rind of 1 lemon
225g/8 oz plain flour
2 teaspoons baking powder
4 medium bananas
50g/2 oz chopped walnuts

Preheat oven to 350°F/180°C/Gas Mark 4
Grease a loaf tin – 8.5cm x 19cm/3½" x 7½"
   – and line the bottom with greaseproof paper.

Place the margarine, sugar and beaten egg in a mixing bowl, then sift in the flour and baking powder. In another bowl, slice the bananas and mash them with a fork to a pulp. Whisk the sugar, fat and flour thoroughly and add the orange and lemon rind, mashed bananas and chopped walnuts. Mix the ingredients further before placing in the prepared tin. Level the top.

Bake on the centre shelf of the oven for about 50 minutes until the loaf has risen and a skewer placed in the centre comes out clean. Serve sliced and buttered.

PICNIC CHICKEN DRUMSTICKS

SERVES 4

8 chicken drumsticks
Seasoned flour
Lightly beaten egg
Fresh white breadcrumbs
Fat for deep frying

Remove and discard the skin from the chicken. Then roll the drumsticks in the seasoned flour, dip them in the beaten egg and roll them in the breadcrumbs. Chill the chicken for 1 hour so that the breadcrumbs become firm.

Fry the coated drumsticks in deep fat for about 8 – 10 minutes or until golden-brown and crisp. Drain on kitchen paper and leave to cool.

CHICKEN LIVER PÂTÉ

A smooth pâté, ideal as a first course served with hot toast.

SERVES 4 – 6

225g/8 oz chicken livers
175g/6 oz butter
2 tablespoons brandy or brown sherry
1 clove garlic
1 level teaspoon fresh chopped thyme
  (or ¼ teaspoon dried thyme)
Salt
Freshly ground black pepper

Remove any stringy bits from the chicken livers. Using a heavy based frying pan, melt about 50g/2 oz of the butter and fry the chicken livers and crushed garlic for about 5 minutes over a medium heat, turning them frequently. Do not overcook. Add salt and pepper. Remove from the pan and put into an electric blender or food processor or press through a sieve.

Melt 100g/4 oz of the butter and add this to the livers together with the brandy or sherry and thyme. Blend to a smooth purée. Either press it into one pot or six individual ramekins. Allow to cool completely and cover with cling film or foil. If it is to be kept for any length of time melt an additional 50g/2 oz of butter and pour over the surface of the pâté. Keep in the refrigerator.

COUNTRY PÂTÉ

Providing you give him sufficient warning, your butcher will probably mince the meats for you. Otherwise, use a food processor or the medium blade of a mincer

SERVES 10 – 12

300g/12 oz lean minced beef
250g/10oz lean bacon, finely chopped
450g/1 lb fat belly pork, minced
225g/8 oz pigs' liver, minced
1 clove garlic, crushed
10 black peppercorns
10 juniper berries
120ml/4 fl oz dry white wine
30ml/1 fl oz brandy
1 teaspoon salt

Preheat oven to 300°F/150°C/Gas Mark 2

Place all the meats in a large bowl and mix thoroughly. Crush the peppercorns and juniper berries

Chicken Liver Pâté (left) and Country Pâté (right).

and add to the bowl together with the salt and garlic. Pour in the wine and brandy and continue to mix well. Cover bowl and leave for at least an hour, two if possible.

Transfer mixture to a 900g/2 lb loaf tin. Place in a roasting tin half-filled with hot water and put in the preheated oven. Bake for 2 hours, remove from oven and allow to cool. A certain amount of shrinkage will have occurred, this is quite normal. When cold, place a double strip of foil across the top and compress with weights. Leave for a few hours.

Delicious for a picnic with French bread, or an informal lunch as a first course with hot toast.

PARSLEY SCOTCH EGGS

A traditional picnic dish that, if well made, is always delicious. Homemade mayonnaise or chutney is a good accompaniment.

SERVES 4

4 hard-boiled eggs
225g/8 oz sausage meat
1 tablespoon chopped parsley
Seasoned flour
1 egg, beaten
Salt and pepper
Oil for frying
Breadcrumbs

Place the eggs in a pan with sufficient cold water to cover them, bring them to the boil and simmer for about 8 minutes, then plunge them into cold water. Mix the sausage meat with the parsley and season well. Shell the cooked eggs and coat evenly with seasoned flour.

Divide the sausage meat into 4 portions and gently shape around each egg, covering completely. Pat the egg and sausage meat into shape then dip them evenly into the beaten egg. Cover very thoroughly in breadcrumbs.

Heat 5cm/2″ of oil in a deep frying pan until very hot and fry eggs for 8 – 10 minutes, turning them frequently. When the Scotch eggs are a nice brown colour, drain them on kitchen paper or greaseproof paper. These are nice served hot or cold.

CORNISH PASTIES

SERVES 4

350g/12oz chuck steak
100g/¼ lb potatoes, peeled and diced
1 small onion, skinned and chopped
Salt and freshly milled pepper
350g/12oz shortcrust pastry

Preheat oven to 425°F/220°C/Gas Mark 7

Cut the steak into small pieces, add the potatoes and onion and season well. Divide the pastry into 4 and roll each piece into a circle about 20cm/8″ in

diameter. Divide the meat mixture between the pastry rounds, damp the edges, draw the edges of the pastry together to form a seam across the top and then flute the edges with your fingers. Place the pasties on a baking tray and glaze them with beaten egg, then place them in the oven.

After ten minutes, remove the pasties from the oven and glaze them again. Turn the heat down to 325°F/160°C/Gas Mark 3 and cook for a further hour. Serve hot or cold.

AMERICAN CLUB SANDWICHES

Triple-decker sandwiches packed full of interesting fillings are a good idea for lunch, especially with hungry children about!

INGREDIENTS FOR 4

B.L.T. (the traditional one with bacon, lettuce and tomato)

12 slices white bread
50g/2 oz butter
4 medium tomatoes, sliced
Lettuce
12 rashers bacon, fried or grilled till crisp
Mayonnaise
Cocktail sticks with olives, onions
    or gherkins to garnish

Toast the bread and cut off the crusts. Butter 8 slices on one side, 4 on both. On the bottom slices, arrange the tomatoes. Season to taste. Cover with slices of toast. Next arrange the lettuce and spoon on mayonnaise. Cover with more toast and on the final layer put the bacon. Finish with remaining toast. Press the sandwiches firmly together and spear each one with a cocktail stick. Garnish with an olive, an onion or gherkin.

CHEESE, CHICKEN AND COLESLAW

12 slices brown or white bread
8 slices cooked chicken
100g/¼ lb coleslaw
75-100g/3 - 4 oz Cheddar cheese, grated

Toast and butter the bread as for B.L.T. and layer up the club sandwiches with the 3 different ingredients.

TUNA, CUCUMBER AND EGG

12 slices brown or white bread
200g/7 oz tin tuna fish, drained
2 tablespoons mayonnaise
24 slices cucumber
3 hard-boiled eggs, chopped
1 tablespoon chives, chopped
Salt and pepper

Toast and butter bread as above. Blend together the tuna fish with 1 tablespoon mayonnaise. Season

with salt and pepper. Mix the eggs with the other tablespoon of mayonnaise and the chopped chives and season with salt and pepper. Then layer the tuna fish, cucumber and eggs.

American Club Sandwiches.

PIPERADE

This is equally delicious served hot or cold. Especially recommended for a picnic or cold buffet.

SERVES 2 – 4

4 eggs
Salt and pepper
2 tomatoes, skinned, deseeded and sliced
1 medium onion chopped
1 medium green pepper, cored, deseeded and chopped
1 tablespoon oil
25g/1 oz butter
Pinch dried or fresh marjoram and thyme
1 clove garlic crushed

Crack eggs into a bowl and whisk thoroughly with the salt and pepper and herbs.

Heat the oil in a frying pan and add the chopped onion, green pepper and garlic. Fry gently until soft

but not brown. Add the tomatoes and cook for a further three minutes. Remove from the heat and add to the egg mixture.

Heat the butter in the frying pan and when frothing add the omelette mixture. Cook gently until the underside is golden brown. Slide out onto a plate and return to the frying pan on the reverse side. Cook for a minute or two more. Do not over cook.

Serve hot immediately or allow to get cold and cut into wedges for a picnic or cold buffet.

SPLIT FRENCH LOAF

An easy picnic idea

Fill a fresh, crusty French loaf with different combinations of cold meats and salads. Wrap up with cling film.

WHOLE SNAPPER WITH SAVOURY RICE FILLING

Although snapper tends to be a fairly expensive fish, its flavour and imposing appearance is well worth the money.

1 x 1kg/2-2½ lb snapper
½ cup long-grain rice
¼ teaspoon saffron or turmeric
1 cup water
10g/½ oz butter
½ medium-sized onion, finely chopped
1 clove garlic, crushed
1 stick celery, finely sliced
½ red pepper, finely chopped
100g/4 oz cooked prawns, peeled and chopped
1 tablespoon chopped chives
¼ teaspoon each marjoram and basil
Salt and black pepper

Put rice, saffron and water in a saucepan, bring to the boil, reduce heat and simmer for 12 minutes or until all the water has evaporated.

In another pan, melt the butter and gently fry the onion, garlic, celery and pepper until tender. Add the prawns and herbs and season to taste. Add to the rice, mix well and use this stuffing to fill the cavity of the fish. Wrap in foil and barbecue until cooked.

CORN ON THE COB

ALLOW ONE COB PER PERSON

Cook the frozen or fresh corn cobs for 5 minutes in salted boiling water. Lay each one on a piece of buttered foil, season to taste with salt and black pepper and add a knob of butter. Sprinkle with mixed spice. Lay them on the barbecue until tender and nicely browned.

BROCHETTES OF MONKFISH WITH COURGETTES AND LEMON

SERVES 4

Allow 225g/8 oz of monkfish, without bones, per person
4 small courgettes cut into 4cm/1½ " slices
2 large lemons
Marinade of oil and lemon juice (about 150ml/¼ pint)
Fennel seeds

Cut the fish into large pieces about 4cm/1½ " square and put into a shallow dish, together with the courgettes. Pour over the marinade and sprinkle with fennel seeds. Leave for at least 2 hours.

Thread the fish, courgettes and lemon wedges onto skewers. Place them on the barbecue grill and cook for about 8 minutes, turning and basting frequently. Serve at once.

BROCHETTES OF SCALLOPS WITH PRAWNS AND LIME

SERVES 6

24 large scallops
24 large prawns with shells on
4 limes
Black pepper

Thread scallops, prawns and lime wedges onto skewers. Season and spread a little lime butter sauce on the fish. Barbecue quickly until tender.

BARBECUED TROUT WITH PINE-NUT STUFFING

FOR 4 PEOPLE

4 whole trout

STUFFING

2 bacon rashers, chopped
50g/2 oz pine-nuts
2 tablespoons chopped chives
50g/2 oz white breadcrumbs
2 tablespoons cream
Salt and black pepper

Fry bacon until crisp, add the pine-nuts and cook for a further minute before adding the rest of the ingredients. Remove from the heat.

Use this stuffing to fill the fish. Barbecue until the fish is tender.

GOOSEBERRY SAUCE

A tangy accompaniment to mackerel.

450g/1 lb gooseberries
25g/1 oz butter
Caster sugar to taste
A little grated nutmeg
4 tablespoons water

Barbecues can be so much more imaginative than may be thought. Corn on the Cob, Barbecued Trout with Pine-Nut Stuffing, Whole Snapper with Savoury Rice Filling, Red Mullet, Brochettes of Monkfish with Courgettes and Lemon, and Brochettes of Scallops with Prawns and Lime make a delicious outdoor feast.

Wash the fruit and place in a saucepan with the water. There is no need to top and tail the gooseberries. Simmer for about 10 minutes or until they are cooked. Drain and pass through a sieve. To the resulting purée add the butter, nutmeg and sugar to taste.

LIME BUTTER SAUCE WITH DILL

SERVES 6

2 egg yolks
1 tablespoon lime juice
Grated rind of 1 lime
125g/5 oz butter
1 tablespoon finely chopped fresh dill

If you do not have a double saucepan put the egg yolks, juice and rind in a bowl in a saucepan of simmering water and stir for 1 minute. Gradually whisk in small pieces of the butter until the sauce thickens. Remove from the heat and add the dill. Allow to cool.

Use the sauce on prawns, monkfish etc. for barbecuing. It can be made in advance and lemon could be substituted for the lime.

HERB BUTTER

Can be made up in advance and frozen. Spread on fish or serve as pats on steak.

100g/4 oz butter
1 tablespoon parsley, finely chopped
1 tablespoon chives, finely chopped
1 teaspoon lemon juice

Add the herbs and lemon juice to the softened butter until well blended.

Experiment with other herbs you might have growing in your garden.

SAUSAGES WITH PRUNES AND BACON

Although many people profess not to like prunes, served this way they contrast beautifully with the sausages and bacon.

250g/1 lb thick herb sausages
   (or your own favourites)
4 rashers bacon
8 pitted prunes, halved
Wooden cocktail sticks

Slit the sausages along one side and stuff each one with 2 halves of prune. Wrap the sausage with half

a bacon rasher and secure with a wooden cocktail stick. Barbecue until golden brown and cooked through thoroughly.

FAMILY HAMBURGERS

A variation on a theme! Serve with creamed potatoes and a green vegetable.

MAKES 4

450g/1 lb good minced beef
1 small onion, finely diced
¼ teaspoon mixed dried herbs
1 tablespoon fresh chopped parsley
1 dessertspoon tomato purée
Dash of Worcestershire sauce
Salt and black pepper
1 egg, beaten
Fat or oil for frying
Flour for rolling burgers

Into a large bowl, put the minced beef, onion, herbs, tomato purée and Worcestershire sauce. Season with salt and pepper and combine all the ingredients with a lightly-beaten egg.

Divide the mixture into 4 and form each one into a hamburger shape. Roll in a little flour and fry for 4 – 5 minutes on each side in shallow fat or oil.

VEGETABLE KEBABS

SERVES 4

12 button mushrooms
4 tomatoes, quartered
1 large onion, segmented
2 green peppers, cut into pieces
1 red pepper, cut into pieces
Bay leaves (optional)

MARINADE

6 tablespoons vegetable oil
1 tablespoon lemon juice
1 clove garlic, crushed
2 tablespoons fresh herbs
Salt and pepper

Thread the pieces of vegetable onto skewers and lay them in a shallow dish.

Put all the ingredients for the marinade into a screw-top jar, shake vigorously and pour over the kebabs. Leave them in a cool place for at least 2 hours, turning them occasionally.

Barbecue for about 8 – 10 minutes, turning frequently, until nicely browned. Serve at once.

Candlelight and a late summer evening barbecue.

HERB AND GARLIC BREAD

A good accompaniment to barbecued food or salads.

1 French stick
100g/4 oz butter, softened
2 cloves garlic, crushed
2 tablespoons of fresh, chopped herbs
   (e.g. parsley, chives, tarragon, thyme) or
   1 teaspoon dried herbs
Pinch of salt

Preheat oven to 400°F/200°C/Gas Mark 6

In a small bowl, mix together the butter, garlic, herbs and salt. Using a bread knife, slice the loaf diagonally at approximately 4cm/1½″ intervals, but without slicing right through. Spread the butter on both sides of each slice and, if there is any left, spread it along the top and sides of the loaf. Wrap the loaf loosely in foil and bake in a preheated oven for 15 – 20 minutes. Serve at once.

HAMBURGERS FOR THE BARBECUE

MAKES 4 100g/¼ lb BURGERS

450g/1 lb chuck steak
Salt and black pepper

Either put the meat through your mincer twice or grind in a food processor or ask your butcher to mince the meat for you. Put the meat in a bowl, season (a large teaspoon salt) then divide the mixture into 4 equal portions and, with your hands, shape the mince into a hamburger shape. Barbecue on a hot grill for about 4 – 5 minutes per side.
   Serve with tomato sauce or ketchup.

PORK SPARE RIBS IN A BARBEQUE SAUCE

A gloriously tasty and messy dish for a barbecue. This dish can be started in the oven and finished off on the barbecue grill.

SERVES 4

12 pork spare ribs
1 tablespoon oil
1 small onion, finely chopped
3 tablespoons wine vinegar
1 tablespoon soy sauce
1 tablespoon soft brown sugar
1 tablespoon tomato purée
1 tablespoon tomato ketchup
1 teaspoon made mustard
1 tablespoon Worcestershire sauce

Preheat oven to 400°F/200°C/Gas Mark 6

Put the spare ribs in a preheated oven in a shallow roasting tin. Roast for 30 minutes.
   In the meantime, heat the oil in a small saucepan and gently fry the chopped onion until it softens. Add all the other ingredients to the pan and bring to the boil, stirring continuously. Remove from the heat. Pour off any fat from the spare ribs and pour over the barbecue sauce, coating the meat well. Reduce the oven temperature to 375°F/190°C/Gas Mark 5 and cook for a further 1 – 1½ hours, basting the meat frequently with the sauce. This last stage can, if wanted, be done on the barbecue.
   To be eaten with fingers only, so plenty of paper napkins should be provided!

STUFFED PITTA BREAD

Slit through pitta bread – white or wholemeal – and fill with a mixture of crisp lettuce, watercress, cottage cheese, radish and tomato for serving with barbecued food – or let your imagination run riot and create a variety of savoury fillings, hot or cold.

CHICKEN AND FRESH PINEAPPLE KEBABS

FOR 4 KEBABS

4 chicken breasts
1 small pineapple
2 green peppers

MARINADE

4 tablespoons soy sauce
4 tablespoons white wine
1 clove garlic, crushed
1 tablespoon tomato purée
Black pepper
1 tablespoon sesame oil (or good cooking oil)
4 long barbecue skewers

Cut the chicken and pineapple into 4cm/1½″ pieces. Deseed the peppers and cut into similar sized chunks.
   Blend all the marinade ingredients together. Put the chicken, pineapple and pepper into a bowl and pour over the marinade. If time permits leave for several hours.
   Thread the ingredients onto the skewers and place on a hot barbecue. Baste with the remaining marinade.

Hamburgers for the Barbecue (top), Herb and Garlic Bread (bottom left) and Pork Spare Ribs in a Barbecue Sauce (bottom right).

CURRIED PORK BROCHETTES WITH COURGETTES AND LEMON

Delicious served with a savoury rice and crisp green salad.

SERVES 6

675g/1½ lb pork fillet
3 small courgettes
2 lemons

MARINADE

4 tablespoons vegetable oil
1 tablespoon curry powder
1 small onion, finely chopped
1 tablespoon tomato purée
Salt and black pepper

Cut the pork into 2.5cm/1″ pieces, the courgettes and lemons into 1cm/½″ slices.

Put all the marinade ingredients in a large bowl and mix well. Add the meat, making sure it is well coated. Cover and leave for at least 2 hours.

Thread the pork, courgettes and lemon slices on skewers. Brush the courgettes with oil and place the skewers on the barbecue grill. Cook for about 15 minutes, turning and basting frequently with the excess marinade, until the pork is tender. Serve at once.

PEPPER AND BEEF KEBABS

SERVES 4

900g/2 lbs rump steak
2 medium onions, quartered
2 green peppers, cut into large pieces
1 tablespoon of freshly chopped parsley

SAUCE

5 tablespoons dry wine
5 tablespoons soy sauce
1 tablespoon tomato purée
1 teaspoon mustard powder
1 clove garlic, crushed
1 tablespoon soft brown sugar
Freshly milled black pepper

4 kebab skewers

Cut the meat into 4cm/1½″ even-sized cubes. Thread the meat onto the skewers, followed by a piece of onion, then pepper, until all the ingredients are used up.

Line the grill pan with foil and turn the heat to

Lamb and Lemon Kebabs (left), Pepper and Beef Kebabs (centre) and Chicken and Fresh Pineapple Kebabs (right).

high. Place the kebabs on the grill pan and brush with the sauce. Place the kebabs under the grill and cook under a high heat for 5 minutes. Reduce heat to moderate, turn kebabs, brush again with the sauce and replace under grill. Cool for about 15 minutes or until cooked as required. Turn often for even cooking and brush each time with the sauce.

When cooked, serve on a bed of buttered rice with any remaining sauce poured over the kebabs. Sprinkle with the parsley and serve at once.

LAMB AND LEMON KEBABS

SERVES 4

900g/2 lb neck fillet of lamb
4 medium onions, cut into quarters
1 tablespoon chopped parsley
2 lemons

MARINADE

3 tablespoons oil
2 tablespoons white wine
1 large clove of garlic, crushed
1 teaspoon dried rosemary
Salt and freshly milled black pepper

4 kebab skewers

Trim the excess fat from the lamb and cut into 4cm/1½″ even-sized cubes. In a bowl, mix together the ingredients for the marinade, add the cubed lamb and turn well with a spoon until the lamb is coated. Cover and leave the lamb to marinate for 6 hours or overnight.

Line grill pan with foil and turn the heat on to moderately high. Thread the meat on 4 skewers with a few pieces of onion in between. Place the skewers on the grill pan and brush with the marinade. Grill for about 20 minutes, turning evenly and brushing with the marinade. Serve the kebabs on a bed of rice sprinkled with parsley and with lemon wedges to squeeze over the lamb.

BANANAS WITH RUM AND ORANGE

SERVES 4

4 firm bananas
75g/3 oz butter
3 tablespoons frozen concentrated orange juice
2 tablespoons dark rum
2 level tablespoons brown sugar

Place all ingredients except the bananas in a small pan and bring to the boil, stirring occasionally. Simmer until syrupy.

Place each banana on a square of foil and drizzle over the sauce.

Wrap tightly, twisting ends to contain sauce. Barbecue until bananas are golden brown.

FRUIT KEBABS

SERVES 4

4 peaches/apricots
Small punnet strawberries
3 – 4 kiwi fruit, sliced
3 – 4 slices fresh pineapple, segmented
Lemon juice
Honey
Mint leaves (optional)

Thread pieces of fruit onto skewers, interspersed with fresh mint leaves. Sprinkle with lemon juice and brush with honey. Barbecue for about 8 minutes.

GREEK FETA SALAD

Crunchy and eye-catching, this salad is a substantial one and, with the addition of crusty bread and a bottle of cold, dry white wine, an easy summer lunch!

1 crisp lettuce
Half a cucumber, sliced or cubed
4 tomatoes, cut into segments

1 green pepper, chopped
1 small onion, thinly sliced
100 – 175g/4 – 6 oz Greek feta cheese, cubed
50g/2 oz black olives
Chopped parsley
150ml/¼ pint French dressing

Tear the lettuce into bite-sized pieces and, in a salad bowl, mix with the cucumber, tomato and pepper. Arrange onion rings on top, then the cheese and olives. Just before serving, pour over dressing and sprinkle liberally with parsley.

SAVOURY RICE

225g/8 oz easy-cook rice
½ teaspoon saffron
Small bunch spinach
50g/2 oz pinenuts

Cook rice with saffron in boiling salted water for about 12 minutes, until tender but firm. Drain.

Meanwhile, cook spinach, drain and chop finely.

In a warm serving dish rake the spinach and pinenuts through the rice with a fork, and serve while still hot with kebabs of your choice laid on top.

MUSTARD BREAD

An interesting addition to a barbecue or salad meal and a change from the usual garlic bread. Try it with a long brown loaf – the granary type is nice.

1 small baguette or French loaf
2 tablespoons whole grain French mustard
3 garlic cloves, crushed
2 tablespoons fresh mixed herbs (parsley, dill, basil etc), chopped
100g/4 oz butter

Preheat oven to 350°F/180°C/Gas Mark 4

Slash the loaf at intervals. Mix the other ingredients and spread on one side of each section. Wrap the loaf in greased foil and bake in a preheated oven for about 15 minutes. Serve hot.

MEATBALL KEBABS

For approximately 4 skewers

Facing page: (clockwise from top) Mustard Bread, Vegetable Kebabs, Curried Pork Brochettes with Courgettes and Lemon, Meatball Kebabs, Savoury Rice, Stuffed Pitta Bread, and Sausages with Prunes and Bacon.

Above: Bananas with Rum and Orange (top left), Greek Feta Salad (top right) and Fruit Kebabs (bottom).

450g/1 lb lean minced beef
225g/8 oz pork sausage meat
2 slices brown bread soaked in
    2 tablespoons cream
1 onion, finely chopped
1 egg
1 dessertspoon chilli sauce
1 tablespoon chopped parsley
Salt and black pepper
Flour for rolling

In a large bowl, thoroughly mix together all ingredients. Shape into large meatballs with floured hands and leave to rest (covered) for a few hours in the refrigerator.

Spear onto skewers and brush with olive oil before barbecuing.

Serve with a spicy tomato sauce.

A Cocktail Party

CELERY FILLED WITH SMOKED SALMON PÂTÉ

225g/½ lb smoked salmon trimmings
50g/2 oz softened butter
1 tablespoon olive oil
2 tablespoons lemon juice
2 tablespoons plain yoghurt
2 tablespoons double cream
Pinch of cayenne pepper
White of 1 egg

Wash and scrub the celery and cut into 5cm/2″ lengths.

In a blender, mix together the smoked salmon, butter, oil and lemon juice. Then add the yoghurt, cream and cayenne pepper. Process until smooth. Turn pâté into a bowl. Whip the egg white until stiff and fold into the pâté. Fill the celery with the pâté. Keep chilled until required. This pâté also freezes well.

CHOUX BUNS WITH FRESH SALMON AND DILL

Fill small choux buns with flaked, poached fresh salmon combined with a light mayonnaise flavoured with fresh dill, salt and black pepper.

SMALL ONION TARTS

The ingredients make approximately 15 small tarts or 1 x 20cm/8″ tart

100g/4 oz shortcrust pastry

FILLING
450g/1 lb onions, finely sliced
50g/2 oz butter
Salt and pepper
Grated nutmeg
3 large eggs
150ml/5 fl oz soured cream

Preheat oven to 375°F/190°C/Gas Mark 5

Roll out the pastry on a floured board and line small tartlet tins or one large tart tin. Prick the base of each tart and bake blind for a few minutes in a preheated oven until the pastry "sets". Remove from the oven.

Melt the butter in a saucepan and sauté the onions gently (with a lid on) until soft. Cook for a further few minutes, uncovered, until they just start to go brown. Remove from the heat and season with salt and pepper and a little grated nutmeg.

Lightly beat the eggs and soured cream together and add to the onions. Spoon the mixture into the tartlet cases and bake for a further 10 minutes until the filling is set.

For the large tart, bake blind for 15 minutes, fill and cook for a further 30–40 minutes.

CHERRY TOMATOES FILLED WITH CREAM CHEESE AND CHIVES

Slice off the top of the tomatoes and, with a small teaspoon, remove some of the pulp. Either buy a commercial brand of cream cheese and chives or make up a quantity of your own and pipe the cheese into the tomatoes.

HAM AND CREAM CHEESE CUBES

Horseradish and cream cheese makes a tasty filling for the ham and these little cubes are an attractive addition to a platter of finger food.

5 slices of "square" packet ham
200g/7 oz Philadelphia cream cheese or
    equivalent
2 dessertspoons horseradish sauce
Squeeze lemon juice
2 dessertspoons double cream or soured cream
Black pepper

Clockwise from top right: Kumquats Filled with Cream Cheese, Ham and Cream Cheese Cubes, Choux Buns with Fresh Salmon and Dill, Celery Filled with Smoked Salmon Pâté, Small Onion Tarts and (centre) Cherry Tomatoes Filled with Cream Cheese and Chives, and Prawn Barquettes.

In a bowl, blend together the cream cheese, horse-radish sauce, lemon juice and cream. Season with black pepper. Spread this mixture evenly between the slices of ham, finishing with a slice of ham on the top. Transfer to the freezer for 2 – 3 hours until firm but not completely frozen. With a sharp knife, cut the "sandwich" into 16 squares. Refrigerate until needed.

KUMQUATS FILLED WITH CREAM CHEESE

Kumquats, those tiny oranges that are appearing in the shops now at various times of the year, make a colourful contribution to a tray of finger food. Simply take a thin slice off the top of each one and pipe with a "blob" of cream cheese.

Covered with fondant icing, they make delicious petits fours.

CRUDITÉS

This crunchy assortment of raw vegetables makes a colourful and healthy start to a meal, or can be served as an alternative to crisps and nuts with drinks.

Choose a variety of vegetables that look good together and select ones that are in prime condition.

Sliced red and green peppers, cauliflower florets, sticks of carrots and celery, fennel, cucumber, spring onions, even tiny cherry tomatoes, are just a few to choose from. Prepare the vegetables and keep in a bowl of cold water in the refrigerator until needed, then drain and pat dry before arranging on a large platter or in individual bowls. Serve with one or more dips or with a very thick, home-made mayonnaise.

CHEESE AND CHUTNEY DIP

SERVES 6

225g/½ lb cream cheese
2 tablespoons double cream
2 level teaspoons curry powder
1 rounded tablespoon tomato ketchup
2 teaspoons lemon juice
4 tablespoons finely chopped chutney or sweet
    pickle

Blend together the cream cheese and double cream, then add the curry powder, ketchup and lemon juice. Finally fold in the chutney or sweet pickle until well mixed and chill for at least half an hour.

TUNA FISH DIP

175g/6 oz tuna, flaked
2 tablespoons mayonnaise
1 – 2 tablespoons tomato ketchup
Juice of 1 lemon
1 small stick of celery, finely sliced
Salt and black pepper

Mix all the ingredients together. For a smoother dip use a blender or food processor.

GREEN ONION DIP

50g/2 oz spring onions
25g/1 oz parsley
25g/1 oz fresh coriander
1 tablespoon fresh ginger
½ tablespoon soy sauce
150ml/5 fl oz soured cream
1 tablespoon mayonnaise

Chop very finely the spring onions, parsley, coriander and ginger and mix together with the other ingredients.

SLIMMER'S DIP

225g/½ lb cottage cheese
150ml/5 fl oz thick yoghurt
1 spring onion, finely sliced
1 stick celery, finely sliced
Pinch cayenne pepper

Combine all the ingredients. Use a blender or food processor for a smoother dip.

TAPENADE

A Spanish dip, excellent with crudités

8 anchovy fillets
200g/7 oz tuna fish
10 black olives
150ml/¼ pint olive or groundnut oil
2 tablespoons brandy
1 teaspoon lemon juice
Freshly ground black pepper

In a blender or food processor, combine all the ingredients until smooth.

Crudités with an assortment of dips.

TARAMASALATA

SERVES 4

100g/4 oz smoked cod roe
Juice of half a lemon
1 clove of garlic, crushed
150ml/¼ pint olive or groundnut oil
Freshly ground black pepper
1 tablespoon parsley, finely chopped

In a blender, combine the cod roe and garlic to a smooth paste. Add the lemon juice and parsley and then the oil, a drop at a time. If the mixture seems too stiff, add a little boiling water to lighten it.

CAMEMBERT FRITTERS

Although deep-fat frying should not be too regular a part of our everyday cooking, once in a while it is a much appreciated treat. Apart from fruit and vegetable fritters and my childhood favourite, jam sandwich fritters, deep-fried Camembert, where the cheese is incorporated into a Béchamel sauce, makes a delicious starter.

MAKES APPROXIMATELY 20 FRITTERS

BÉCHAMEL SAUCE
300ml/½ pint milk
Small onion
1 bay leaf
10 black peppercorns
50g/2 oz butter
50g/2 oz flour

225g/½ lb Camembert cheese
3 egg yolks
Large teaspoon Dijon mustard
Salt and black pepper
Oil for deep frying

COATING
Seasoned flour
2 eggs, beaten
75-100g/3-4 oz fresh white breadcrumbs

Put the milk, onion, bay leaf and peppercorns into a medium-sized saucepan and bring gently to the boil. Remove from the heat, cover with a lid and allow to infuse for 30 minutes. Strain the milk into a jug. Melt the butter in a saucepan, add the flour and stir continually for a minute. Gradually add the strained milk and beat until the sauce is smooth. Meanwhile, remove the rind from the cheese and discard. Chop the cheese into small pieces and add to the Béchamel sauce together with the egg yolks. Simmer for 2-3 minutes, stirring, until the cheese has melted. Remove from the heat and add the seasonings. Pour into a cake tin or Swiss roll tin to a depth of 1cm/½ " and allow to cool. The fritters can be made a day in advance and kept in the refrigerator, or they can be frozen until needed.

Using a small pastry cutter approximately 4cm/1½ " round, cut out the cheese mixture. Dip the rounds in the seasoned flour, then into the beaten egg and finally coat with the breadcrumbs, pressing the crumbs in lightly with your fingers.

Heat the oil in a deep fryer or large saucepan with a draining basket to 350°F/180°C and fry the fritters, a few at a time, until golden (1½-2 minutes will probably be about right). Remove from the oil, drain on kitchen paper and keep them warm on a serving dish whilst frying the rest.

Serve by themselves, garnished with a little parsley or watercress, or with a cranberry or red-currant sauce.

PRAWN BARQUETTES

Half fill crisp boat-shaped pastry cases or tartlets with a sharp lemon sauce and top with plump peeled prawns.

CROQUE MONSIEUR

This simple fried sandwich makes an ideal hors d'oeuvre or snack

8 slices white bread ⅓ " thick
75g/3 oz butter
4 slices lean ham
100g/4 oz Cheddar cheese, grated
Oil for frying

Butter the bread and lay the ham and cheese on 4 of the slices. Cover with the remaining slices. Press firmly together. Cut off the crusts and cut each sandwich into 3 fingers. Fry in hot oil until golden. Drain on kitchen paper and serve at once.

SMOKED SALMON PUFFS

Instead of making a starter, produce a plateful of these tasty canapés to hand around with a pre-dinner drink.

MAKES 8 – 10

450g/1 lb puff pastry
Smoked salmon trimmings
175g/6 oz cream cheese
Cayenne pepper
Oil for deep or shallow frying

Roll out the puff pastry very thinly and cut into rectangles approximately 7.5 x 15cm/3 x 6". On one half of each rectangle put a piece of smoked salmon,

Clockwise from top: Croque Monsieur, Savoury Bacon Bites, Cheese Aigrettes, Camembert Fritters, Kefthedes, and Smoked Salmon Puffs (centre).

a small spoonful of cream cheese and a dusting of cayenne pepper. Dampen the edges of the pastry with cold water, fold it over and seal the edges tightly. Refrigerate. (They can be made the day before you need them.)

Deep or shallow fry in hot oil until puffed up and golden brown.

Serve at once.

KEFTHEDES (SAVOURY MEATBALLS)

A speciality of Greece. Can be served as a cocktail snack, first course or, if made larger, a tasty main course.

1 medium sized onion, finely chopped
Butter or oil
450g/1 lb lean steak, finely minced
Parsley or mint, chopped
1 egg, beaten
Flour
Salt and pepper
Cocktail sticks

Fry the chopped onion in the butter or oil until golden brown. In a bowl, combine the onion, steak and herbs with the beaten egg. Season. With your hands, roll the mixture into balls about the size of marbles. Coat lightly with flour and fry in hot oil until golden brown. Transfer to cocktail sticks and serve with a tomato sauce dip.

SAVOURY BACON BITES

Another tasty cocktail snack

MAKES APPROXIMATELY 12

1 medium sized onion, chopped
225g/8 oz bacon rashers
25g/1 oz butter or dripping
150ml/¼ pint chicken stock
75g/3 oz breadcrumbs
Freshly ground black pepper
1 egg, beaten
Fat or oil for deep frying
Cocktail sticks

Mince together the onion and bacon. In a saucepan, melt the butter or dripping, stir in the flour and cook for 1 minute. Add the chicken stock and stir until it comes to the boil. Cook for a further minute. Remove from the heat, add half the beaten egg, black pepper and 50g/2 oz of the breadcrumbs. Mix well and add the bacon and onion. Divide this mixture into 12 small balls and refrigerate for about 30 minutes. Brush the bacon bites with the rest of the egg, roll in the remaining breadcrumbs and deep-fry in hot fat or oil for about 8 minutes. Drain on kitchen paper. Serve on cocktail sticks.

CHEESE AIGRETTES (BEIGNETS)

These make excellent cocktail savouries or an interesting starter.

SERVES 4 AS A STARTER

CHEESE CHOUX PASTRY
150ml/¼ pint water
50g/2 oz butter
60g/2 ½ oz plain flour, sifted
2 eggs
50g/2 oz Gruyère or Cheddar cheese, diced
Salt and pepper
Pinch dried mustard

To serve: Parmesan cheese (optional)

Deep fat for frying

In a heavy-based saucepan, boil the water and butter together. When bubbling, draw to one side and shoot in the sifted flour all at once. Beat vigorously until smooth. Allow to cool slightly before beating in the eggs one at a time until the mixture is glossy. Add the cheese and season to taste with the salt, pepper and mustard. This pastry can be prepared a few hours in advance and kept in the refrigerator, covered with a damp cloth.

Meanwhile, heat the deep fat until moderately hot. Drop in the mixture a teaspoonful at a time. Do not try to fry too many at once as they need space to swell. Slightly increase the temperature of the fat and cook the Aigrettes for 5 – 6 minutes until puffed and golden brown. Lift out with a draining spoon onto kitchen paper and dust with grated Parmesan cheese. Repeat until all the mixture has been used. Serve hot.

Christmas Fare

ROAST TURKEY

Although turkey in its various forms is now a familiar sight in our supermarkets and shops throughout the year, a turkey with all the traditional trimmings is unbeatable on Christmas Day, when a large number of people is to be catered for.

Allow about 175g/6 oz meat per person but, as turkey is so good cold, a larger bird than you need will provide additional meals.

Always choose a bird that is white with plump breast and drumsticks. Turkey varies in price according to whether it is fresh, chilled, frozen, self-basting etc, so select a bird to suit your individual needs and pocket.

If you freeze or buy a frozen bird, allow plenty of time for it to thaw out completely before cooking, to avoid the risk of salmonella poisoning. All but the smallest turkeys should be thawed in the refrigerator, up to 3.6kg/8 lb can be thawed at room temperature.

Thawing Times			
Size		Fridge	Room Temp.
2.7kg-3.6kg	6lb-8lb	36-48 hrs	30 hrs
3.6kg-4.5kg	8lb-10lb	48-56 hrs	Not advisable
4.5kg-5.4kg	10lb-12lb	56-60 hrs	Not advisable
5.4kg-6.8kg	12lb-15lb	60-70 hrs	Not advisable
6.8kg-7.7kg	15lb-17lb	3 days	Not advisable
7.7kg-9kg	17lb-20lb	4 days	Not advisable
9kg-11.3kg	20lb-25lb	4-5 days	Not advisable

Roasting Times for Turkey

Ovens and turkeys vary. I have tried roasting birds at a fairly high temperature and at a moderately hot temperature. Both ways were successful, especially with frequent basting and the birds well protected with bacon, butter and foil. If a forcemeat stuffing has been used, then extra cooking time may be needed. As a guide, however, with the oven set to 350°F/180°C/Gas Mark 4, allow 20 minutes per 450g/1lb plus 15 minutes for birds weighing up to 4.5kg/10lb. For larger birds, allow a little extra but test with a skewer inserted into the thickest part of the leg. If the juices run clear then the turkey is cooked. Use this test on all size birds.

GIBLET GRAVY

Wash the giblets and place them in a pan with a piece of onion, a bay leaf, some parsley stalks and salt and pepper. Cover with water and bring to the boil. Skim the surface, cover the pan and simmer the giblets for about half an hour. Remove from the heat and strain into a jug. This can be done the day before the turkey is to be roasted.

When the bird has been transferred to a serving dish, pour off the excess fat from the roasting tin and then place it over a low heat. When the juices are bubbling, stir in about a tablespoon of flour and cook for a further minute, stirring constantly with a wooden spoon. Gradually add the turkey giblet stock and some white wine. If it is too thick, add a little water. Cook for 3 or 4 minutes until smooth. Check the seasoning before straining the gravy into a sauce boat. (If the gravy is not to be used immediately, pour it into a thermos jug to keep hot.)

ROAST TURKEY WITH TWO STUFFINGS

SERVES 12 – 15

1 turkey 4.5kg/10 lb (oven weight)
Streaky bacon rashers
Butter, softened
Seasoning
150ml/¼ pint white wine or stock

CHESTNUT STUFFING

50g/2 oz butter
1 small onion, finely chopped
Turkey liver, chopped
225g/8 oz chestnut purée
100g/4 oz mushrooms, sliced
1 stick celery, finely chopped
100g/4 oz bacon, chopped
Finely grated rind of 1 lemon
1 tablespoon parsley, chopped
50g/2 oz fresh white breadcrumbs
1 egg, beaten
Salt and black pepper

Melt the butter in a saucepan and sauté the onion for a few minutes until softened. Add the turkey liver and bacon and cook for a further 2 minutes, followed by the sliced mushrooms, celery and parsley. Blend in the chestnut purée and remove from the heat. Add the lemon rind and breadcrumbs, beaten egg and seasoning. When completely mixed, leave to get cold before filling the breast end of the turkey.

SAUSAGE MEAT STUFFING

450g/1 lb pork sausage meat
225g/8 oz veal, minced
1 large onion, finely chopped
1 clove garlic, crushed
1 apple, grated
50g/2 oz fresh white or wholemeal breadcrumbs
¼ teaspoon dried sage
¼ teaspoon dried thyme
¼ teaspoon dried marjoram
1 tablespoon parsley, finely chopped
Salt and black pepper
1 egg, lightly beaten

In a large bowl, combine all the ingredients well. Use the sausage meat stuffing to fill the body cavity. Do not pack in too tightly. Any excess stuffing can be cooked separately.

To Roast the Turkey

Preheat oven to 425°F/220°C/Gas Mark 7

Make sure the turkey is at room temperature. Pluck out any remaining quills that might have been left on and clean the bird inside and out with damp kitchen paper or a cloth.

Push the stuffing into the body cavity and neck end, pushing it up well but not too tightly. Truss or skewer the flaps. Spread the bird with butter, sprinkle with salt and pepper and lay the bacon over the breast. Lay the bird on its side on a rack in the roasting tin, pour in the stock or wine and cover the turkey loosely with foil.

Put into the preheated oven for 30 minutes at the above temperature and then reduce the oven heat to 350°F/180°C/Gas Mark 4 for the rest of the cooking time (about 2-2 ½ hours). Turn the turkey from one side to another and then on to its back during cooking and baste it at regular intervals. Remove the foil 30 minutes before the end of the cooking so the skin browns and becomes crispy.

Remove the bird carefully to a hot carving dish and allow to stand for at least 15 minutes while you finish off the gravy.

BREAD SAUCE

MAKES 1 PINT

1 onion
6-8 cloves
1 bay leaf
600ml/1 pint milk
75g/3 oz fresh white breadcrumbs
Salt and black pepper
1-2 tablespoons cream (optional)

Peel the onion and stud it with cloves. Put the onion, bay leaf and milk into a saucepan and bring to the boil. Remove from the heat and cover. Leave to infuse for about 15-20 minutes. Then add the breadcrumbs and butter and cook over gentle heat for 15 minutes, stirring from time to time (bread sauce is liable to

stick!), then remove the onion and bay leaf and any cloves that might have fallen out. Season to taste and, just before serving, stir in a little cream.

Apart from roast potatoes, try serving such things as spiced red cabbage and sprouts with chestnuts (if you haven't used a chestnut stuffing). Purées of celeriac and carrot make a nice change.

Spiced cranberry relish, bacon rolls and chipolatas are traditional accompaniments.

Other stuffings you could use instead of the ones above are sage and onion or apricot.

SPICED CRANBERRY RELISH

Excellent served with roast turkey, chicken, venison, gammon etc.

SERVES 8

350g/12 oz fresh cranberries
225g/6 oz caster sugar
Rind and juice of 1 orange
150ml/¼ pint water
1 cinnamon stick
¼ teaspoon ginger
3 cloves
2 tablespoons port

Place all the ingredients in a saucepan, stir until the sugar dissolves and then bring to the boil. Reduce the heat and simmer without a lid until the cranberries pop, about 4 – 5 minutes. Remove from the heat.

For Christmas dinner the relish can be made in advance and kept in the refrigerator. It can be served hot or cold but remember to remove the cinnamon stick and cloves first.

CHRISTMAS PUDDING

This is a recipe that dates back to 1870!

Enough for 2 puddings in 2 x 1 litre/2 pint basins

350g/12 oz plain flour
350g/12 oz breadcrumbs
675g/1½ lb raisins
450g/1 lb currants
100g/4 oz chopped peel
675g/1½ lb chopped beef suet
   or 550g/1¼ lb shredded suet
450g/1 lb soft brown sugar
4 eggs lightly beaten

Facing page: Roast Turkey and Spiced Cranberry Relish.

Overleaf: Mulled Wine (left) and Mince Pies (right).

Christmas Pudding.

Juice and grated rind of an orange and a lemon
½ teaspoon salt
½ teaspoon mixed spice
½ teaspoon ginger ⎱ to
½ teaspoon nutmeg ⎰ taste
450ml/¾ pint stout (Guinness)

In a large bowl, mix all the dry ingredients, add the beaten egg, fruit juice and stout and stir well. Leave to stand overnight, covered with a cloth. The following day divide the mixture into 2 x 1 litre/2 pint greased pudding basins, packing the mixture well down. Cover each basin with greaseproof paper and either tin foil or a pudding cloth tied securely with string around the rim.

Steam the puddings for 8 hours or pressure cook according to booklet instructions. Top up from time to time with boiling water, which should come half way up the sides of the basins. Store in a cool cupboard until needed.

To serve, steam for a further 2 hours, remove and invert onto a hot serving dish. Top with a piece of holly and flame with a tablespoon of warm rum or brandy.

Serve with brandy butter, rum sauce or cream.

MINCE PIES

The original mince pies really did contain minced meat, but nowadays we regard them as a sweet addition to Christmas fare.

TO MAKE 18 – 20 PIES

350g/12 oz shortcrust pastry
   or 450g/1 lb puff pastry
450g/1 lb fruit mincemeat
1 egg
Caster sugar to dust

Preheat oven to 425°F/220°C/Gas Mark 7

Roll out the pastry thinly into about 8cm/3″ rounds and line patty tins with these. Fill to about half their depth with mincemeat. Cut slightly smaller rounds for the tops of the pies. Dampen the rims with cold water, place on top of the bases and press down, sealing the edges together. Make a slit in the top of each pie to allow the steam to escape, brush each one well with beaten egg and sprinkle with caster sugar.

    Bake in a preheated oven for about 20 minutes until golden. Remove from the tins and allow to cool on a wire rack. Serve with cream, custard, brandy or rum butter.

BRANDY BUTTER

This can be made in advance and kept in the refrigerator or frozen, to lessen the work load at Christmas.

75g/3 oz unsalted butter
75g/3 oz caster sugar
Grated rind of half an orange
3 – 4 tablespoons brandy (more or less according
   to taste!)

Simply cream together the butter and sugar until light and fluffy. Beat in the orange rind and gradually add the brandy. Transfer to a serving dish, cover and refrigerate until needed.

MULLED WINE

Greet your guests on a chilly winter's night with a glass of hot mulled wine.

FOR 6 – 8 GLASSES

300ml/½ pint water
1 stick cinnamon
6 cloves
Juice and rind of 1 lemon
75g/3 oz brown sugar
1 bottle of red wine (a cheap red table wine
   will do – not your best bottle!)
Slices of orange and lemon

Put the water, cloves and cinnamon into a large saucepan and simmer for 10 minutes. Add the juice and rind of the lemon and the sugar and stir until the sugar is dissolved. Add wine and fruit slices and heat almost to boiling point. Remove the spices and serve in heat-proof glasses.

RUM SAUCE

An alternative to brandy butter for serving with the Christmas pudding.

40g/1½ oz butter
40g/1½ oz plain flour
40g/1½ oz caster sugar
450ml/¾ pint milk
3 tablespoons rum

In a saucepan, melt the butter over low heat, add the flour and mix well with a wooden spoon. Allow to cook for a minute before gradually adding the milk, stirring continually until a smooth sauce is achieved. (If any stubborn lumps form, a balloon whisk can work miracles.) Bring to the boil then reduce the heat. Add the sugar and cook for a further 5 minutes. Add the rum before serving.

RICH FRUIT CAKE

Suitable for Christmas, birthday or wedding cakes.

MAKES 1 x 23CM/9″ ROUND OR 20CM/8″ SQUARE CAKE.

225g/8 oz butter
225g/8 oz soft brown sugar
6 small eggs
250g/9 oz self-raising flour ⎫
150g/5 oz plain flour   ⎬ sieved together
Pinch of salt   ⎪
¼ teaspoon mixed spice ⎭
50g/2 oz ground almonds
900g/2 lb mixed dried fruit (sultanas, currants,
   seedless raisins)
50g/2 oz mixed peel
100g/4 oz glacé cherries (washed, dried and
   halved)
Juice of half a small lemon and grated rind of
   whole lemon
2 tablespoons black treacle (optional – darkens
   mixture and keeps cake moist)

Preheat oven to 275°F/140°C/Gas Mark 1

Grease and line a 23cm/9″ round or 20cm/8″ square cake tin. In a large mixing bowl, cream together the butter and sugar until light and fluffy. Add the eggs one at a time and include a little flour with the last egg to avoid curdling. Fold in the dry ingredients i.e. flours, spice and ground almonds. Stir in the treacle and lemon juice and finally add the fruit and grated lemon rind.

    Put the mixture into the prepared tin and smooth the top with the back of a wet spoon.

    Bake the cake on the lower shelf of the oven for about 3½ hours. Leave until cool before turning out onto a wire rack. Store in an airtight tin until needed. If you like, a little brandy can be added to the cake during storage. To do this, make a few holes with a large needle and pour over a little brandy. This can be done once a week.

A Chinese Meal

PRAWN TOAST WITH SESAME SEED TOPPING

Makes a delicious starter or appetizer to hand around with drinks.

SERVES 6 – 8

450g/1 lb raw prawns without heads
2 slices back bacon
1 egg white
1 tablespoon cornflour
½ teaspoon salt
8 – 10 slices white bread
2 tablespoons white sesame seeds
Oil for deep frying

Peel and de-vein prawns. Finely mince with knife or food processor. De-rind bacon, separate fat from lean. Finely dice bacon fat and add to minced prawns. Add egg white, cornflour and salt and mix thoroughly.

Neatly trim crusts from bread. Cut each slice into 7.5 cm/3″ rounds or triangles. Cut lean bacon into strips or decorative shapes. Spread equal portions of prawn mixture onto slices of bread. Smooth over the top and decorate with the bacon strips. Sprinkle with the sesame seeds (best done on a sheet of greasproof paper) and press lightly into the prawn mixture.

Heat oil in a wok, saucepan or deep fat fryer until hot (350°F/180°C) and deep-fry for 2 – 3 minutes, turning twice until golden brown.

Drain on kitchen paper and serve immediately.

FRIED VERMICELLI (SINGAPORE NOODLES)

SERVES 6 – 8

225g/½ lb dried vermicelli
100g/4 oz bean sprouts or chinese leaves, finely shredded
100g/4 oz prawns (fresh or frozen)
100g/4 oz cooked meat (chicken, pork or beef, finely sliced)
2 cloves garlic, finely chopped
4 small shallots OR 1 small onion, finely chopped
1 egg, beaten
2 spring onions, finely chopped
2 fresh chillies, finely sliced
2 teaspoons soy sauce
2 teaspoons curry powder made into a paste with A little hot water
Salt and pepper
Stock or water
Corn/sunflower/groundnut oil

Soak dried vermicelli in warm water for 30 minutes. Drain. Deep-fry the chopped shallots or onion until light brown and crispy. Drain and set aside.

In 1 tablespoon hot oil make a light omelette with the beaten egg. When cold, cut into fine strips.

If fresh prawns are being used, shell, de-vein and cut into two pieces. Frozen prawns should be defrosted thoroughly and well drained to get rid of any accumulated water.

Heat 3 tablespoons oil in a wok or large non-stick saucepan. Add garlic and stir-fry until golden. Add curry paste and cook for 2 minutes, then add meat, prawns and vermicelli together with ½ cup stock or water. Toss vermicelli and other ingredients with 2 spatulas over medium heat until the liquid is nearly all absorbed. Add bean sprouts and continue cooking for a further 2 minutes. Transfer to a warm serving dish and garnish with shredded omelette, chopped spring onions, sliced chillies and crispy fried onions.

WHOLE STEAMED FISH WITH GINGER

SERVES 6

1 whole fish 900-1125g/2 – 2 ½ lbs such as sea bass or grey mullet
2 large dried mushrooms
50g/2 oz finely shredded pork (uncooked), bacon or ham
2.5 cm/1″ knob of ginger, finely shredded
4 spring onions
3 tablespoons thin soy sauce
5 tablespoons corn oil or similar

Facing page: Fried Vermicelli (top) and Prawn Toast with Sesame Seed Topping (bottom).

Overleaf: Whole Steamed Fish with Ginger.

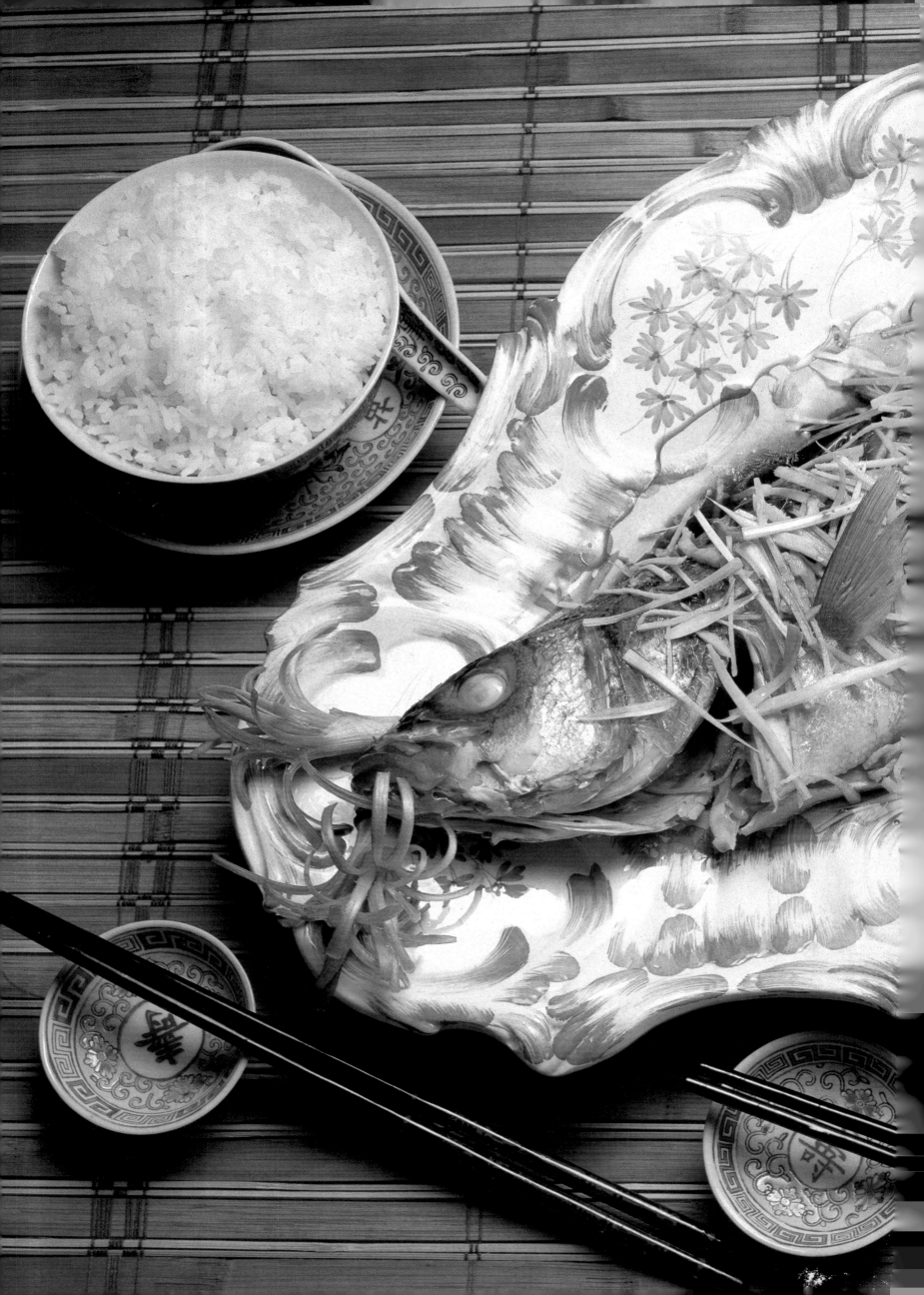

Pour boiling water over the mushrooms and leave to soak for 20 minutes, then squeeze out the mushrooms to remove soaking liquid. Cut off and discard stalks and slice mushrooms thinly.

Scale and clean the fish, but leave head and tail intact. Dry fish with kitchen paper and make 2 diagonal cuts on each side. Put on a large dish to steam. Sprinkle over the meat and mushrooms and steam over high heat in steamer or wok for 10 – 15 minutes until just cooked.

Remove from heat and, if necessary, transfer to a warmed serving plate. Sprinkle over ginger and spring onions.

Heat oil in a saucepan until very hot and pour over the fish, this will briefly cook the ginger and spring onions, releasing their flavours. Add soy sauce and serve immediately.

CHICKEN SATAY

This recipe comes in 2 parts and makes a delicious starter or an original dish to hand around with drinks.

ENOUGH FOR 3 – 4 DOZEN SKEWERS

PART 1: MARINATED CHICKEN ON SKEWERS

1.6kg/3 ½ lb chicken
2 tablespoons mild curry powder
2 cloves garlic
1½ tablespoons sugar
2 tablespoons oil
1 tablespoon soy sauce
3 tablespoons coconut milk (buy 1 large tin and use the rest for sauce)
1 tablespoon lemon juice
3 – 4 dozen bamboo skewers (available from Chinese shops or good hardware stores)

PART 2: SATAY SAUCE

350g/12 oz salted roasted peanuts
225g/8 oz onions
2 cloves garlic
8 dried red chillies or 2 teaspoons chilli powder
2 tablespoons mild curry powder
1 tablespoon lemon grass powder
    OR 2 stalks fresh lemon grass
    OR 1 tablespoon grated lemon rind
1 large tin coconut milk (less 3 tablespoons for the chicken)
3 tablespoons lemon juice
4 tablespoons sugar
3 tablespoons oil (sunflower, corn or groundnut)
¾ cup water
2 tablespoons peanut butter
2 tablespoons dark soy sauce

To prepare chicken: Empty the tinned coconut milk into a small pan and heat gently to mix to liquid with the solids. Do not boil. Leave to cool.

Skin and bone the chicken and cut into bite-sized pieces.

Finely chop garlic, mix with the rest of the ingredients and pour over chicken pieces. Cover with foil or cling film and leave to marinate in the refrigerator for 3 hours. Thread onto skewers, 3 – 4 pieces on each skewer.

To prepare sauce: Deseed and soak dried chillies in hot water for 20 minutes.

Finely chop (by hand or in a food processor) the onions, garlic, chillies and lemon grass (if used). Mix curry powder, lemon grass powder and chilli powder (if used) into a thick paste with hot water. Finely chop peanuts in food processor or coffee grinder.

Heat the oil in a saucepan, gently fry the onion mixture until soft but not coloured, add curry paste and continue frying for another 2 minutes.

Add peanuts, water and coconut milk, bring gently to the boil, add the rest of the ingredients and bring to the boil again, stirring all the time. Simmer until the oil separates from the satay sauce (about 5 minutes). Remove from heat.

Heat the grill to very hot and quickly grill the chicken on the skewers until golden. Serve with the satay sauce, chunks of onion and cucumber. Before eating, dip the skewers into the sauce.

STIR-FRIED BEEF WITH VEGETABLES

SERVES 6 – 8

175g/6 oz rump steak
1 red pepper
1 green pepper
4 large carrots
100g/4 oz mangetout
3 sticks celery
2 courgettes
2 slices ginger
1 clove garlic, crushed
3 tablespoons corn oil
2 tablespoons soy sauce
1 tablespoon sherry
2 tablespoons water
1 teaspoon sugar
1 teaspoon cornflour

1 wok, saucepan or frying pan

Slice beef thinly across the grain into 6 x 1 x .5 cm/ 2 ½ x ½ x ¼ ″ strips and marinate in 1 teaspoonful each of soy sauce, sherry, cornflour and corn oil.

Deseed and cut the peppers into 5 x 1 cm/2 x ½ ″ strips. Scrape and cut carrots into roughly same size pieces as the peppers. Cut courgettes to the same size. Wash and cut celery into diagonal pieces 1.25 cm/½ ″ thick. Wash and top and tail mangetout – leave whole. Peel and crush garlic in press or with knife blade.

Chicken Satay.

234

Heat 1 tablespoon oil in the pan, add ginger and garlic, stir-fry for ½ minute. Add beef and cook rapidly, stirring continuously in order to separate the pieces. Remove beef, garlic and ginger to one side. Reheat rest of oil in pan until hot. As the vegetables cook at different rates, add in the following order, leaving about 15 seconds between each addition – carrots, courgettes, celery, mangetout and peppers. Keep stirring so that all the vegetables are evenly coated with oil. Add the rest of the ingredients, soy sauce, sherry, sugar and water. Cover and leave to cook for 2 more minutes (no more!). Add the beef, heat through and serve immediately. If liked, thicken sauce with 1 tablespoon of water mixed to a smooth paste with 1 teaspoon cornflour.

Below: Casseroled Leg of Pork with Chestnuts and Mushrooms.

Facing page: Stir-Fried Beef with Vegetables.

CASSEROLED LEG OF PORK WITH CHESTNUTS AND MUSHROOMS

SERVES 6 – 8

½ leg of pork (about 1.6 – 1.8kg/3 ½ – 4 lbs) with bone in and skin on and, if leg comes with trotter, so much the better
½ teacup dry sherry (or rice wine)
½ teacup dark soy sauce
3 tablespoons golden syrup
4 whole star anise
2.5 cm/1″ piece of ginger in 4 slices
24 fresh (preferable) or dried chestnuts
24 medium-sized, dried black mushrooms

Pour boiling water over the mushrooms and leave to soak for 20 minutes. Then squeeze to extract soaking liquid. Cut off and discard stalks but leave mushroom caps whole. Reserve soaking liquid.

Slash the base of each chestnut, if fresh, and put into a hot oven and bake for 5 – 10 minutes. Peel and skin when cool. If using dried chestnuts, put into a pan of cold water and soak overnight.

Place leg of pork (and trotter) in a large saucepan and add water to cover. Bring water to boil, simmer for 5 minutes and drain. This will prevent scum from forming in the casserole later on, thus giving a clear gravy.

Return leg to saucepan and add 1.4 litres/2½ pints water, including the liquid used to soak mushrooms. Add the rest of the ingredients except for the mushrooms and chestnuts. Bring to the boil,

reduce heat to a simmer and cover. Continue simmering for 2 hours, taking care to turn meat over three or four times to ensure even cooking and to prevent sticking. Uncover and continue cooking for another 1½ hours, adding the mushrooms and chestnuts in the last hour.

Remove meat, chestnuts and mushrooms. Strain liquid into another saucepan, discard spices, and cook over a high heat, stirring often, until sauce is syrupy and reduced to about 300ml/½ pint. Cut meat into thin slices and arrange on a warmed plate with the mushrooms and chestnuts. Pour over gravy and serve with rice.

Mexican Specialities

TACO SHELL FILLING (REFRIED BEANS WITH CRUMBLY CHEESE AND CRISPY BACON)

Beans supply a valuable amount of the much needed protein in Latin American countries. In Britain many varieties are readily available in supermarkets and health food stores, either dried or canned and are relatively cheap to buy.

Refried beans, frijoles refritos, are beans that are first boiled until tender and then refried with the addition of such ingredients as onion, garlic and tomato.

TO FILL 12 TACO SHELLS

450g/16 oz black pinto or red kidney beans
2 medium onions, finely chopped
2 cloves garlic, crushed
1 chilli, finely chopped
1 bay leaf
2 tablespoons vegetable oil
1 large tomato, peeled and chopped
Salt
225g/8 oz crumbly cheese (Cheshire, Wensleydale or Feta would be ideal) cubed
6 rashers bacon, grilled until crisp
Few onion rings
Tomato sauce

Preheat oven to 350°F/180°C/Gas Mark 4

Put the beans into a large saucepan and cover with cold water to 2.5 cm/1″ above the level of the beans. Add half the onions, one clove of garlic, the chilli and the bay leaf. Cover the pan, bring to the boil and simmer for 1½ – 3 hours, until the beans are tender. (You may have to top up the liquid with hot water.) Add salt and simmer for another 30 minutes until soft and very little liquid is left. Turn off the heat. Remove the bay leaf.

In a large frying pan, heat the oil, add the remaining onion and garlic and cook until soft. Add the tomato and sauté for a further 3 – 4 minutes. Add the beans gradually, mashing them with a wooden spoon over a moderate heat until they form a heavy paste. Add a little more oil if necessary.

Heat the taco shells for 5 – 10 minutes and fill with the refried beans. Top with small cubes of cheese, pieces of crispy bacon, onion rings and tomato sauce. Serve at once.

TACO SHELL FILLING (LAMB WITH ALMONDS)

FILLS 12 TACO SHELLS

450g/1 lb minced lamb
1 large onion, finely chopped
1 large clove garlic, crushed
1 teaspoon cumin
1 teaspoon chilli powder
2 teaspoons paprika
50g/2 oz flaked almonds
2 tablespoons tomato purée
150ml/5 fl oz stock
Salt and black pepper

Preheat oven to 350°F/180°C/Gas Mark 4

In a pan, fry the onion in a little oil until soft, add the minced lamb, garlic and spices and fry quickly until the meat is lightly browned. Stir in the tomato purée and stock and season to taste. Cook gently for a further 15 – 20 minutes, stirring occasionally. Whilst the lamb is cooking, place taco shells in the oven for 5 – 10 minutes. Remove and fill with the cooked mixture. Top with grated cheese, some tomato sauce or chilli sauce.

TACO SHELL FILLING (CREAM CHEESE AND CHICKEN)

FILLS ABOUT 6 TACO SHELLS

100g/4 oz cream cheese
225g/8 oz cooked chicken, chopped
4 tablespoons double cream
Salt and black pepper

GARNISH
Shredded lettuce and tomato or chilli sauce

Preheat oven to 350°F/180°C/Gas Mark 4

Courgettes with Sweetcorn and Peppers (top), Broad Bean Salad (centre right) and filled Taco Shells (bottom).

Blend together the cheese, chopped chicken and cream. Season to taste. Warm through the taco shells for 5 – 10 minutes and fill with the cheese mixture. Garnish with the shredded lettuce and a sauce of your choice.

CEVICHE (SEVICHE)

With the emphasis on healthy eating today, ceviche, which is literally raw fish marinated in lime or sometimes lemon juice, certainly fits the bill.

A variety of fish "cooked" in this fashion constitutes a tasty and simple hors d'oeuvres.

Try some of the following fish served on a bed of lettuce leaves (radicchio leaves are pretty).

CEVICHE OF HADDOCK

SERVES 4

350g/¾ lb haddock (other whitefish can be used)
150ml/¼ pint lime or lemon juice
Salt and pepper
1 teaspoon paprika
½ a small onion, finely chopped

Cut the fish into 2.5 cm/1″ pieces and put in a large bowl together with the lime juice, onion and seasonings. Cover and refrigerate for at least 3 hours until the fish becomes opaque. Serve on a bed of lettuce leaves.

CEVICHE OF OYSTERS

SERVES 4

2 dozen oysters
150ml/¼ pint lime or lemon juice
1 large tomato, peeled, deseeded and chopped
1 small onion, finely chopped
1 tablespoon fresh mint
Salt and pepper

Marinate the oysters in the lime juice for 5 – 6 hours. Add the other ingredients. Strain off most of the liquid but leave enough to keep the oysters moist. Serve on a bed of lettuce leaves.

CEVICHE OF PRAWNS

SERVES 4

350g/¾ lb peeled prawns
150ml/¼ pint lime juice
Juice of 1 large orange
½ small onion, finely chopped
1 large tomato, peeled, deseeded and chopped
1 fresh hot red or green pepper, deseeded and finely chopped
1 tablespoon vegetable oil
½ teaspoon Worcestershire sauce
A few drops of tabasco

Pour the fruit juices over the prawns in a large bowl. Cover and leave for three hours or overnight, turning the fish occasionally. Add the rest of the ingredients, mix well and serve on a bed of lettuce leaves.

CEVICHE OF MACKEREL

SERVES 4

350g/¾ lb mackerel fillets
150ml/¼ pint lime or lemon juice
1 small hot green pepper, deseeded and finely chopped
1 tomato, peeled, deseeded and chopped
3 – 4 spring onions, chopped
Salt and pepper
½ teaspoon oregano

Cut the mackerel into small bite-sized pieces and put into a bowl together with the lime juice. Cover and leave it for about 3 hours, turning the fish occasionally. Add the other ingredients and serve on a bed of lettuce leaves.

GUACAMOLE (MEXICAN AVOCADO DIP)

Ideal as a first course or as a tasty dip to serve with drinks. Hot toast, taco chips or pieces of raw vegetable are good accompaniments.

SERVES 6

2 medium-sized ripe avocados
2 ripe tomatoes
½ small onion
1 fresh green chilli
1 clove garlic
1 tablespoon fresh coriander
    or 2 tablespoons parsley
Juice of ½ lemon or lime
Salt and pepper to taste

Skin and deseed the tomatoes and chop finely together with the onion, chilli and coriander. Crush the garlic. Mix together all the ingredients except for the avocados. Cover with cling film until needed.

No more than 30 minutes before serving, halve the avocados, remove the stones and spoon out the flesh. Mash with a fork and add to the other ingredients. Mix well. For a smoother Guacamole put the ingredients into a food processor. Re-cover with cling film until required. I believe that if the stone is put back into the centre of the dip it slows down the discolouring process.

COURGETTES WITH SWEETCORN AND PEPPERS

A good dish to make in late summer or early autumn when all ingredients are plentiful and cheap.

SERVES 4

2 corn on the cob (or 100g/4 oz frozen corn kernels)
1 small onion, finely chopped
50g/2 oz butter
450g/1 lb courgettes
1 green pepper
1 tablespoon tomato purée
150ml/¼ pint chicken stock
Salt and pepper

Cut the corn cobs into 2.5cm/1″ rounds, slice the courgettes and deseed and slice the pepper.

In a large pan, melt the butter and fry the onion and green pepper for a few minutes until soft. Add the sweetcorn, courgettes, tomato purée and chicken stock and season according to taste. Simmer the ingredients for about 10 minutes or until the corn is tender. Serve hot.

BROAD BEAN SALAD

SERVES 4

450g/1 lb young broad beans
25g/1 oz butter
1 dessertspoon fresh herbs, e.g. parsley and
   tarragon
Salt and pepper
1 tablespoon lemon juice

Shell the broad beans and cook in a very little salted water for about 5 – 8 minutes until tender. Drain and cool. Melt the butter in a saucepan, add the beans and herbs, season to taste and cook for about a minute. Remove the pan from the heat and pour in the lemon juice. Stir and serve warm.

Ceviche (left) and Guacamole (right).

A Wedding Cake

WEDDING CAKE

Commercially-made cakes are quite expensive and, providing you can smooth-ice well (or ask a friend), there is no reason at all why, with the addition of pretty silk flowers and ribbons, a home-made cake should not be more than acceptable.

The Rich Fruit Cake recipe would provide between 30-40 portions, so you might well need a 2 or 3 tier cake.

For a 2 tier cake use 1 x 18cm/7″ and 1 x 25.5 cm/10″ square tin
For a 3 tier cake use 1 x 13cm/5″, 1 x 18cm/7″ and 1 x 25.5 cm/10″ square tin

Cooking times for each size tin:
13cm/5″   –   3 hours approximately
18cm/7″   –   3½ – 4 hours approximately
25.5 cm/10″   –   5 – 5¼ hours approximately

Almond Paste and Royal Icing for Single Tier Cake (see recipes)

Almond Paste for Two Tier Cake:

1kg/2 lb 4 oz ground almonds
500g/1 lb 2 oz icing sugar
500g/1 lb 2 oz caster sugar
3-4 large eggs
2 teaspoons lemon juice
1 teaspoon almond essence

Almond Paste for Three Tier Cake:

1.175kg/2lb 9 oz ground almonds
600g/1 lb 5 oz icing sugar
600g/1 lb 5 oz caster sugar
4 large eggs
3 teaspoons lemon juice
1 teaspoon almond essence

Royal Icing for Two Tier Cake

1.575kg/3 lb 8 oz icing sugar
7 egg whites (approximately)
4 drops lemon juice
2 small teaspoons glycerine

Royal Icing for Three Tier Cake:

2kg 25g/4 lb 8 oz icing sugar
9 egg whites (approximately)
5 drops lemon juice
2 small teaspoons glycerine

ROYAL ICING

Sufficient for icing a 23cm/9″ round or 20cm/8″ square cake.

675g/1½ lbs icing sugar (sieved)
3 egg whites
2 drops lemon juice
1 small teaspoon glycerine

Place egg whites in a bowl and beat lightly until frothy. Add icing sugar gradually, beating between each addition, until mixture is smooth, shiny and white. It should be easily spreadable, but thick enough to hold its shape.

Beat in glycerine and lemon juice.

For a Christmas cake with peaked icing, make icing slightly stiffer (more icing sugar). Cover cake thickly then lift icing into peaks with palette knife.

ALMOND PASTE

This is sufficient to cover the top and sides of a 23cm/9″ round or 20cm/8″ square cake.

450g/1 lb ground almonds
225g/8 oz icing sugar (sieved)
225g/8 oz caster sugar
4 drops almond essence
2 teaspoons lemon juice
1 large egg, beaten
Apricot jam

Mix dry ingredients. Add almond essence, lemon juice and enough beaten egg to mix into a fairly dry paste. Knead until smooth to form a round ball. Roll out to shape on a board dusted with sieved icing sugar, using ⅓ for the top and ⅔ for the sides.

Melt a little apricot jam with 2 tablespoons water and pass it through a sieve. Brush the top and sides of the cake with the jam before covering with almond paste. Leave to dry for 1 – 2 days before icing.

Wedding Cake (see Rich Fruit Cake recipe on page 229).

BAILIE WALLACE

A Pink Party

PRAWN COCKTAILS WITH CREAM DILL SAUCE

Prawn cocktails are still a firm favourite with people when they eat out. The dill sauce in this recipe makes it just a little different.

SERVES 6

350g/12 oz shelled prawns
Lemon juice
Tabasco
Ground black pepper
1 lettuce

SAUCE

150ml/¼ pint mayonnaise
150ml/¼ pint thick cream
50g/2 tablespoons chopped dill
Salt and pepper
Paprika to dust

Marinate the prawns in lemon juice and a few drops of tabasco. Season with black pepper.

Wash and shred the lettuce and place about a tablespoon in the bottom of each glass or dish. Pile on the prawns. Blend together the mayonnaise, cream, dill and seasoning and spoon over the prawns. Dust with paprika.

BORTSCH

Hot or cold, this soup is a winner.

SERVES 4 – 6

4 uncooked beetroots
900ml/1½ pints beef stock
225g/½ lb carrots, thickly sliced
100g/¼ lb turnips, thickly sliced
100g/¼ lb onions, roughly chopped
1 stick celery, chopped
1 small bunch parsley
1 sprig fresh dill
Juice of half a lemon
Salt and black pepper
4 – 6 tablespoons soured cream

GARNISH

Chopped fresh herbs

In a large saucepan, put 3 of the beetroots, roughly chopped, plus the other vegetables, the herbs and beef stock. Bring to the boil and then reduce heat and simmer for an hour. Strain the soup into another saucepan, pressing the vegetables well to extract all their juices. Peel the fourth beetroot, grate finely, add to the liquid and simmer for an additional 10 – 15 minutes. Allow to cool and then add the lemon juice, salt and pepper and, at the very last moment, swirl in the soured cream. Scatter with finely chopped fresh herbs.

SALMON MOUSSE

A colourful addition to a buffet table or a substantial first course served with hot toast.

SERVES 6 – 8

2 x 213g/7½ oz cans red salmon
25g/1 oz butter
3 level tablespoons plain flour
300ml/½ pint milk
2 eggs
150ml/¼ pint double cream
2 tablespoons tomato ketchup
1 teaspoon anchovy essence
1 teaspoon lemon juice
Salt and pepper
10g/½ oz gelatine
4 tablespoons hot water

Drain the cans of salmon, remove any skin and bones. Flake the fish into a small bowl. (You could use a food processor or blender for a smoother texture, but I personally prefer the fish flaked.)
In a saucepan, melt the butter, add the flour, stir well and cook for a minute. Gradually add the milk, stirring continuously. (If any lumps appear, a balloon whisk works like magic.) Bring to the boil and allow to cook for a further minute.

Separate the egg yolks from the whites and add the yolks to the sauce. Allow the mixture to cool slightly. Whip the cream to a floppy consistency and fold into the sauce, together with the ketchup, anchovy essence and lemon juice. Season to taste with salt and pepper. Add the flaked salmon. Dissolve the gelatine in the hot water. If not completely smooth, stand the bowl in a saucepan of hot water until the gelatine mixture becomes clear. Do not let it boil. Stir into the salmon mixture. Whisk the egg whites until stiff and gently fold into the mixture with a metal spoon.

Pour into a dampened 600ml/1 pint mould or individual ramekins. Refrigerate until firm. This mousse also freezes well, but allow 3 – 4 hours

to thaw at room temperature or overnight in the refrigerator before serving. Turn out onto a bed of lettuce and garnish with slices of cucumber and lemon.

Above: Baked Glazed Gammon.

Overleaf: a birthday spread, including Pink Fondant Cakes, Bortsch, Pink Meringues, Salmon Mousse, Prawn Cocktails with Cream Dill Sauce, Strawberries Romanov, Mary's Ambrosia, Pink Party Radicchio and Endive Salad, and Baked Glazed Gammon.

BAKED GLAZED GAMMON

In this recipe the gammon is cooked mainly in liquid but for the last 45 minutes goes into the oven, studded with cloves and brushed with honey, mustard and brown sugar to give a tempting golden finish.

SERVES 8 – 12

1.4-1.8kg/3-4 lb middle cut gammon
Few peppercorns
1 bay leaf
3 tablespoons wine vinegar
2 dozen cloves
1 tablespoon freshly made English mustard
1 tablespoon honey
2 tablespoons demerara sugar

Soak the gammon for several hours in cold water or, if very salty, overnight. Place it in a large pan and cover with fresh cold water with a few peppercorns, a bay leaf and 3 tablespoons wine vinegar added. Bring to the boil and reduce the heat immediately. Cover and simmer (the water should be only just moving otherwise the meat tends to shrink), allowing 30 minutes per 450g/1 lb. This applies to joints up to 4.5kg/10 lbs in weight. For joints of over 4.5kg/10 lbs, allow 25 minutes per lb. Forty-five minutes before the end of the cooking time remove the gammon to a large roasting tin. Allow it to cool slightly. While it is cooling, preheat oven to 400°F/200°C/Gas Mark 6. Strip the skin off the gammon, leaving a thin layer of fat over the meat. With a sharp knife, score the fat into diamond shapes.

Mix together the mustard and honey and brush this over the outside of the gammon. With your fingers press on the demerara sugar and stud a clove at the corners of each diamond.

Put the meat into the preheated oven and bake

for 45 minutes, basting occasionally until the sugar has melted and the surface is golden brown.

Remove to a hot serving dish, garnish with watercress and serve with a variety of vegetables.

Alternatively, leave to get cold and serve with salads and new potatoes.

PINK PARTY RADICCHIO AND ENDIVE SALAD

Combine the bitter, frilly leaves of endive (also known as chicory in America) with the rich, dark red leaves of radicchio to make a pretty salad.

Add plenty of fresh herbs and a classic French vinaigrette.

MARY'S AMBROSIA

This lovely combination of ingredients is a child's

The Rich Fruit Cake recipe on page 229 may be used for a variety of 'occasion' cakes, such as the birthday cake above.

dream (and most adults find it hard to resist). Using Greek yoghurt instead of double cream is one way of making it less wicked! Vary the ingredients according to what you have in the cupboard.

SERVES 10

600ml/1 pint double cream or thick Greek yoghurt (or half and half)
1 x 375g/13 ¼ oz can crushed pineapple
3 bananas
1 tablespoon lemon juice
25g/1 oz mixed peel
25g/1 oz glacé cherries
25g/1 oz sultanas
16 marshmallows

Drain the crushed pineapple, reserving the juice for another recipe. Put the sultanas in a cup and pour over boiling water. Leave until they plump up and then drain off the water. Peel and slice the bananas into a small bowl and sprinkle on the lemon juice. Quarter the cherries and the marshmallows.

In a large bowl, whip the double cream until stiff, fold in the drained pineapple and all the other ingredients. Transfer to a large, glass dish or individual glasses. Top with any spare marshmallows. Chill for at least an hour before serving.

PINK FONDANT CAKES

Mouthwatering little cakes for a special occasion.

MAKES 24 CAKES

GENOISE SPONGE

100g/4 oz plain flour, sifted
3 eggs
2 egg yolks
100g/4 oz caster sugar
1 teaspoon vanilla essence
50g/2 oz unsalted butter

FONDANT ICING

150ml/¼ pint water
450g/1 lb caster sugar
Pinch of cream of tartar OR 25g/1 oz glucose

Preheat oven to 350°F/180°C/Gas Mark 4

Genoise Sponge Grease the base and sides of a 20cm/8″ sandwich tin with melted butter. Line the base with a circle of buttered greaseproof paper and lightly flour the sides and base of the tin, removing any excess flour. Melt the butter until it is runny and put to one side to cool. Break the eggs into a large bowl, add the sugar and vanilla essence and stand the bowl in a pan of boiling water. Reduce heat. Whisk the ingredients together over a simmering heat until the mixture is light and creamy and twice its original bulk.

Remove the bowl from the heat and whisk for a further 5 minutes until the mixture is cool. The whisk should leave a trail when drawn across the surface of the mixture. Quickly but lightly fold in the sifted flour followed by the melted butter, and pour at once into the prepared sandwich tin.

Cook in the preheated oven for about 30 minutes. The cake is ready when it shrinks away slightly from the sides of the tin and springs back into shape when pressed. Allow to stand in the tin for a couple of minutes, then remove and turn onto a wire rack to cool. Peel off the greaseproof paper. Cut into rectangles ready for icing.

Fondant Icing Pour the water into a heavy-based saucepan, add the sugar and dissolve it to a syrup over low heat. Dip a pastry brush in cold water and wipe round the sides of the pan to remove any undissolved sugar crystals. Put a lid on the pan and bring to the boil. Uncover and add the cream of tartar or glucose dissolved in a little water and continue to

boil steadily to the "soft ball" stage or 240°F/116°C on a sugar thermometer.

Remove the pan from the heat and, after the bubbles have subsided, pour the syrup into a heat-resistant bowl. When a skin forms on the top, use a wooden spatula to work the icing in a figure-of-eight movement until it becomes opaque and firm i.e. becomes fondant. Knead until smooth and store in an airtight tin until needed.

To use, warm gently with a little sugar syrup, add colouring or flavouring as required before covering the genoise sponge fingers. Decorate the cakes with crystallized violets or silver balls.

STRAWBERRIES ROMANOV

A good way to serve strawberries for a change.

Strawberries
Orange juice
Orange liqueur such as Grand Marnier or Curaçao

Quarter the strawberries and put into a bowl. Pour over orange juice and sprinkle on the orange liqueur. Cover with cling film and marinate for several hours.

PINK MERINGUES

Be careful not to use too much pink food colouring – the result could be less than subtle!

MAKES APPROXIMATELY 12 SMALL MERINGUES

3 egg whites
175g/6 oz caster sugar
One or two drops pink food colouring
Extra caster sugar for dusting

To fill: 300ml/½ pint double cream

Ideally the egg whites should be at room temperature when used – they will whisk up to a greater volume than if they are taken straight from the refrigerator. Put the egg whites in a bowl and whisk them until stiff and dry. Make sure that there are no lumps in the sugar and add half the sugar only at first, together with food colouring. Whisk in until the whites stand in peaks. Lightly but evenly fold in the remaining sugar with a metal spoon. Do not over mix.

Spoon or pipe the meringues onto baking trays lined with non-stick paper. Sprinkle the meringues with a little extra caster sugar and dry them out in a very cool oven – 225°F/110°C/Gas Mark ¼ – for 2–3 hours. Rotate the trays so the meringues dry evenly. Remove from the oven and cool on wire racks. Unfilled, they will keep perfectly in an airtight tin for several weeks. They also freeze well.

Sandwich together with stiffly-whipped double cream which could also be tinted pink.

A Children's Party

TOFFEE CHOCOLATE DIAMONDS

This rich biscuit is a favourite with children and adults alike.

BASE
100g/4 oz margarine
50g/2 oz sugar
175g/6 oz plain flour

TOFFEE CENTRE
100g/4 oz margarine
100g/4 oz sugar
1 tablespoon syrup
½ tin condensed milk

CHOCOLATE TOPPING
100g/4 oz dark chocolate (cooking chocolate could be substituted)

Preheat oven to 325°F/160°C/Gas Mark 3

Base Cream together the margarine and sugar and add the flour. Press into an 18cm/7″ square tin with your finger tips. Bake for 30 minutes until pale and crisp.

Toffee Centre Melt all the ingredients in a small, heavy-based saucepan over a low heat. When the sugar is dissolved, bring to the boil and boil for 5 – 7 minutes, stirring from time to time to prevent the bottom of the pan from burning. Allow to cool slightly and pour over base.

Chocolate Topping Melt 100g/4 oz of chocolate in a small bowl placed in a pan of simmering water and pour over the base and toffee centre.

Allow to cool and remove from the tin. With a sharp knife, cut the biscuits into diamond shapes.

GINGERBREAD MEN

MAKES ABOUT 18

225g/8 oz plain flour
Pinch salt
2 teaspoons ground ginger
150g/5 oz butter, in small pieces
1 egg, separated
25g/1 oz caster sugar
2 tablespoons treacle
Few currants

Additional 25g/1 oz caster sugar for glazing

To decorate: white glacé icing

Preheat oven to 350°F/180°C/Gas Mark 4

Sieve the dry ingredients, flour, salt and ginger, into a large mixing bowl. Add the butter and rub into the flour with your fingertips until the mixture resembles fine breadcrumbs – this can be done in a food processor. Add the egg yolk, sugar and treacle, mix well and then knead lightly and turn out onto a floured board. Roll out to about 5mm/¼″ thick and then cut out the gingerbread men (special cutters are easily available, or else let children cut out their own shapes). Transfer them to greased baking sheets, brush with the egg white and sprinkle with the additional sugar. Press on the currants to form eyes and buttons.

Bake in a preheated oven for 12-15 minutes, until golden brown. Allow to cool slightly before lifting off the baking sheets and placing them on wire racks. If liked, decorate with white glacé icing.

CHOCOLATE TRAIN BIRTHDAY CAKE

This is an effective birthday cake that is fairly quick and easy to assemble.

2 chocolate sponge cakes made in 2 Swiss roll tins (see recipe for Victoria Sandwich Cake and add 1 tablespoon cocoa powder to the dry ingredients)
450g/1 lb cooking chocolate
6 small chocolate-covered Swiss rolls
1 large chocolate-covered Swiss roll
1 chocolate marshmallow biscuit

Enough to satisfy any child's appetite! Shown facing page is a tempting party spread featuring: Chocolate Train Birthday Cake, Party Loaf, Fresh Fruit Party Kebabs, Toffee Chocolate Diamonds, Raisin Cornflake Crispies, Mini Pizzas, Savoury Party Kebabs, Gingerbread Men, Fancy Sandwiches, Peanut Butter Cookies, Sausages on Sticks, Decorated and Named Biscuits, and Small Party Cakes.

BUTTER ICING

50g/2 oz softened butter
100g/4 oz icing sugar, sieved
50g/2 oz plain chocolate, melted or 2 tablespoons
    cocoa powder

Smarties
Chocolate buttons
Cocktail sticks

Using one of the chocolate sponges, cut out a base for the train, slightly longer and wider than the large Swiss roll, and cover with melted chocolate. Put 3 small Swiss rolls on a long, rectangular cake board (or use 2 x 30cm/12″ boards) and place the sponge base on top of them. Place the large Swiss roll on the base as the engine and cut a small square from the sponge cake for the cab. Cover the cab with chocolate and press into the engine with a little butter icing. Stick on a couple of chocolate buttons as illustrated and 2 on the front of the train. Fix half a small Swiss roll onto the engine and the chocolate marshmallow just behind.

From the other sponge cake, make the truck by cutting a base and 4 sides. Secure with cocktail sticks and butter icing and cover with melted chocolate. (Take care to remove the cocktail sticks before serving.) Place the truck on top of 2 more small Swiss rolls behind the train. Fill with Smarties.

Complete the birthday cake by piping the butter icing around the edges.

PARTY LOAF AND FANCY SANDWICHES

Take 1 large white or wholemeal loaf and cut off the crusts. Slice it lengthways into about 6 slices. Butter the slices and use a variety of fillings to sandwich the slices together. Cream cheese with a variety of flavourings is a good idea, but tuna fish or salmon creamed with a little mayonnaise also works well. Hard-boiled egg, banana, peanut butter etc. are other favourites. Garnish the loaf with mustard and cress, sliced tomatoes, chopped lettuce etc.

Use shaped pastry cutters to make small sandwiches. Vary the bread, or sandwich a slice of white with one of brown.

SMALL PARTY CAKES

MAKES 18 CAKES

100g/4 oz margarine
175g/6 oz caster sugar
2 eggs
225g/8 oz self-raising flour
150ml/¼ pint milk

Preheat oven to 400°F/200°C/Gas Mark 6

In a bowl, cream margarine and sugar until light and fluffy. Add one egg and a teaspoon of flour and then the other egg. Fold in the rest of the flour and the milk. Transfer the mixture into 18 paper cake cases and bake in a preheated oven for 12–15 minutes.

Decoration Either decorate with butter icing and smarties or with glacé icing and the new icing pens. The icing can be coloured or flavoured e.g. with cocoa or lemon juice.

Glacé Icing

175g/6 oz icing sugar
5 teaspoons warm water – (boiling water makes the
    finished icing dull)
Mix together until smooth and coats the back of a spoon.

Butter Icing

100g/4 oz soft margarine or butter or a mixture of both
225g/8 oz sieved icing sugar
Few drops vanilla essence

Beat together until creamy.

FRESH FRUIT PARTY KEBABS

Add a touch of sophistication to a children's party with fresh fruit kebabs.

Simply thread whole strawberries, pineapple pieces, grapes, cherries, bananas etc. onto long wooden skewers and use whole grapefruits as firm bases for displaying the kebabs.

RAISIN CORNFLAKE CRISPIES

An old-time favourite for children.

MAKES 20

280g/10 oz bar chocolate (milk or plain)
2 tablespoons syrup
50g/2 oz butter
25g/1 oz demerara sugar
100g/4 oz cornflakes
50g/2 oz raisins

Small paper cases

In a bowl over hot water, melt the chocolate. In a small saucepan, melt the butter, syrup and demerara sugar, stirring continuously. Combine the chocolate and syrup mixture and transfer it to a large bowl. Add the cornflakes and raisins and mix well until the cornflakes are completely covered. Spoon the mixture into the paper cases and leave to cool and set. Crispies keep well in an airtight tin.

PEANUT BUTTER COOKIES

MAKES 45 – 50

100g/4 oz butter
100g/4 oz caster sugar
100g/4 oz crunchy peanut butter
1 egg, beaten
175g/6 oz plain flour
½ teaspoon baking powder } sieved together
Peanut halves for decoration
Milk for glazing

Preheat oven to 375°F/190°C/Gas Mark 5

Cream together the butter, sugar and peanut butter in a mixing bowl. Add the beaten egg and mix well. Add the sieved flour and baking powder and fold into the peanut butter mixture. Incorporate well until it forms a firm smooth dough. Dust a board with flour and roll out the dough until 5mm/¼" thick. With a 3.75cm/1½" pastry cutter, cut out small rounds and place them on a greased baking tray. Press a peanut into each one. Brush with milk, place the tray in a preheated oven and bake for 15 – 20 minutes. Cool the peanut cookies on a wire tray.

SAUSAGES ON STICKS

Always a favourite, but vary them a little by tying strips of puff pastry in a knot around each sausage and baking in a hot oven until both sausages and pastry are golden brown.

SAVOURY PARTY KEBABS

Thread pieces of sausage, cubes of cheese, celery, cocktail onions, gherkins etc. onto cocktail sticks.

PIZZA AND MINI PIZZAS

A firm favourite with all ages. Mini pizzas make a tasty addition to a children's party.

FOR 2 LARGE OR 12 SMALL PIZZAS

BASE

1 x 283g/10 oz packet of white or wholemeal
    bread mix
1 tablespoon olive oil or good cooking oil

TOPPING

2 x 400g/14 oz tins tomatoes
2 teaspoons dried oregano or basil
Black pepper
4 cloves garlic, crushed
450g/1 lb mozzarella, Cheddar or Gruyère cheese
2 x 50g/2 oz tins anchovy fillets
12 black olives, pitted

ALTERNATIVE TOPPINGS
Pepperoni, salami, prosciutto, sliced mushrooms
    or green peppers etc.

Preheat oven to 425°F/220°C/Gas Mark 7

Make up the base according to the packet instructions. Knead it for 5 minutes by hand or for a couple of minutes if you have a dough hook attachment on your mixer. Roll the dough out into 2 x 25cm/10" rounds or 12 x 12.5cm/5" rounds.

Transfer them to greased baking sheets or pizza plates, turn in 1cm/½" of each dough base to make a rim and brush each one with the olive oil. Cover the baking sheets with a damp tea towel or an oiled polythene bag and allow to rise in a warm place for about half an hour.

Drain the tomatoes, chop them finely and spread them over the top of each base. Sprinkle over the oregano, black pepper and crushed garlic. Thinly slice the cheese and place it on the tomatoes, followed by the drained anchovies arranged in a lattice pattern. Decorate with the olives. If liked, drizzle a little more oil over the pizzas before placing in a preheated oven.

For the large pizzas, bake for 20 – 25 minutes and for the mini pizzas 15 – 20 minutes, until golden and bubbling.

DECORATED AND NAMED BISCUITS

Great fun for a children's party, when each guest has a personalised biscuit.

100g/4 oz plain flour
60g/2½ oz hard margarine
50g/2 oz caster sugar
1 teaspoon lemon rind, finely grated
1 egg yolk
1 egg white

Preheat oven to 350°F/180°C/Gas Mark 4

Sieve the flour into a bowl. Rub in the margarine lightly with your fingers. Stir in the sugar and lemon rind. Add the egg yolk and mix to a dough. Wrap in foil and chill for 30 oven mintes. Roll out to about 3mm/⅛" thick and cut into various shapes.

Decorated Biscuits Press glacé cherries and angelica into the shapes. Bake for 15 minutes then brush with lightly-beaten egg white and sprinkle with caster sugar. Bake for a further five minutes until crisp and golden.

Named Biscuits Roll and cut as above, but bake for a full 20 minutes. When cool, pipe names on the biscuits with butter icing made with:

50g/2 oz margarine
100g/4 oz icing sugar
1 dessertspoonful milk

Beat together until creamy.

Almond and Apricot Meringue Cake 156
Almond Orange Gateau 136
Almond Paste 242
Almond Petits Fours 192
American Club Sandwiches 204
Apple Dumplings 177
Apple Pancake Layer with Apricot Sauce 122
Apricot and Soured Cream Flan 164
Apricot Cream with Brandied Grapes 156
Asparagus on Toast 23
Baked Avocados with Chicken 17
Baked Glazed Gammon 245
Baked Pears in Cider 162
Baked Salmon Trout 32
Baked Stuffed Peaches 152
Baked Trout 32
Bakewell Tart 177
Bananas with Rum and Orange 213
Barbecued Trout with Pine-Nut Stuffing 206
Barm Brack 180
Beef Fondue 50
Beef Stroganoff 64
Beetroot, Onion and Soured Cream Salad 110
Blackcurrant Ice Cream 141
Blender Gazpacho 10
Blue Stilton Chicken 77
Bortsch 244
Brandy Butter 229
Brandy Snaps 194
Bread Sauce 224
Broad Bean Salad 241
Brochettes of Monkfish with Courgettes and Lemon 206
Brochettes of Scallops with Prawns and Lime 206
Brussels Sprouts with Chestnuts 108
Camembert Fritters 220
Caramelized Oranges 160
Carbonnade of Beef 43
Carrot and Orange Soup 30
Carrot Salad with Raisins and Nuts 104
Casseroled Leg of Pork with Chestnuts and Mushrooms 236
Cassoulet 60
Cauliflower Cheese 100
Cauliflower with Mustard Seed 72
Celeriac Remoulade with Prosciutto 8
Celery Filled with Smoked Salmon Pâté 216
Celery, Swede and Carrot Bake 101
Ceviche 240
Ceviche of Haddock 240
Ceviche of Mackerel 240
Ceviche of Oysters 240
Ceviche of Prawns 240
Cheese Aigrettes 222
Cheese and Chutney Dip 218
Chef's Salad 104
Cherry Bites 189
Cherry Ice Cream 141
Cherry Tomatoes Filled with Cream Cheese and Chives 216
Chicken and Avocado Pear Salad with Grapes and Tarragon 68
Chicken and Avocado with Green Peppercorns served with Tagliatelle 112
Chicken and Fresh Pineapple Kebabs 210
Chicken and Spring Vegetable Salad 104

Chicken Breasts with Cream and Fresh Tarragon 77
Chicken Ham and Leek Pie 73
Chicken Kiev 79
Chicken Kromeskies 79
Chicken Liver Pâté 202
Chicken Provençale 77
Chicken Salad with Mangetout and Pine Nuts 106
Chicken Satay 234
Chilled Chocolate Layer Pudding 136
Chilled Lettuce Soup 20
Chilli Con Carne 46
Chilli Hot Pot 52
Chinese Salad 88
Chocolate Cream Pie 148
Chocolate Crunch Biscuits 186
Chocolate Fruit and Nut Cookies 195
Chocolate Fudge 189
Chocolate Fudge Cake 184
Chocolate Mousse 154
Chocolate Pears 161
Chocolate Profiteroles 148
Chocolate Pudding 174
Chocolate Roulade 132
Chocolate Sponge Pudding 177
Chocolate Train Birthday Cake 250
Chop Toad in the Hole 56
Choux Buns with Fresh Salmon and Dill 216
Christmas Pudding 224
Churros 170
Cinnamon Squares 180
Coconut 72
Coeur à la Crème 142
Coffee Meringue Cake 136
Coffee Ring Cake 192
Coleslaw 108
Continental Gateau 162
Coq au Vin 82
Coquilles Saint-Jacques 20
Coriander Chicken 68
Corn on the Cob 206
Corned Beef Hash 198
Cornish Pasties 204
Coronation Chicken 67
Country Pâté 202
Courgettes au Gratin 88
Courgettes with Sweetcorn and Peppers 241
Cream of Carrot Soup 14
Cream of Chayote Soup 10
Cream of Senegalese Soup 20
Crème Brulée 144
Crème Pâtissière 124
Crêpes Suzette 119
Crêpes with Black Cherries and Flaked Almonds 121
Crêpes with Nectarines and Orange Liqueur 123
Crêpes with Pineapple and Kirsch 122
Crispy Chicken Bake 68
Croque Monsieur 220
Crudités 218
Crumpets 181
Crunchy Chocolate Meringue Cake 158
Cucumber Cups with Prawns 24
Cucumber Mousse 23
Cucumber Salad with Yoghurt and Mint 94
Curd Cheesecake 193
Curd Tartlets 179
Curried Parsnip Soup 14
Curried Pork Brochettes with Courgettes and Lemon 213

Curried Smoked Fish Ramekins 18
Custard Cream Biscuits 190
Dainty Chocolate Éclairs 181
Decorated and Named Biscuits 253
Deep-Fried Apple Puffs 170
Deep-Fried Mushrooms 86
Deep-Fried Onion Rings 88
Dhal 72
Duck Breasts in Black Cherry Sauce 80
Easy Raspberry Mousse 148
Escalopes of Veal in a Tomato and Tarragon Sauce 38
Family Hamburgers 208
Five Bean Salad 102
Flapjacks 192
Florentines 179
Frangipane Tarts 193
French Apple Flan 172
French Bean and Mushroom Salad 104
French Onion Soup 13
French Tuiles Biscuits 193
Fresh Asparagus 23
Fresh Asparagus Quiche 98
Fresh Fruit Flan Fillings 124
Fresh Fruit Party Kebabs 252
Fresh Fruit Salad 144
Fresh Peach and Hazelnut Meringue 152
Fried Courgettes 86
Fried Vermicelli 230
Fruit Fritters 171
Fruit Kebabs 214
Game Chips 67
Giblet Gravy 223
Gigot d' Agneau 60
Ginger and Advocaat Cream 130
Gingerbread 180
Gingerbread Men 250
Ginger Ice Cream 130
Gooseberry Fool 156
Gooseberry Sauce 206
Gratin of Turnips 110
Greek Feta Salad 214
Green Onion Dip 218
Grilled Kippers with Scrambled Egg 198
Grilled Quail with Sautéed Mushrooms 83
Guacamole 240
Ham and Cream Cheese Cubes 216
Hamburgers for the Barbecue 210
Heavenly Pie 130
Herb and Garlic Bread 210
Herb Butter 208
Honeyed Apple Mousse 158
Hot Cucumber and Tarragon in a Lemon Sauce 94
Hungarian Goulash 58
Iced Lebanese Soup 26
Individual Steaks in Puff Pastry with Mushroom Sauce 56
Italian Pancakes 121
Jam Sandwich Fritters 170
Jelly Oranges 134
Jerusalem Artichoke Soup 14
Kate's Carrot Cake 189
Kedgeree 196
Kefthedes 222
Kidneys Turbigo 54
Kumquats Filled with Cream Cheese 218
Lamb and Lemon Kebabs 213
Lamb Chops in Caper Sauce 60
Lancashire Hot Pot 43
Lasagne 114
Layered Pasta Salad 114